Jan Hus

Czech Theological Perspectives

Series Editors: Dr. Jan Blahoslav Lášek, Charles University, Prague; Dr. Jacob Marques Rollison, independent scholar

This series aims to constitute a distinguished forum for research issuing from or concerning Czech theology in the broadest sense of this compound term. Examples of research sought and welcomed under this umbrella include: high-quality original monographs and edited volumes presenting research conducted by Czech scholars, in Czech universities, or in Czech territory; research conducted by non-Czech scholars or outside of Czech universities and territory which examines contemporary or historical theological trends and events linked to the Czech lands, people, and church (such as the Bohemian Reformation, the legacy of Jan Hus, etc.); and scholarly translations of both contemporary research and works of enduring theological or historical value which aim to fill out the currently sparse anglophone resources on these same topics. While anglophone discussion is well acquainted with the historical and theological contours of the Reformation in Western Europe (especially France, Switzerland, and Germany), it has yet to fully attend to the importance of Czech theological history and Czech voices in contemporary theology. Wider recognition that this history and these voices are important in their own right (and not merely as precursors to Luther or Calvin) drives the posture of inquiry, listening, and dialogue this series aims to embody.

Titles in the Series

Jan Hus: Faithful Witness to Truth, by Jan Blahoslav Lášek and Angelo Shaun Franklin

The Four Articles of Prague within the Public Sphere of Hussite Bohemia: On the 600th Anniversary of Their Declaration (1420–2020), by Kamila Veverková

Jan Hus

Faithful Witness to Truth

Jan Blahoslav Lášek and
Angelo Shaun Franklin

LEXINGTON BOOKS
Lanham • Boulder • New York • London

Published by Lexington Books
An imprint of The Rowman & Littlefield Publishing Group, Inc.
4501 Forbes Boulevard, Suite 200, Lanham, Maryland 20706
www.rowman.com

86-90 Paul Street, London EC2A 4NE

British Library Cataloguing in Publication Information available

Library of Congress Cataloging-in-Publication Data available

ISBN 9781793637420 (hardcover) | ISBN 9781793637437 (epub)

♾™ The paper used in this publication meets the minimum requirements of American
National Standard for Information Sciences—Permanence of Paper for Printed Library
Materials, ANSI/NISO Z39.48-1992.

Contents

Preface

In addition to his research on Jan Amos Komenský, Czech modernism, and the beginnings of Christianization among the Eastern Slavs,[1] Dr. Jan Blahoslav Lášek has devoted a significant amount of time throughout his illustrious teaching career to writing articles, overseeing exhibitions and symposiums, editing major publications, and sharing his extensive knowledge about Jan Hus and other personalities and aspects of the Bohemian Reformation in various public speaking engagements.[2] This work aims to consolidate some of Lášek's expertise into an original and accessible presentation of key elements of Hus's life and teaching for anglophone readers. It seeks to offer an original proposition for how to approach studying Hus and makes a new contribution to English-language resources on Hus.

The tone, content, and layout of this unconventional volume can be explained with reference to Hus's didactical and ethical emphasis on *truth*. While this work is certainly not the first to highlight Hus's dedicated focus on truth, failing to properly understand his emphasis on truth will result in misreading this book. For Hus, the idea of "truth" was far from being cold, abstract, detached, or merely theoretical; truth represented a personal challenge, confrontation, and call. Similar to Martin Luther's later underscoring of the *pro nobis* and *pro me* aspects[3] of the gospel—the "promeity" of the gospel message, in the sense of being truly "good news"—Hus's teaching on "truth" can never be approached without reference to his own life, nor properly understood without an accompanying challenge for the hearer to pursue truth as one who, like Hus, is being challenged, confronted, and called.

After a political "turning of the tide" when the Communist regime was overthrown during the Velvet Revolution in Czechoslovakia in 1989, Professor Lášek wrote a short booklet in Czech entitled *Kristův Svědek Mistr Jan Hus* (*Jan Hus: Faithful Witness of Jesus Christ*). While expectations for political change had been thankfully realized to a great extent, an increasing sense of personal accountability linked with longings of profound hope for social change was sweeping through the nation. It was a transitional time of newly discovered freedom and radical change in many aspects following a momentous turning point for all of Europe. Along with these changes came a renewed search for truth accompanied by a need to confront existential concerns connected with individual and collective hope for the future of the nation. It was within this unique context that Lášek offered a simple reminder that the struggle for truth had a rich tradition for the Czech people. The purpose and aim of his booklet was to encourage people from his homeland to become more acquainted with at least a basic outline of Jan Hus's life in order to help them orient their own lives in the direction of living in truth.

The present text began with my encouraging Professor Lášek to revise and expand his original popular account into an introductory academic text. Ultimately, our discussion and cooperation was realized in our composing this work together. We hope it will provide a helpful and appropriate foundation for understanding just a few of the major themes related to the background, life, events, writings, and significance of Jan Hus, and that it will serve as a stimulus for further research.

I have translated and expanded Lášek's original booklet, adding explanatory comments, clarifications, and endnotes, and have also provided annotated translations of two of Hus's important texts. The first is a new translation of Hus's *Appellacio ad Supremum Iudicem* (*Appeal to the Supreme Judge*),[4] which we have placed here as chapter 3 in order to coincide with the flow of the material presented in previous chapters. The annotations are not necessarily to be construed as an attempt to offer a particular interpretation of the appeal itself or its role in Hus's ongoing legal battles, since both Jiří Kejř and Thomas Fudge have already put forward helpful research in this regard, whether or not one accepts their conclusions.[5] My hope in providing this translation of the text with relevant supplementary references is to facilitate further research from interested readers, encouraging them to reach their own informed conclusion of both the appeal's personal importance and legal significance for Hus. I hope the reader will find herself in agreement with Czech philologist and literary historian Václav Flajšhans (1866–1950), who enthusiastically appraised Hus's appeal to Christ with these memorable words: "From among the entire extensive literary activities of Hus, there is no more impressive and powerful declaration than his renowned *Appellacio ad Jesus Christum Supremum Judicem*."[6] The second text is Hus's *Homily on the Feast Day of the Holy Trinity*, which is a biblical exposition of John 3:1–15 drawn from Hus's *Czech Sunday Postil* (see appendix). While among Hus's sermons there are others which are surely more theologically profound, more emotionally engaging, or perhaps even more historically interesting, Hus's treatment of this most well-known Johannine pericope was chosen as exemplary of Hus's overall homiletical style, manner of exposition, and theological concerns.

In addition to situating Hus under the category of a reformer, Lášek reminds us that Hus was primarily a Christian man whose undying commitment to the truth was "demonstrated in his dedication to developing true, pure, authentic, and moral lives of both individuals and society as a whole." He also notes that "the significance of the truth" which has the power to captivate and inspire us "has still not made its full impact in terms of our own personal witness in society." Following from Hus's humble approach to truth, Lášek's admonition should be heard as a personal challenge for each of us to consider not only that the truth for which Hus lived and died remains a necessary question and a vital matter of concern for every culture, but that seeking and savoring the truth is arguably also the greatest need of our contemporary society, just as it was for Hus many centuries ago.

Contemporary views of Hus demonstrate that the often paradoxical nature of truth catches the undivided attention of those slumbering in mediocrity and captures the minds and hearts of those who seem to have the least in common with one another. Indeed, which other historical personality besides Jan Hus has ironically inspired two major heads of state from entirely opposed philosophical and political viewpoints to each write a book praising the Bohemian reformer as an outstanding leader worthy of admiration? In 1913, the future Italian Prime Minister Benito Mussolini (1883–1945) published a book entitled *Giovanni Hus: Il Veridico* (*Jan Hus: The Truthful One*),[7] in which he portrayed Hus not merely as a fierce critic of ecclesiastical abuses, but as a truth-speaking revolutionary figure who "unites all endeavors, brings together all aspirations, concentrates and directs all the forces of religious and moral liberation."[8] While we are not entirely sure how to evaluate Mussolini's motivations for writing about Hus, we simply note the historical irony that a fascist dictator, master of propaganda, and self-professed atheist who seemingly had nothing in common with a truth-driven medieval Christian priest and theologian of Hus's character somehow considered the Bohemian reformer worthy of his opinion journalism.[9]

Nearly twenty years earlier Tomáš Garrigue Masaryk (1850–1937), a philosopher who would later become the first president of the newly created sovereign state of Czechoslovakia in 1918, composed a work entitled *Jan Hus: Naše obrozeni a naše reformace* (*Jan Hus: Our Renaissance and Our Reformation*).[10] In it he expressed a deep appreciation for Hus as a reformer, noting that "Hus's reform, precisely because it was religious, had such a profound reach and significant impact and such influence; and that is why Hus's thought ultimately prevailed, perhaps because from the beginning everyone was against it—everyone against only one."[11] On July 6, 1915, the five-hundredth anniversary of Jan Hus's martyrdom, Masaryk delivered a speech in Geneva, asserting that Hus and other reformers provided a "living agenda" and that "our reformation, like other reformations, was not and is not finished; reformation means perpetual reform, continual renewal, a desire for superior development and progress."[12] He specified that Hus's greatest teaching and the main lesson which we can learn from his life should be expressed in the imperative mood: "Stand in the known truth! Defend the truth unto death."[13] In another speech given two days earlier he posed the following questions: "What does the death of Hus mean? Considering what Hus desired, why did he die? What did Hus teach?"[14] He noted that the Bohemian Reformation represented "an endeavor to resolve questions of authority" and maintained that any Czech who is honestly informed and aware of the contemporary situation should not only admire Hus, but also that any Czech "who understands the history of his own nation must follow along Hus's path."[15] Five years earlier, in his July 1910 speech "Master Jan Hus and the Czech Reformation," Masaryk had felt urged to present the audience with a few probing questions concerning Hus's legacy and his impact on Czech culture and history:

> Now we must come to the heart of the matter. Why are we here, what do we want, what does the Reformation mean to us today? Are we here just to listen politely to a speaker—or are we troubled and stirred by Hus; is he still a living force in our lives? Did he die in vain, were the long, bloody Hussite wars in vain, were the bitter internal struggles in vain, the Reformation, the counter-reformation?[16]

In the spirit of Masaryk's questions, in this book we suggest that serious consideration of Jan Hus should not leave us unaffected, but should indeed trouble us, stir us, and exert some living force in our lives. Our admiration for Hus is not in any way lessened merely because he was a flawed human being who was martyred for his faith during a medieval time rife with political and ecclesiastical troubles: *Hus should trouble us.* Our understanding of Hus is not in any way diminished merely because his person and message have been interpreted, used, and misused in a multitude of different ways by countless groups: *Hus should stir us.* Our appreciation of his life and teachings is not in any way undermined merely because our often-faltering commitment to truth pales in comparison to his incomparable passion for the truth: *Hus should exert some living force in our lives.* One author has rightly stated that "Hus stands 'between confessions, nations, and centuries' and only ecumenical, international, and interdisciplinary dialogue can uncover a new path towards a greater understanding of his personality and work."[17] Such an approach toward dialogue surely presents opportunities for offering fresh appraisals of a controversial figure whose life and teachings will hopefully continue to inspire many people from vastly different walks of life.

For Jan Hus, the undeniable reality of Jesus Christ—the one who according to Hus is the Truth—led him to a martyr's stake with a blazing fire intended to extinguish Hus's convictions of "truth." The indelible thread running throughout his entire life was a passion for seeking, understanding, loving, and proclaiming the truth. And although it may appear that "truth has stumbled in the public square, and honesty finds no place there,"[18] humanity today needs the courage and hope to realize that the "truth which conquers all" is by no means dead at all. Truth is still alive and well, and in the remarkable case of Jan Hus, both his living and dying for the truth bear witness to the fact that "we cannot do anything against the truth, but only for the truth."[19]

Angelo Shaun Franklin
Prague, Czech Republic, 2021

NOTES

Translator's Note: All source material cited in the notes that was originally composed in German or Czech has been translated into English.

1. See: Jan B. Lášek, *Počátky křesťanství u východních Slovanů* (Praha: Síť, 1997); "Význam náboženství starých Slovanů a proces christianizace Evropy," in *Bohové dávných Slovanů*, ed. Martin Pitro and Petr Vokáč (Praha: ISV, 2002), 177–183; "Comenius als Prediger," in *Comenius als Theologe: Beiträge zur Internationalen wissenschaftlichen Konferenz "Comenius' Erbe und die Erziehung des Menschen für das 21. Jahrhundert" (Sektion VII): anläßlich des 400. Geburtstages von Jan Amos*, eds. Vladimír Dvořák and Jan Blahoslav Lášek (Praha: Nadace Comenius, 1998), 166–173; "Teologické předpoklady pro mír a pokoj v Komenského Všeobecné poradě," in *"Rýžoviště zlata a doly drahokamů". Sborník pro Václava Huňáčka* (Červený Kostelec: Pavel Mervart, 2006), 493–504; Norbert Kotowski and Jan Blahoslav Lášek, eds., *Johann Amos Comenius und das moderne Europa* (Fürth: Flacius-Verlag, 1992).

2. For example, see: Jan Blahoslav Lášek, *Kristův Svědek Mistr Jan Hus* (Praha: Blahoslav, 1991); "Aktuální Husův apel na svědomí," in *Jan Hus: 600 let od smrti*, ed. Marek Loužek (Václav Klaus Institute, 2015), 19–22; "Mistr Jan Hus," in *Mistr Jan Hus v proměnách času a jeho poselství víry dnešku*, compiled by Tomáš Butta and Zdeněk Kučera (Praha: Církev československá husitská, 2012), 9–19; "Preface," in *Jan Hus mezi epochami, národy a konfesemi: Sborník z mezinárodního sympozia konaného 22.–26. září v Bayreuthu*, ed. Jan Lášek (Praha: Česká křesťanská akademie, 1995), 12–15; "Některé specifické úkoly husovského bádání," in *Jan Hus mezi epochami, národy a konfesemi*, 305–310; "Konzultace o teologii M. Jana Husa," in *Mediaevalia Historica Bohemica* 4 (1997): 408–409; *Husitství ve východních Čechách* (Praha: 1996); "K ekumenické diskusi o životě a díle M. Jana Husa," in *Český zápas* 76/14 (1996): 3; "Ke 'sporu' o Husovo pojetí večeře Páně. Zpráva o literatuře," in

Theologická revue 67/3 (1996): 40–41; "Liturgická a svátostná teologie mistra Jana Husa: Byl Jan Hus reformátorem liturgie?" in *Theologická revue*, 67/1 (1996): 9–11; "Jak je to s husitstvím?" in *Český zápas* 77/14 (1997): 1; Jan Lášek, "Preface," in Daniel Larangé, *La Parole de Dieu en Bohème et en Moravie: La tradition de la prédication dans l'Unité des Frères de Jan Hus à Jan Amos Comenius* (Paris: L'Harmattan, 2008); Jan Lášek *et al.*, *Mistr Jan Hus 1415–2005* (Praha: Sdružení Tradice, 2005), 8–13, 19–24, 52–53; see also his articles in *The Encyclopedia of the Reformation*, ed. Hans J. Hillerbrand (Oxford: Oxford University Press, 1996), 1:97–98; 2:323–324; 3:458–459; "Luther und die Reformation in Böhmen," in Michael Hrubá, Jan Royt, Petr Hrubý *et al.*, *Sola fide—Pouhou vírou: Luterská šlechta na Ústecku a Děčínsku a její kulturní dědictví: Katalog výstavy konané na zámku v Děčíně 25. dubna–30. září 2018* (Dolní Břežany: Scriptorium, 2019), 27–38; "Christliche Vordenker der europäischen Idee in Böhmen," in *Theologen—Europäer—Brückenbauer*, eds. Jan B. Lášek, Thomas Kothmann, and Stephen James Hamilton (Neuendettelsau: Freimund, 2020), 20–46.

3. See Sasja Emilie Mathiasen Stopa, "'Seeking Refuge in God against God': The Hidden God in Lutheran Theology and the Postmodern Weakening of God," *Open Theology* 4/1 (2018): 658–674.

4. There are several Czech translations of Hus's appeal. See: *M. Jana Husi Korespondence a dokumenty*, ed. Václav Novotný (Praha: Nákladem komise pro vydávání pramenů náboženského hnutí českého, 1920), 134–136; *Husova výzbroj do Kostnice*, eds. F.M. Dobiáš and Amedeo Molnár (Praha: Kalich, 1965), 28–33; *Sto listů M. Jana Husi*, trans. and ed. Bohumil Ryba (Praha: Jan Laichter, 1949), 77–81; M. Jan Hus, *Obrany v praze: (r. 1408–1412). Obran Husových*, vol. 1, trans. Václav Flajšhans (Praha: J. Otto, 1916), 1:73–78; *Husitské manifesty*, trans. and ed. Amedeo Molnár (Praha: Odeon, 1980), 43–47. For a modern German translation, see "Appellation des Magisters Johannes Hus gegen die Urteilssprüche des römischen Bischofs an Jesus Christus, den höchsten Richter (1412)," trans. Armin Kohnle, in *Johannes Hus Deutsch*, eds. Armin Kohnle and Thomas Krzenck (Leipzig: Evangelische Verlagsanstalt, 2017), 249–254. An older translation in English was included in John Foxe's *Acts and Monuments*. See Stephen Reed Cattley, ed., "The Copy and Tenor of the Appeal of John Huss," in *The Acts and Monuments of John Foxe*, vol. 3 (London: Seeley, Burnside & Seeley, 1844), 467–468.

Church historian Matthew Spinka included his English translation of Hus's *Appellatio* in two of his major works: *The Letters of John Hus* (Manchester: Manchester University Press, 1972), 215–219, and *John Hus at the Council of Constance* (New York: Columbia University Press, 1965), 237–240. Although a very useful translation overall, Spinka did not employ the legal terminology which underscores Hus's appeal and which is all-important for understanding the significance of his case. Due to the polysemy of many Latin words, the text itself is hard to determine at times when Hus was intending to use a personal, moral, or legal example and emphasis. One must determine Hus's intentions based on the historical context, exceptional circumstances, personal theology, and unique diction. Under the rubric of what Jiří Kejř labeled as Hus's "legal-theological" (*rechtstheologische*) understanding and approach to law, it should be noted that "for Hus and his students

the legal standard was transformed into a moral standard." See Jiří Kejř, *Dvě studie o husitském právnictví* (Prague: ČSAV, 1954), 5; "Johannes Hus als Rechtsdenker," in Jan Hus—*Zwischen Zeiten, Völkern, Konfessionen: Vorträge des internationalen Symposions in Bayreuth vom 22. bis 26. September 1993*, Ferdinand Seibt et al., eds. (Munich: R. Oldenbourg, 1997), 219.
The translation offered here will aim to help the reader discern the legal terminology and context of Hus's appeal. Specific references to relevant canon law will thus appear as endnotes, although as Brian Tierney has aptly demonstrated, there were multitudes of different interpretations of canon law, each of course leading to different scholarly conclusions. See Brian Tierney, *Foundations of the Conciliar Theory: The Contributions of the Medieval Canonists from Gratian to the Great Schism* (Cambridge: Cambridge University Press, 1955), 199–219. Although he certainly would not have agreed with many aspects of canon law, Hus was a studious reader of legal texts available and often cited canon law in his works; however, during the last few years of his life he ultimately rejected canon law, which is evidenced primarily by the actual appeal itself.
5. See: *The Trial of Jan Hus: Medieval Heresy and Criminal Procedure* (Oxford: Oxford University Press, 2013); Jiří Kejř, *Husovo odvolání od soudu papežova k soudu Kristovu* (Ústí nad Labem: Albis International, 1999); idem, *Husův proces* (Praha: Vyšehrad, 2000); idem, "Husův proces z hlediska práva kanonického," *Theologická revue* 71 (2000): 33–39; idem, "Husův proces z hlediska práva kanonického," in *Jan Hus na přelomu tisíciletí: Mezinárodní rozprava o českém reformátoru 15. století a o jeho recepci na prahu třetího milénia Papežská lateránská univerzita Řím 15.–18. prosince 1999*, eds. Miloš Drda, František J. Holeček, and Zdeněk Vybíral (Tábor: Husitské museum, 2001), 303–311; idem, *Die Causa Johannes Hus und das Prozessrecht der Kirche,* trans. Walter Annuss (Regensburg: Pustet, 2005).
6. Václav Flajšhans, "Husovo odvolání ke Kristu," in *Český časopis historický* 39 (1933): 237.
7. See Benito Mussolini, *Giovanni Hus: Il Veridico* (Rome: Podrecca e Galantara, 1913); Benito Mussolini, "Giovanni Huss il veridico," in *Opera omnia, vol. 33: Opere giovanili: 1904–1913,* eds. Edoardo and Duilio Susmel (Firenze: La Fenice, 1961), 271–327. Mussolini's work has been translated into English and Czech. See: *John Huss,* trans. Clifford S. Parker (New York: Albert & Charles Boni, 1929); *Jan Huss, the Veracious* (New York: Italian Book Co., 1939); *Mussoliniho kniha o Janu Husovi, muži pravdy,* trans. Anežka Loskotová (Turnov: Jiránek, 1937); Pavel Helan, *Duce a kacíř: Literární mládí Benita Mussoliniho a jeho kniha Jan Hus, muž pravdy* (Brno: L. Marek, 2006).
8. Parker, trans., *John Huss,* 149.
9. On the origin of Mussolini's book on Hus, see Pavel Helan, "Mussolini Looks at Jan Hus and the Bohemian Reformation," *The Bohemian Reformation and Religious Practice* 4 (2002): 309–316 [trans. Zdeněk V. David].
10. Tomáš Garrigue Masaryk, *Jan Hus: Naše obrození a naše reformace* (Prague: Čas, 1896). There are nine editions, with the critical edition being found in volume six of his collected works. See *Spisy T. G. Masaryka, vol. 6: Česká otázka. Naše nynější krize. Jan Hus,* ed. Jiří Brabec (Prague: Ústav T. G. Masaryka, 2000),

310–372. For Masaryk's views on Hus, see Zdeněk David, "Masaryk's View of Jan Hus and the Bohemian Reformation," *Kosmas: Czechoslovak and Central European Journal* (2016): 149–171; see also Marie L. Neudorflová, "Mistr Jan Hus v pojetí T. G. Masaryka," *ČAS: Časopis Masarykova demokratického hnutí* 23, no. 110 (2015): 17–22; Henry Wickham Steed, "Jan Hus and T. G. Masaryk," *Spirit of Czechoslovakia* 4, no. 9–10 (1943): 85–86; *Hus a Masaryk: Hedání národní tradice a identity: Sborník projevů pronesených na slavnostním setkání u příležitosti 163. výročí narození Tomáše Garrigua Masaryka v budově Poslanecké sněmovny Parlamentu České republiky a dalších příspěvků*, eds. Zdeněk Kučera, Tomáš Butta, and Olga Nytrová (Praha: Církev československá husitská, 2013).

11. *Spisy T. G. Masaryka, vol. 6: Česká otázka. Naše nynější krize. Jan Hus*, 317.

12. *Spisy T. G. Masaryka, vol. 30: Válka a revoluce I: Články—memoranda—přednášky—rozhovory. 1914–1916,* ed. Karel Pichlík (Praha: Ústav T. G. Masaryka, 2005), 82.

13. Ibid., 83.

14. Ibid., 77–81.

15. Ibid., 80. Masaryk made mention of Hus in several of his speeches. For example, see T. G. Masaryk, *V boji o náboženství* (Praha: ČIN, 1947).

16. Tomáš Garrigue Masaryk, "Hus and Czech Destiny," in *The Spirit of Thomas G. Masaryk (1850–1937): An Anthology*, ed. George J. Kovtun (Houndmills: Macmillan, 1990), 91.

17. Tomáš Halík, "Hus a český katolicismus," in *Jan Hus mezi epochami, národy a konfesemi: Sborník z mezinárodního sympozia konaného 22.–26. září v Bayreuthu*, ed. Jan B. Lášek (Praha: Česká křesťanská akademie, 1995), 312.

18. Isaiah 59:14.

19. 2 Corinthians 13:8.

Preface to the 1991 Czech Edition

The little booklet which you hold in your hands now should not be construed as a replacement for a much more in-depth study of Jan Hus's life and works from other scholarly sources. It only seeks to continue in our exceedingly high-spirited tradition from the time of Tomáš Garrigue Masaryk's First Czechoslovak Republic[1] when dozens of little pamphlets and brochures about Jan Hus were published. Their goal was always to provide up-to-date information about Hus, to "actualize" Hus by representing him realistically, and to draw attention to the specific ways in which his legacy is still alive and well in the twentieth century. Our own Czechoslovak Hussite Church has even published these kinds of texts, many of which have unfortunately already faded out of existence. In the fifties this tradition was violently interrupted and a restricted and severely diminished Marxist point of view was forced upon both the nation and the churches. We can thank God that now the time of "real socialism" and communism is already behind us. We endorse the tradition of publishing popular brochures, and so we contribute this little booklet in order to strengthen the awareness of the Hussite movement in our religious communities. We may safely assume that the ecumenical and cultural Czech scene at large will once again be led to clashing interpretations of Hus; who knows how many times it has already happened, and who knows how many times a new struggle for truth will continually emerge? Perhaps these new struggles will even lead to a reappraisal of Hus's life and work by the Catholic Church. Any new developments will not only require the proficient expertise of specialists but also a cultivated approach from our churches and the general public. This present essay is issued now at the beginning of a new Czech struggle concerning Hus and the Hussite movement; therefore, it should provide a strong initiative in our religious communities for the Czechoslovak Hussite Church to engage with its current theological views in light of Jan

Hus's legacy and also Hussite theological thought as a whole. Finally, I would like thank Dr. Noemi Rejchrtová for looking over the original manuscript.

Dr. Jan Blahoslav Lášek
Prague, Czechoslovakia
September 1, 1991

NOTE

1. Tomáš Garrigue Masaryk founded Czechoslovakia and became its first Czech president after the end of the First World War. Czechoslovakia was established by the Czechoslovak National Council in Prague on October 28, 1918. It basically came to an end in 1938 when Czechoslovakia was forced to cede the Sudetenland to Germany after Edvard Beneš (1884–1948) signed the Munich Agreement. Although diverse problems existed, the so-called First Republic is usually seen as a sort of lively golden age for culture, industry, and economic prosperity.

Preface to the 2022 English Edition

Since the original text was aimed at a popular audience who needed to be reminded that the pursuit of truth is intensely personal, I wanted to compose a short sketch of Hus's life intended for people of various backgrounds. This new expanded version should be perceived as a brief introductory academic text for those who are interested in acquiring important foundational knowledge about Jan Hus. There are, of course, other good popular introductions as well as lengthier academic monographs concerning the life and works of Hus which are highly commendable. Anyone who has studied Hus at all is quite aware that there are ongoing debates concerning multiple issues, and it is not necessary to rehearse all of the pertinent details regarding those here in this work; in fact, each major event in the life of Hus is worthy of a monograph in itself, and since more research concerning Hus is now becoming available in English, even those who are not familiar with our most important events and significant personalities can still gain an awareness of our rich, long and storied Czech history.

It is worth noting that any attempt to approach Hus must contend with centuries of controversial issues which have been debated from various denominational perspectives, with the result that scholarly discourse on Hus often lacks the amicable, dialogical character which research often aims to embody. Contrary to popular belief, the number of published articles and books does not make one an expert on Hus. Rather, having a kindred spirit with Hus and following his own example should be one's goal: keeping an inexhaustible desire to learn coupled with an incessant pursuit of gaining a deeper understanding of the truth while doing research. Therefore, despite the inexpedient and pedantic practice of scholars who constantly critique anyone who disagrees with their interpretations, I prefer to encourage anyone who seeks to engage in legitimate research and offer their findings for both the academy and the public at large; indeed, each side should serve the other with a mutual sense of deep appreciation.

I am convinced that two of the main keys to understanding Jan Hus revolve around comprehending his extraordinary appeal to Jesus Christ and gaining at least a simple appreciation of his passion for preaching and the underlying *logos*, *ethos*, and *pathos* of his sermons.[1] For more completeness of detail, several significant monographs which discuss historical events in more detail and offer a deeper investigation into specific aspects of Hus's life are recommended.[2] As well, there are already several fine biographies on the life of Hus.[3] This work will include some chapters which are basic and straightforward in terms of content (chapters 1, 2, 4, and the conclusion), while others will explain more-detailed considerations (chapters 3, 5, 6, and the appendix). This careful presentation is supplemented with endnotes providing references to important original sources in order to stimulate further research from the primary and international secondary literature.

Since the original publication of the shorter Czech version of this work, there have been several major developments in the field of Hussite studies, and it would be inappropriate if I failed to mention them here. In addition to the ongoing project to make Hus's *Opera Omnia* available,[4] the publication of several critical editions of Hus's works has thankfully already been realized, as well as translations of some of Hus's major works which now appear in other foreign languages.[5] Another good example is the 1993 international colloquium held in Bayreuth, Germany, called "Jan Hus among Epochs, Nations, and Confessions." Norbert Kotowski, Z.R. Ditrich, Zdeněk Kučera, Ferdinand Seibt, and others helped me to co-organize the symposium, whose main aims were to encourage irenic scholarly interaction, to promote research interests, and to forge a path forward for studying the personality of Jan Hus from a variety of perspectives.[6]

I also need to make an important clarification about my statement written in the original preface concerning the reevaluation or rehabilitation of Hus by the Roman Catholic Church, since in 1999 another International Symposium on Master Jan Hus was held at the Pontifical Lateran University in Rome.[7] Several more conferences which aim to promote scholarly research related to the Bohemian Reformation have also taken place in Prague every other year.[8] There will no doubt be necessary future endeavors and research projects focusing on a host of other pertinent issues, historical questions, and theological concerns in relation to the life and work of our great Bohemian reformer.[9] Keeping in mind the humble intention of the authors, it is my sincere hope and prayer that this work may serve as a valuable introduction for certain theology students and historians and will inspire many others to engage in further research about one of our most beloved Czechs—the unforgettable Jan Hus.[10]

Dr. Jan Blahoslav Lášek
Prague, Czech Republic, 2021

NOTES

1. On Hus's preaching, see Thomas A. Fudge, "'Feel This!' Jan Hus and the Preaching of Reformation," *The Bohemian Reformation and Religious Practice* 4 (2002): 107–126; see also Reid S. Weber, "The Knowledge and Eloquence of the Priest is a Gift from God." *The Homiletic Self-Promotion of Jan Hus," The Bohemian Reformation and Religious Practice* 10 (2015): 28–48.

2. In English, see Thomas A. Fudge, *Jan Hus: Religious Reform and Social Revolution in Bohemia* (London: I. B. Tauris, 2010). In addition to his other works on Hus and the Hussites, Fudge has written numerous academic articles, with two of the most important concerning Hussite historiography. See Thomas A. Fudge, "The State of Hussite Historiography," *Mediaevistik* 7 (1994): 93–117; *idem*, "Jan Hus in English Language Historiography, 1863–2013," *Journal of Moravian History* 16, no. 2 (2016): 90–138.

3. For example, see: Matthew Spinka, *John Hus: A Biography* (Princeton: Princeton University Press, 1968); Václav Novotný, *M. Jan Hus: Život a učení*, 2 vols. (Prague: Jan Laichter, 1919–1921); Paul de Vooght, *L'hérésie de Jean Huss, 2nd ed.* (Louvain: Publications Universitaires de Louvain, 1975); Peter Hilsch, *Johannes Hus (um 1370–1415): Prediger Gottes und Ketzer* (Regensburg: Verlag Friedrich Pustet, 1999); Amedeo Molnár, *Jan Hus: Testimone della verità* (Torino: Claudiana, 1973); František Šmahel, *Jan Hus: Život a dílo* (Prague: Argo, 2013); Ernst Werner, *Jan Hus. Welt und Umwelt eines Prager Frühreformators* (Weimar: Hermann Böhlaus, 1991); Thomas Krzenck, *Johannes Hus. Theologe, Kirchenreformer, Märtyrer* (Gleichen/ Zürich: Muster-Schmidt, 2011); Pavel Soukup, *Jan Hus: The Life and Death of a Preacher* (West Lafayette: Purdue University Press, 2020).

4. Hus's *Opera Omnia* is being published by the prestigious academic Belgian publishing house Brepols.

5. *Johannes Hus Deutsch*, eds. Armin Kohnle and Thomas Krzenck (Leipzig: Evangelische Verlagsanstalt, 2017); Jan Hus, *O Kościele*, trans. Krzysztof Moskal (Lublin: Towarzystwo Naukowe Katolickiego Uniwersytetu Lubelskiego, 2003).

6. The proceedings were later published in Czech and German: *Jan Hus mezi epochami, národy a konfesemi: Sborník z mezinárodního sympozia konaného 22.–26. září v Bayreuthu*, ed. Jan Lášek (Praha: Česká křesťanská akademie, 1995); *Jan Hus: Zwischen Zeiten, Völkern, Konfessionen (Vorträge des internationalen Symposions in Bayreuth vom 22. bis 26. September 1993)*, ed. Ferdinand Seibt (München: Oldenbourg, 1997). Hana Pátková provided a summary of the conference in *Mediaevalia Historica Bohemica* 3 (1994): 348–351. See also Norbert Kotowski, "Magister Johannes Hus im Gespräch mit Prag, Kiew, Rom und Wittenberg. Bericht über das internationale Hus-Symposion," *Una Sancta* 2 (1994): 145–152.

7. See *Jan Hus na přelomu tisíciletí: Mezinárodní rozprava o českém reformátoru 15. století a o jeho recepci na prahu třetího milénia Papežská lateránská univerzita Řím 15.–18. prosince 1999*, eds. Miloš Drda, František J. Holeček, and Zdeněk Vybíral (Tábor: Husitské museum, 2001). For a consideration of the same issue from the previous generation, see Milan Machovec, *Bude katolická církev rehabilitovat*

Jana Husa? (Praha: NPL, 1965). See also Fudge's comments in *Jan Hus: Religious Reform and Social Revolution in Bohemia*, 227–240.

8. For example, the Bohemian Reformation and Religious Practice is a biennial international symposium which focuses on issues related to the Bohemian Reformation. Its scholarly journal, *The Bohemian Reformation and Religious Practice*, is published under the auspices of the Philosophical Institute of the Czech Academy of Sciences. Articles from the journal may be accessed on the internet at www.brrp.org.

9. On prospects of further research, see Kamila Veverková, "Co a proč stojí u Husa za další bádání?" *Theologická revue* 86/2 (2015): 152–157; see also Dušan Coufal, "Vědecké bádání o Janu Husovi," in *Praha Husova a husitská 1415–2015: Publikace k výstavě: Clam-Gallasův palác, 25. září 2015 – 24. ledna 2016* (Praha: Scriptorium, 2015), 241–247.

10. Depending on one's criteria for assessing greatness, calling Hus "unforgettable" is certainly not engaging in an undue hagiographical appraisal of his life, nor is it dismissing his many faults. I merely acknowledge that whether or not Czech people actually understand Hus's contribution to history or share his convictions, they have consistently ranked Hus high on the list of "great" Czechs in public surveys. See Martin Štoll, "Is Kafka a Greater Czech Than Freud? The Global TV Format 100 Great Britons in Czech Translation (A Case Study)," *Czech and Slovak Journal of Humanities* 1 (2017): 68–87 [trans. Richard Olehla].

1

Historical Background: The Context of the Medieval Church

INTRODUCTION: JAN HUS & CZECH HISTORY

Without any degree of unwarranted exaggeration, it is possible to say that for the Czech people our relationship with Jan Hus not only indicates and describes our ecclesial affiliation, but it also determines our personal attitude towards our national history. We could elaborate here upon the extensive history of the Hussite movement and even describe the way in which this history has been presented as undoubtedly the most distinctive tradition in all of Czech history. That pivotal issue, however, is not our particular aim at the moment; we simply want to remind the reader of Jan Hus himself. The great Bohemian "Goose"[1] was the unique spark that ignited the "blazing flames" of the Hussite movement and the entire Bohemian Reformation out of the pervasive social and spiritual crisis of the fourteenth century. In this essay we will take a closer look at the situation and circumstances which Hus himself encountered, paint a picture of the development and main course of events in his life, offer a brief evaluation of his preaching, and conclude with an attempt to broadly reconstruct the foundational pillars of his thinking which illustrate for us the special ways in which Jan Hus has been perceived in our Reformed churches: mainly *as a faithful witness to truth.*

THE CONTEXT OF THE MEDIEVAL CHURCH

Jan Hus usually appears in our minds as one who castigated the wicked immorality and the extreme worldliness of the church. This is certainly true, even as it is also true that he was following in the footsteps of a church reform movement which had already originated in Bohemia at the end of the reign of Emperor Charles IV. However, there are even deeper roots which are directly related to the overall spiritual situation in Christian Europe at that time—roots which must be mentioned here.[2] Approximately one hundred years before Hus was born, the leading spirit of high scholasticism died. Thomas Aquinas (1225–1274) was an Italian Dominican friar and influential Christian theologian whose two most famous works are *Summa Contra Gentiles*[3] and *Summa Theologiae*.[4] Aquinas adopted the principles of Aristotelian logical reasoning, utilized it for his theological conceptions, and formed a specific integrative system which later came to be known as Thomism. This philosophical school, which aspired for an explanation of the biblical message with the help of terms and expressions drawn from ancient philosophy, was the culmination of a long and gradual development. However, even though an impressive philosophical-theological system emerged, the biblical message was thereby distorted. Under the influence of Roman legal thought (i.e., the heritage of Thomism), Rome's "biblical" message was not primarily concerned with salvation in Christ, but rather noted a mere affiliation to the Roman Church whose visible sign was baptism. Rome's "biblical" message did not seem to be concerned with personal faith and obedience to Jesus Christ, but subservience to the priesthood and the Roman pope above all else.

Nevertheless, the enduring mystery of the church is that whenever she faces either an impending or an actual crisis, she always finds the strength to rise above the *status quo* and return to her essential mission. It was certainly no different in the European churches at the end of the thirteenth century and at the beginning of the fourteenth century. European schools of thought resonated with the extremely vibrant spiritual and highly political situation which was quickly unfolding in certain historical events involving many nations. First of all, in 1309 the so-called Babylonian captivity of the papacy[5] began in Avignon. Despite the fact that the doctrine of papal infallibility was not promulgated as official dogma until the First Vatican Council (1869–1870),[6] it was surely experienced as a concrete reality in the Middle Ages. Consequently, a reform movement called conciliarism emerged as a response against the exercise of unrestricted papal power (both spiritual and political).

Conciliarism promoted the theory that the highest authority in the church should not be the pope but rather a general council.[7] Two of the most important spiritual fathers of conciliarism include Jean Quidort (1255–1306) and Marsilius of Padua (1275–1347). In his treatise *De Potestate Regia et Papali* (*On Royal and Papal Power*), Quidort described the relationship between spiritual and temporal power and explained how both spiritual and secular rulers derive their authority from God and how each has recognizably different goals.[8] In his world-renowned book *Defensor Pacis* (*The Defender of the Peace*), which remains widely read today, Marsilius taught that in both spiritual and secular affairs the rightful "plenitude of power" (*plenitudo potestatis*) belongs to secular authority. He was one of the first scholars to deny the validity of canon law, and in anticipation of the Bohemian and the ensuing European Reformation, he emphasized the Augustinian doctrine that the church is *congregatio fidelium*: a congregation, assembly, or fellowship of believers.[9] According to Marsilius, all believers are equal from the point of view of sharing this common faith; canon law and the temporal power or jurisdiction of the church cannot be derived or deduced from Christ's commands. Two other eminent thinkers who disputed the legal understanding of late scholasticism were William of Ockham (1285–1349) and John Duns Scotus (1265–1308). Scotus in particular emphasized the superiority of Christ's love and the human will in following him over the accent that Thomas of Aquinas had placed on law and reason.[10]

Now it is worth remembering that these two scholars were proponents of a philosophical movement known as nominalism—a view which teaches that universal concepts or abstract objects are mere names.[11] In order not to lose the chronological correlation with the Bohemian lands, we will mention that when all of these ideas emerged in Europe, Václav was born as the son of the Bohemian king Jan of Luxembourg (1296–1346) and Eliška Přemyslovna (1292–1330). Václav later adopted the name Charles at his confirmation and entered the annals of world history as Emperor Charles IV (1316–1378). When Charles arrived in Bohemia as a sixteen-year-old after being raised abroad, he found that great havoc had been wreaked upon the land, an unfortunate fact which he admitted in his autobiography.[12] This young Moravian margrave later became the king of Bohemia and the holy Roman emperor.

For the sake of objectivity, we must remember that his personal admission in *Vita Caroli* (*The Life of Charles*) concerning the desolate and decadent state of the Kingdom of Bohemia was an accurate portrayal, and not only as it pertained to the realm of material culture. After the extinction of the Přemyslid dynasty and even beforehand—approximately since the death of Přemysl Otakar II (ca. 1233–1278)—there had been a significant decline in the quality and condition of education. Thus, the commencement of a broad cultural restoration at that time was only due to the diligent efforts and leading endeavors of Charles IV. Two of his main accomplishments included the establishment of the Archbishopric in Prague in 1344 and the founding of the University of Prague in 1348. Thus, after more than a hundred years of decay, Bohemia was becoming one of the centers of European politics and eventually a cultural focal point as well. Without losing sight of the monarch's skilled and experienced leadership and political realism, we can say that Charles was a very devout medieval Christian. As a devoted member of the church, he did not view the church merely as an instrument or tool for controlling his subjects, but he sincerely desired to see the overall flourishing of the church. However, this expansion of cultural development did not only bring certain positive aspects along with it; unfortunately, some of the negative aspects which we have mentioned above also began to dominate Prague's cultural and political horizons from the second half of the 1450s. Although dissident ideas of ecclesiastical reform certainly appeared, they arrived later and needed a longer period of time to develop into a more mature form.[13]

A distinctive response in this era of prosperity (often called "early humanism" by some historians) was a reform movement known as *devotio moderna* (modern devotion), which originally proliferated in the city of Deventer in the Netherlands.[14] The Dutchmen Gerard Groote (1340–1384) and John van Ruysbroeck (1293–1381) stand out as important characters from the origin of the movement. Groote promoted the idea of a religious community known as the Brethren of the Common Life (*Fratres Vitae Communis*). The main aspiration of the community was to seek the renewal of the church by leading each individual member to cultivate a rich inner devotion and prayer life. His pupil Florens Radewijns (1350–1400) studied in Prague for five years and received the degree of Master of Arts in 1378. The members of these brotherhoods primarily consisted of secular clergy and laymen who were greatly interested in the church's breaking free from its burdensome situation within the contemporary crisis. The spiritual rules adopted by these communities were those of Saint Augustine (354–430),[15] Saint Bernard (1090–1153), and Saint Bonaventure (1221–1274). Augustine was particularly significant and especially influential due to his theological and practical emphasis on God's grace. A younger contemporary of Hus named Thomas à Kempis (1380–1471) also belonged to this movement. The devotional book which best represented the aims of the modern devotion is entitled *De Imitatione Christi (The Imitation of Christ)*.[16] This work, whose origin dates from between 1418 and 1427, emphasizes humbly following or imitating Christ, epitomizes everything the movement was seeking to promote, and is rightly attributed to Thomas à Kempis. The four main sections of this spiritual classic are entitled as follows: (1) Useful Counsels on the Spiritual Life; (2) Instructions for the Inner Life; (3) Inner Consolation; and (4) The Blessed Sacrament.

All of the above-mentioned streams of medieval thought found a lively reception in Prague; the emergence of a similar reform movement which began with the Austrian preacher Konrád Waldhauser (ca. 1326–1369), culminated with Jan Hus and later continued to develop in the theological efforts of the Hussites and the Czech Brethren until 1620.[17] Although this history is perhaps already public knowledge for most of our modern Czech churches, we will simply mention a few important predecessors of Hus.[18] Konrád Waldhauser was a church reformer who preached in German and Latin in the Church of Saint Havel and later in the Church of Our Lady before Týn in the Old Town of Prague.[19] He wrote *Postilla studentium sanctae Pragensis universitatis* [*Homiliarium of the Students of the Sacred University of*

Prague],[20] a collection of homilies which the author of *Dicta de Tempore* was undoubtedly familiar with since he quoted it often.[21] Jan Milíč of Kroměříž (ca. 1325–1374) was another reformer whose influence was so great that he has justifiably been called the "father of the Czech Reformation."[22] One of Milíč's well-known accomplishments from among his wide range of social activities was establishing a kind of halfway house for converted prostitutes, which he named Jerusalem.[23] A distinguished theologian of the Czech reform movement named Matěj of Janov u Mladé Vožice (ca. 1350–1394) wrote a major theological work entitled *Regulae Veteris et Novi Testamenti* [*The Rules of the Old and the New Testament*].[24] Janov's *Regulae* not only "prepared the way for Hus and his Bohemian followers, but it also stands as a monument of the universal desire for reform which touched Europe as a whole."[25] An interesting and insightful layman named Tomáš Štítný (ca. 1333–ca. 1401) not only translated several works dealing with spiritual themes, but also composed several works concerning Christian faith and morality.[26] His writings on the Eucharist warrant "being numbered among the foundation stones of the sacramental revival which made the Bohemian church unique in late medieval Europe" and "were an important instrument in propagating a reformed sacramental piety" reflected in further developments of lay participation in the chalice.[27] We must remember that efforts to reform the church not only followed the currents and direction already indicated, but the leading representatives of spiritual life also tried to make major improvements as well. Jan of Jenštejn (ca. 1350–1400), who was the Archbishop of Prague from 1379 to 1396, and the king's court preacher, Vojtěch Raňkův of Ježov (1320–1388), serve as two good examples. Jenštejn served as the third archbishop of Prague from 1378 to 1396. He supported Czech education and tried to reform corruption within the clergy by forbidding them from charging fees for merely administering the sacraments.[28] Raňkův studied in Paris and was chosen to be the rector of the University of Paris in 1355. He received a doctorate there and later preached the funeral oration of Emperor Charles IV. He also established fellowships for native Bohemian students to study theology and philosophy in Paris and Oxford.[29] Unfortunately, although both of these men made valiant attempts at promoting spirituality, neither experienced much success due to conflicts with the king and the church and perhaps personal defects of character.

NOTES

1. The word *husa* in the Czech language means goose. Hus used the moniker "goose" to refer to himself on numerous occasions. See *Korespondence*, 149–150, 154, 222, 235, 249, 255–258.

2. See Jennifer Kolpacoff Deane, *A History of Medieval Heresy and Inquisition* (Lanham: Rowman & Littlefield Publishers, 2011), 247–288.

3. For the Latin text, see *Sancti Thomae Aquinatis Doctoris Angelici Liber de veritate Catholicae fidei contra errores infidelium, qui dicitur Summa contra gentiles*, ed. P. Marc, C. Pera, and P. Caramello, 3 vols. (Turin: Marietti, 1961–1967). The standard English translation is Thomas Aquinas, *Summa Contra Gentiles*, 5 vols., trans. Anton Pegis, James F. Anderson, Vernon J. Bourke, and Charles J. O'Neil (Notre Dame: University of Notre Dame Press, 1975).

4. Thomas Aquinas, *Summa Theologiae: Latin Text and English Translation, Introductions, Notes, Appendices, and Glossaries*, 61 vols. (London: Blackfriars; Eyre & Spottiswoode, 1964–1980); see also Thomas Aquinas, *Summa Theologica*, trans. Fathers of the English Dominican Province (Westminster: Christian Classics, 1981).

5. This phrase was used in a letter by Italian scholar and poet Francesco Petrarch (1304–1374) to describe the corruption and decadence of the Avignon papacy. See *Readings in European History, vol. 1*, ed. James Harvey Robinson (Boston: Ginn & Company, 1904), 502–504. Though writing in much different circumstances, Martin Luther (1483–1546) later used the same term in 1520 in his work *De Captivitate Babylonica Ecclesiae Praeludium*. See *Martin Luther's The Church Held Captive at Babylon: Latin-English Edition with a New Translation and Introduction*, ed. Denis R. Janz (Oxford: Oxford University Press, 2019).

6. See *Pastor aeternus* in *Decrees of the Ecumenical Councils*, ed. Norman Tanner (London: Sheed & Ward, 1990), 2:815–816: "Therefore, faithfully adhering to the tradition received from the beginning of the Christian faith, to the glory of God our savior, for the exaltation of the Catholic religion and for the salvation of the Christian people, with the approval of the Sacred Council, we teach and define as a divinely revealed dogma that when the Roman Pontiff speaks EX CATHEDRA, that is, when, in the exercise of his office as shepherd and teacher of all Christians, in virtue of his supreme apostolic authority, he defines a doctrine concerning faith or morals to be held by the whole Church, he possesses, by the divine assistance promised to him in blessed Peter, that infallibility which the divine Redeemer willed his Church to enjoy in defining doctrine concerning faith or morals. Therefore, such definitions of the Roman Pontiff are of themselves, and not by the consent of the Church, irreformable . . . So then, should anyone, which God forbid, have the temerity to reject this definition of ours: let him be anathema."

7. See Brian Tierney, *Foundations of the Conciliar Theory: The Contribution of the Medieval Canonists from Gratian to the Great Schism* (Cambridge: Cambridge University Press, 1955); idem, *The Crisis of Church and State: 1050–1300* (New York: 1964).

8. John of Paris, *On Royal and Papal Power*, trans. John A. Watt (Toronto: Pontifical Institute of Mediaeval Studies, 1971); Arthur P. Monahan, *John of Paris on Royal and Papal Power: A Translation, with Introduction, of the* De Potestate Regia et Papali (New York: Columbia University Press, 1974).

9. Marsilius of Padua, *The Defender of the Peace*, trans. Annabel Brett (Cambridge: Cambridge University Press, 2005), 145: "This term 'church' is said of the universal

body of faithful believers who call upon the name of Christ, and of all the parts of this body within any community, even the household."

10. Cf. *Duns Scotus on Divine Love: Texts and Commentary on Goodness and Freedom, God and Humans*, ed. A. Vos et al. (New York: Routledge, 2003), 78–87, 89–129.

11. See John Duns Scotus, *Philosophical Writings: A Selection*, trans. Allan B. Wolter (Indianapolis: Hackett Publishing, 1987); see William of Ockham, *Philosophical Writings: A Selection*, trans. Philotheus Boehner (Indianapolis: Hackett Publishing, 1990).

12. See Marie Bláhová, ed., *Kroniky doby Karla IV* (Praha: Svoboda, 1987), 11–54; *Karel IV. Vlastní životopis. Vita Karoli Quatri*, eds. Jiří Spěváček, Jakub Pavel, Bohumil Ryba, and Josef Krása (Praha: Odeon, 1978).

13. Thomas Prügl, "Dissidence and Renewal: Developments in Late Medieval Ecclesiology," *Bulletin du centre d'études médiévales d'Auxerre* (2013): 1–17.

14. On the relationship of the *devotio moderna* with the Bohemian Reformation, see Manfred Gerwing, "Die sogenannte Devotio moderna," in *Jan Hus: Zwischen Zeiten, Völkern, Konfessionen: Vorträge des internationalen Symposions in Bayreuth vom 22. bis 26. September 1993* (München: Oldenbourg, 1997), 49–58; see also Johanna Schreiber, "Devotio moderna in Böhmen," in *Bohemia: Jahrbuch des Collegium Carolinum*, Band 6 (München: Verlag Robert Lerche, 1965), 93–122; Johanna Girke-Schreiber, "Die böhmische Devotio moderna," in *Bohemia sacra. Das Christentum in Böhmen 973–1973*, ed. Ferdinand Seibt (Düsseldorf: Schwann, 1974), 81–91.

15. For the history, influence, and meaning of Augustine and Augustinians in Bohemia, see the following articles in the second part of Henri-Irénée Marrou, *Svatý Augustin* (Řím: Křesťanská akademie, 1979): Franz Machilek, "Augustiniánské mnišství. Řehole sv. Augustina a jejich význam pro řeholní život v církvi," 145–158; Bohumil Zlámal, "Cesta sv. Augustina českými dějinami," 159–165; Franz Machilek, "Augustiniánští kanovníci v Čechách, na Moravě a ve Slezsku," 166–174; Jaroslav Kadlec, "Kláštery Augustiniánů-eremitů v Čechách a na Moravě," 175–190.

16. For a fine English translation, see Thomas à Kempis, *The Imitation of Christ*, trans. Ronald Knox and Michael Oakley (San Francisco: Ignatius Press, 2005).

17. The fateful year 1620 refers to the Battle of White Mountain (*Bílá Hora*), which occurred on the eighth day of November on a hill just outside of Prague. It was the first important battle of the Thirty Years War (1618–1648) and led to Bohemia remaining under Habsburg rule for nearly three centuries.

18. Dominik Duka, "Předchůdci Mistra Jana Husa (Konrád Waldhauser, Jan Milíč z Kroměříže, Matěj z Janova)," in *Jan Hus mezi epochami, národy a konfesemi: Sborník z mezinárodního sympozia, konaného 22.–26. září 1993 v Bayreuthu, SRN*, ed. Jan Blahoslav Lášek (Praha: Česká křesťanská akademie, 1995), 51–53.

19. For an older but still useful biography, see František Loskot, *Konrad Waldhauser, řeholní kanovník sv. Augustina, předchůdce Mistra Jana Husa* (Praha: Volné myšlenky, 1909); see also Jana Zachová, "Waldhauser a Hus," in *Husitství—reformace—renesance: Sborník k 60. narozeninám Františka Šmahela*, 3 vols. (Praha: Historický ústav AV ČR, 1994), 1:287–297.

20. *Staročeské zpracování Postily studentů svaté University pražské Konráda Waldhausera*, ed. František Šimek (Praha: Česká akademie věd a umění, 1947).

21. *Dicta de Tempore Magistro Iohanni Hus Attributa II (Corpus Christianorum Continuatio Mediaevalis 239A)*, ed. Jana Zachová (Turnhout: Brepols, 2011), 1473–1484. Hus's authorship is doubtable.

22. See Miloslav Kaňák, *Milíč z Kroměříže* (Praha: Ústřední církevní nakladatelství, 1975); see also František Loskot, *Milíč z Kroměříže: Otec české reformace* (Praha: Volná myšlenka, 1911).

23. See Peter C.A. Morée, *Preaching in Fourteenth-century Bohemia: The Life and Ideas of Milicius de Chremsir (+1374) and His Significance in the Historiography of Bohemia* (Slavkov: EMAN, 1999), 10, 38, 55–59, 72–75, 249.

24. Vlastimil Kybal, ed., *Matthiae de Janov, Regulae Veteris et Novi Testamenti, I–IV* (Innsbruck: Wagner, 1908–1913); Vlastimil Kybal and Otakar Odložilík, *Regulae Veteris et Novi Testamenti, V* (Praha: ČAVU, 1926); Jana Nechutová et al., *Matthiae De Janov Dicti Magistri Parisiensis Regularum Veteris Et Novi Testamenti Liber V De Corpore Cristi: (editionis Volumen VI)* (München: R. Oldenbourg, 1993). Selected portions have been translated to Czech in Matěj z Janova, *Výbor z Pravidel Starého a Nového Zákona*, trans. Rudolf Schenk (Praha: Blahoslav, 1954). For the standard biography, see Vlastimil Kybal, *M. Matěj z Janova: Jeho život, spisy a učení*, 2nd ed. (Brno: L. Marek, 2000). For a review of scholarly literature on Matěj, see Jana Nechutová, "M. Matěj z Janova v odborné literatuře," *Studia minora Facultatis philosophicae Universitatis Brunensis* E 17 (1972): 119–133.

25. R.R. Betts, "The Regulae Veteris et Novi Testamenti of Matěj z Janova," *The Journal of Theological Studies* 32, no. 128 (1931): 346.

26. Tomáš Štítný, *Knihy naučení křesťanského*, ed. Antonín Jaroslav Vrťátko (Praha: Musea království Českého, 1873); *Knížky šestery o obecných věcech křesťanských*, ed. Karel Jaromír Erben (Praha: K. Jeřábkové, 1852); *Sborník Vyšehradský*, 2 vols., ed. František Ryšánek (Praha: Československá akademie věd, 1960).

27. David Holeton, "The Sacramental Theology of Tomáš Štítný of Štítné," *The Bohemian Reformation and Religious Practice* 4 (2002): 79.

28. See František Michálek Bartoš, *Světci a kacíři* (Praha: Husova československá evangelická fakulta bohoslovecká, 1949), 62–82; *Bohemia Sancta: Životopisy českých světců a přátel Božích*, ed. Jaroslav Kadlec (Zvon: České katolické nakladatelství, 1989), 194–207; see also Ruben Ernest Weltsch, *Archbishop John of Jenstein (1348–1400): Papalism, Humanism and Reform in Pre-Hussite Prague* (The Hague: Mouton, 1968); and Albert Henry Wratislaw, "John of Jenstein, Archbishop of Prague, 1378–1397," *Transactions of the Royal Historical Society* 7 (1878): 30–57.

29. See Jaroslav Kadlec, *Leben und Schriften des Prager Magisters Adalbert Ranconis de Ericinio* (Münster: Aschendorff, 1971); see also Vilém Herold, "Vojtěch Raňkův of Ježov (Adalbertus Rankonis de Ericinio) and the Bohemian Reformation," *The Bohemian Reformation and Religious Practice* 7 (2009): 72–79; and Dominik Duka, "Předchůdci mistra Jana Husa," *Jan Hus mezi epochami, národy a konfesemi*, 51–53.

2

The Life of Jan Hus

Jan Hus was born during the last few years of the reign of Charles IV, at a time when the overall condition of the church and society was very precarious. The year of his birth is not known exactly, but based on one particular reference in his writings where he mentioned his age, 1371 is now generally assumed as being his year of birth.[1] He was probably born in a village called Husinec near Prachatice in southern Bohemia.[2] We also do not know anything with certainty about his early youth, but the most reliable information we have comes from the year 1393, since we know that Hus received a Bachelor of Arts degree in that year, and later in 1396 he became a Master of Liberal Arts. Between 1397 and 1398 he accompanied the court of King Václav IV on a royal diplomatic journey to Reims, France.[3] After his return he began lecturing at the university. He was then ordained as a priest in 1400, and in the winter semester of 1401–1402 he served as the dean of the Faculty of Arts (now the Faculty of Philosophy) of the University of Prague.[4] Hus's crowning moment occurred in 1402 when he became the preacher in Bethlehem Chapel, where he served in the pastoral office for ten consecutive years.

The first years of the fifteenth century were the same in Prague as they were in the majority of European universities: they were years of great conflict concerning the great Oxford professor John Wyclif. Wyclif (1330–1384) was an English philosopher, priest, theologian, and reformer who according to the evaluation of many historians had the greatest influence upon Hus, greater even than all of his other forerunners from Bohemia.[5] Some of the main tenets espoused by Wyclif include philosophical realism and the right of secular lords or rulers to make order in the church. He also argued that secular and ecclesiastical authority depended on being in a state of grace: whoever is not in a state of grace "cannot" govern or rule. Furthermore, in a significant way he anticipated the *formal* principle of the Reformation: that the only infallible standard of Christian doctrine is Holy Scripture.[6] In his treatise *De Eucharistia* [*On the Eucharist*] he advocated the so-called doctrine of remanence over against transubstantiation.[7] The essence of the

9

teaching concerning remanence consists in that it does not stress the transubstantiation of bread and wine into the body and blood of Christ, but places
proper emphasis on the spiritual presence of Jesus Christ which is symbolized
by the elements. He also composed a number of very important philosophical
treatises espousing a philosophical system known as realism.[8] Since Hus's
philosophical commitment also revolved around realism, the intricate relationship between John Wyclif and Jan Hus still remains a complex question
and intriguing area of academic research in terms of recognizing the influence
which the great English philosopher exerted on the great Bohemian preacher.[9]

Czech church historian Miloslav Kaňák explained the interesting relationship between the two with these words:

> Both Hus and Wyclif were distinguished and original, although of course each
> was unique in his own way. They do not overshadow one another, but from a his-
> torical perspective they complement and complete each other. Without Wyclif,
> Hus almost certainly would not have reached his level of maturity in thought
> and assertiveness, and *vice versa*; Wyclif would probably have not attained
> his European renown if it were not for Hus. The providential connections, the
> circumstances of that era, and the socio-economic laws each provided the recip-
> rocal conditions for Hus and Wyclif to become great historical personalities.[10]

In summary, we can add that Hus adhered to many of (some would perhaps say most of) Wyclif's views (except for his assessment on the Lord's
Supper, since Hus did not formally teach the concept of remanence but rather
expressed a viewpoint much in line with transubstantiation).[11] He became
acquainted with most of the theological writings of Wyclif through his friend
Jerome of Prague (1379–1416), who probably brought Wyclif's writings
from Oxford to Prague in 1402.[12] In 1403, a dispute concerning Wyclif arose
in Prague. The Czech masters defended him, while the foreigners implicated
Wyclif as a heretic. Hus increasingly began endorsing Wyclif, despite the
fact that the Archbishop of Prague had forbidden teaching Wyclif's doctrine
of remanence in 1406. However, since it is apparent from his treatise *De
Corpore Christi* (*On the Body of Christ*)[13] that Hus did not exactly adhere to
Wyclif's doctrine concerning the Lord's Supper, he was at that time still in
favor with the archbishop and was chosen twice as the synodal preacher, in
1405 and in 1407.[14]

Bethlehem Chapel became the pivotal and inevitable source of endless
conflict for Hus. As long as he directed his passionate criticism of the church
against his own order of the priesthood and wrote in Latin, he was both a
tolerable and desirable critic for the archbishop and the king. However, when
he began publicly criticizing the *status quo* of the church (i.e., her corruption
and worldly condition) from the pulpit in Bethlehem Chapel in the Czech

language, and when he challenged the common people to take action by correcting their own priests, the spiritual, ecclesiastical, and even political atmosphere started to become very uncomfortable as Hus had now become an inconvenience to them. Some of Hus's Czech hymns and liturgical songs and his plainly written and easily understandable Czech writings derive from the period 1408–1412.[15] For example, he wrote a tract *On Sin*[16] and a very brief text entitled *The Nine Golden Maxims* (reproduced below).[17] Despite its brevity, this text is insightful as it succinctly explains the all-important and paradoxical difference between true Christianity and false Christianity. True Christianity is as a matter of the heart which of course emphasizes deeds done humbly for God and for the sake of others out of love. False Christianity focuses on outward and pompous displays of religion and "ascetical-heroical" deeds which seek the praise of men.[18] Hus's text was later adapted, expanded, and used by the religious and social thinker Petr Chelčický (c. 1390–c. 1460), who definitely differed with Hus in some main areas of theological persuasion, but found much in common with his critiques of the church's domination over the lives of people and exploitation of power in the realm of secular affairs.[19]

The Nine Golden Maxims[20]

Remember the precepts here in these maxims concerning how you should live so that your soul will flourish and prosper.[21]

The first golden maxim: Whoever gives one heller[22] for the sake of God while he is still healthy and alive will honor the Lord God more and his soul will prosper more than if after his death he were to gain and to give away as much gold as would reach between heaven and earth.[23]

The second golden maxim: Whoever suffers and endures one hateful word of opposition for the sake of God[24] will honor the Lord God more and his soul will prosper more than if he were to scourge his own back with as many birches as would grow in the largest forest.

The third golden maxim: Whoever humbles himself before the lowest of the low[25] will honor God more and his soul will prosper more than if he were to journey on a pilgrimage to the ends of the earth and pour out his blood with every footstep.

The fourth golden maxim: Whoever surrenders and gives all of his body and soul to God[26] will honor Him more and his soul will prosper more than if he were to walk throughout the whole world while standing on his head.[27]

The fifth golden maxim: Whoever sheds a single tear for his sins will honor God more and his soul will prosper more than if after his death he were to weep so much that two rivers flowed from his eyes.[28]

The sixth golden maxim: Whoever treasures the Lord God above all creatures and entrusts[29] all of himself to Him will honor God more and his soul will prosper more than if the mother of God along with all the saints were to intercede for him.[30]

The seventh golden maxim: Whoever does not foolishly or rashly condemn anyone will honor God more than if he were to be roasted on a gridiron as Saint Lawrence was.[31]

The eighth golden maxim: Whoever shows mercy to any one of God's creation for the sake of God[32] will honor God more and his soul will prosper more than if he were to be caught up and carried away into the third heaven as Saint Paul was.[33]

The ninth golden maxim: Whoever does not oppose or disobey the will of God will honor God more and his soul will prosper more than if he were to possess the whole world and were give it to God.[34]

HUS'S CONFLICT WITH THE CHURCH

The separation of Archbishop Zbyněk Zajíc of Hazmburk (ca. 1376–1411) from Hus occurred sometime in 1408.[35] Although the archbishop claimed that he did not find any of Wyclif's heresies in his diocese, Hus's enemies increasingly accused him of spreading Wyclif's ideas. At that time there were two rival popes—Benedict XIII (1328–1423) in Avignon and Gregory XII (1326–1417) in Rome. The biblical image and reality of the church being "without spot or wrinkle or any other blemish" (Ephesians 5:27) was always at the forefront of Hus's personal concerns; therefore, he diligently strove for the reform of the church, not only from below (i.e., among the priesthood and believers) but also at her head (i.e., reform of the papacy). The University of Paris proposed that the two popes should surrender their power and that one new pope would then be elected. This proposal was also supported by the French king Charles VI (1368–1422) and the Czech king Václav IV (1361–1419). Unfortunately, the Czech masters could not reach an agreement with the masters of other nations[36] (and especially the Germans), who held the majority at the university. Václav IV wished for at least some measure of accord to exist between the nations, so on January 18, 1409, he issued the *Decree of Kutná Hora*, a royal decree which avouched the right of the majority of votes at the university to the Czech masters.[37] Since the inception of the *Decree*, Hus was actively engaged in advising the king concerning the volatile situation.[38] As a result of the *Decree*, hundreds of German masters departed from Prague and made their way to Leipzig, where a "rival university" was founded in the same year.[39] In the fall of 1409 Hus became the rector of the whole University of Prague,[40] and the overall situation appeared to be moving in a favorable direction; the popes were deposed and Alexander V (1339–1410) was elected as the new pope at the Council of Pisa (1409).

Although the storm seemed to be calming down somewhat, conflict was simply impossible to escape as other important events were moving forward at the same moment. One of the archbishop's priests in Prague, named Jan Protiva (1370–1430), again accused Hus of being a Wyclifite, but the actual prosecution and enhanced persecution of Hus began in 1410. The pope issued a bull which prohibited all preaching outside of the main cathedrals in Prague; this mandate was deliberately directed against Hus and Bethlehem Chapel in an attempt to silence his voice. Unfortunately, this mandate was met with the dark foreboding clouds of another drastic measure against the truth. A truly bleak day in the history of Bohemia occurred on July 16, 1410: following the archbishop's previous order demanding Wyclif's books to be surrendered and burned, the mandate was supinely followed and more than two hundred books of the great evangelical doctor's works (both theological and philosophical) were torched in the archiepiscopal courtyard by the archbishop in front of the ecclesiastical dignitaries.[41] Hus did not dare remain silent now, so he emerged from among the crowd of theologians at the university and presented a defense of Wyclif by composing the short treatise *De Libris Hereticorum Legendis* [*On Reading the Books of Heretics*], where he expressed the conviction that the books of heretics should not be burned, but rather that believers should skillfully engage even with the ideas and writings of heretics in order to more properly discern, appreciate, and defend the truth.[42] Although the blazing fires had reduced the physical books to mere ashes blowing in the wind, they had done nothing at all to destroy the spiritual truths contained within them. In fact, Hus mentioned in a letter to Pope John XXIII that burning Wyclif's books had accomplished nothing good in terms of results except to promote "discord, disputes, hatred, and murder."[43] Hus wrote,

> I declare that the burning of books is evil, and that burning [them] has never yet removed a single sin from the hearts of men (unless proved and rejected by those who are condemned), but it has only destroyed many truths, many noble and refined thoughts written in them, and has multiplied disturbances, envy, defamation, hatred, and murders among the people, and the other regions have foolishly and improvidently regarded the most Christian Kingdom of Bohemia as being under the suspicion of evil.[44]

Hus called for a public university disputation[45] and later composed a few Latin treatises which also presented a defense of some of Wyclif's ideas: *Defensio Libri de Trinitate* [*A Defense of the Book on the Trinity*], *Contra Iohannem Stokes* [*Response Against John Stokes*], and *Contra Occultum Adversarium* [*Response Against a Hidden Adversary*].[46]

The archbishop aggravated the ban and made it more difficult for Hus by having it confirmed by the new Pope John XXIII (c. 1370–1419) and by declaring it in all of the churches in Prague in March 1411. The quick-tempered and unpredictable King Václav IV tried to prevent the wildfire in his own way: he expelled the archbishop from Prague, but he died on his journey to Bratislava, where he intended to meet Sigismund of Luxembourg (1368–1437). Thus, the interdict which he had personally declared was rendered ineffective for the time being.

In the meantime, under the leadership of their courageous preacher, the people of Bethlehem Chapel were moving towards a revolution (i.e., in terms of their political ideology). The situation was further complicated when the new pope sent a vendor of indulgences to Prague in May 1412 because he needed more financial resources for a "personal war" that he was pretentiously waging against King Ladislaus of Naples (1277–1414). On June 7, 1412, a public dispute was organized at the university in which Hus argued against indulgences using Wyclif's ideas again as his inspiration. His response was entitled *Questio de indulgentis sive de cruciata papae Joannis XXIII fulminata versus Ladislaum Apuliae regem* [*A Disputed Question concerning Indulgences or the Crusade which Pope John XXIII Fulminated against Ladislaus the King of Naples*].[47] However, the unity of the Czech masters did not last very long at all. Hus's former friends Štěpán Páleč and Stanislav of Znojmo, masters of the theological faculty, rose up against Hus primarily by condemning Wyclif. Hus then rose to Wyclif's defense with a number of tracts preserved in a compendium entitled *Defensio Articulorum Wyclif* [*A Defense of the Articles of Wyclif*] in the same year.[48] Hus was determined not to cease preaching the truth from the pulpit in Bethlehem Chapel, following his conviction that a preacher of the gospel should obey God and continue preaching even when it is forbidden by papal bulls and injunctions, since Christ himself had commanded his disciples to "go into all the world and preach the gospel to all creation" (Mark 16:15).[49] He protested and spoke out against indulgences even as he had done at the university defense. This, of course, resulted in unlawful gatherings and incited the people, and for their violation of this ban, three of Hus's young listeners at Bethlehem Chapel—the journeymen Jan, Martin, and Stašek—were executed on July 11, 1412.[50] In a real sense, it was the "first blood" poured out for the truth of God and the struggle for a church "without spot or wrinkle" in Bohemia.[51]

THE "MOMENT OF TRUTH"

Hus again proved himself to be a faithful and worthy shepherd of the flock of God. The dead martyrs were buried in Bethlehem Chapel and Hus paid homage to their memories in a special sermon delivered on July 24, 1412.[52] Hus's enemies obviously took notice and the papal curia was immediately informed of what had happened in Prague. A papal interdict was declared throughout Prague, a stricter ban against Hus was enacted, and the pope even threatened that he would pronounce the king a heretic as well. For all intents and purposes, Hus was being forced to leave Prague. Before he left, however, he made a bold and courageous move by which he demonstrated as it were the "monumental style" of the later Reformation and proved himself to be a true reformer in every sense of the word. He did not confide in his king, whose capricious and dubious nature he already knew all too well; nor did he trust the pope, who had already persecuted him; neither did he consult a council in whose objectivity he surely did not believe. He appealed to the only ultimate authority which is determinative and decisive for every Christian, even though that authority was not acknowledged or accepted in the canon law. He appealed ultimately to his personal Savior and Judge—the Lord Jesus Christ.[53] It was precisely in this momentous appeal that Hus nullified the false tradition of the church by abolishing the symbiosis of the heritage of ancient Roman legal thought and the Roman Catholic Church; he was returning to the original faith of the New Testament witnesses of the resurrected Messiah. Therefore, we may declare without any hesitation that Jan Hus's appeal on October 18, 1412, effectively possesses the same level of importance for the Reformation on a worldwide scale as Martin Luther's famous nailing of his *95 Theses* on the door of the Castle Church (*Schlosskirche*) in Wittenberg on October 31, 1517.[54] At the very least, the Council of Constance perceived the remarkable meaning of his appeal as well as its significant future ramifications. This is evidenced by the fact that the definitive sentence of degradation against Hus included the following astonishing statement: "He has excessively scandalized Christ's faithful through his obstinacy, disregarding the ecclesiastical intermediaries by having interposed the Lord Jesus Christ as the supreme Judge with a direct appeal."[55]

NOTES

1. See *Knížky proti knězi kuchmistrovi in Magistri Iohannis Hus Opera Omnia*, 4:315.
2. See Václav Novotný, *Kde se narodil Jan Hus? Přednáška proslovená 8. XI. 1923 na schůzi Historického spolku a Společnosti Husova musea v Praze* (V Praze: Dědictví Husovo, 1923); idem, "Kdy se narodil Jan Hus?," *Časopis Národního musea* 89 (1915): 129–146.
3. Kamil Krofta, *Francie a české hnutí náboženské* (Prague: Melantrich, 1935), 29–30.
4. Ján Liguš, "Jan Hus a pražská univerzita: Její teologická a filozofická perspektiva v Husových rektorských promluvách," *Theologická revue* 87/2 (2016): 151–165.

5. For a discussion of the debate, see Vilém Herold, "How Wyclifite Was the Bohemian Reformation," *BRRP* 2 (1998): 25–37.

6. See the following works by Wyclif: *Tractatus de ecclesia*, ed. Johann Loserth (London: Trübner & Co., 1886); *De veritate Sacrae Scripturae*, 3 vols., ed. Rudolf Buddensieg (1905–1907); *Tractatus de potestate papae*. ed. Johann Loserth (London: Trübner & Co., 1907).

7. Iohannis Wyclif, *De eucharistia tractatus maior: Accedit tractatus De eucharistia et poenitentia sive de confessione*, ed. Johann Loserth (London: Trübner & Co., 1892).

8. For example, *Summa de ente, De individuatione temporis, De ideis, De materia et forma, De logica, De universalibus*, etc.

9. For example, see: Gustav Adolf Benrath, "Wyclif und Hus," *Zeitschrift für Theologie und Kirche* 62, no. 2 (1965): 196–216; David R. Holeton, "Wyclif's Bohemian Fate: A Reflection on the Contextualization of Wyclif in Bohemia," *Communion Viatorum* 32 (1989): 209–222; Miloslav Kaňák, "M. Hus a Viklef," in *Husův sborník: Soubor prací k 500. výročí M. Jana Husa*, ed. Rudolf Říčan and Michal Flegl (Prague: Komenského evangelická fakulta bohoslovecká, 1966), 253–264; Thomas Krzenck, *Jan Hus: Theologe, Kirchenreformer, Märtyrer* (Gleichen: Muster-Schmidt Verlag, 2011), 38–55; Gordon Leff, "Hus and Wyclif: A Doctrinal Comparison," *Bulletin of the John Rylands Library* 50, no. 2 (1968): 387–410.

10. Miloslav Kaňák, *Jan Viklef: Život a dílo anglického Husova předchůdce* (Praha: Blahoslav, 1973), 81.

11. Others have claimed that Hus deviated from transubstantiation and taught a doctrine of the eucharist closer to consubstantiation. For various understandings, see: Jan Sedlak, *Jan Hus*, 170–174, 374; Stanislav Sousedík, *Učení o eucharistii v díle M. Jana Husa* (Praha: Vyšehrad, 1998); Alexander Kolesnyk, "Husovo pojetí eucharistie," in *Jan Hus mezi epochami, národy a konfesemi: Sborník z mezinárodního sympozia, konaného 22.–26. září 1993 v Bayreuthu, SRN*, ed. Jan Blahoslav Lášek (Praha: Česká křesťanská akademie, 1995), 118–125; Olivier Marin, "Hus et l'eucharistie: Notes sur la critique hussite de la Stella clericorum," *The Bohemian Reformation and Religious Practice* 3 (2000): 49–61; Ctirad V. Pospíšil, "Jan Hus a transsubstanciace z hlediska dogmatické teologie," *Acta Universitatis Carolinae Theologica* 5/1 (2015): 9–40; Pavel Soukup, *Jan Hus*, 47–49; Paul de Vooght, *Hussiana* (Louvain: Bureaux de la Revue: Publications universitaires de Louvain, 1960), 263–191. For Hus's own perspective, see *De Corpore Christi (tom.' 1 fasc. 2)* in *Mag. Joannis Hus Opera Omnia: Nach neuentdeckten Handschriften*, vol. 1, ed. Václav Flajšhans (Osnabrück: Biblio-Verlag, 1966), 1–31; ibid., *De Sanguine Christi (tom.1 fasc. 3)*, 1–37.

12. Of course, the dating of the transmission of manuscripts is still a matter of scholarly debate. See Anne Hudson, "From Oxford to Prague: The Writings of John Wyclif and His English Followers in Bohemia," *The Slavonic and East European Review* 75, no. 4 (1997): 642–657.

13. *De Corpore Christi (tom. 1 fasc. 2)*, in Flajšhans, *Mag. Joannis Hus Opera Omnia*.

14. His synodal sermons are *Diligite dominum Deum tuum ex toto corde tuo* (*Historia et monumenta*, 2:39–47) and *State succincti lumbos vestros in veritate* (*Historia et monumenta*, 2:47–56).

15. See František Michálek Bartoš, *Literární činnost M. J. Husi* (Praha: České akademie věd a umění, 1948), 117–118. The texts of the songs are found in *Magistri Iohannis Hus Opera Omnia*, 4:348–359, 423, 563–576.

16. *O hřieše* (*MIHOO*, 4:334–337).

17. Ryšánek observed that the impulse for this work was drawn from Wyclif or at the very least was definitely affiliated to his sermons (ibid., 40). See Johann Loserth, ed., *Iohannis Wyclif Sermones, vol. 4: Sermones Miscellanei* (London: Trübner & Co., 1890), 21 (*Sermo 2*), 244–245 (*Sermo 28*), *Sermo 55* (432–433). Ryšánek also noted that Hus's overall structure borrowed from a citation of Pseudo-Chrysostom found in Wyclif's *Opus evangelicum,* since the same phrases "*parva in opere . . . magna in merito*" and "*magna in opere . . . parva in merito*" are virtually repeated in each maxim (ibid., 43). See Johann Loserth, ed., *Iohannis Wyclif, Opus Evangelicum* (London: Trübner & Co., 1895), 122; Cf. *Depositiones testium contra M. J. Hus anno 1414 (Documenta,* 184–185).

18. František J. Ryšánek, "Husových 'Devět kusův zlatých' a jejich rozbor od Petra Chelčického," *Listy filologické* 49 (1922): 43.

19. See ibid., 32–46, 118–134. The adapted texts by Chelčický are found in *Magistri Iohannis Hus Opera Omnia,* 4:548–551. For biographical information on Chelčický, see Murray L. Wagner, *Petr Chelčický: A Radical Separatist in Hussite Bohemia* (Scottsdale: Herald Press, 1983); see also František Michálek Bartoš, *Petr Chelčický: Duchovní otec Jednoty Bratrské* (Prague: Kalich, 1958).

20. The source for this translation of the text which appears here in its entirety is *Devět kusóv zlatých* (*MIHOO,* 4:346). The title is a play on words since *kus* means a piece of some material (e.g., gold) or a particular article of some written work such as a creed or confession. Thus, the title could also be rendered *Nine Pieces of Gold* or *Nine Golden Nuggets of Truth.*

21. See Ecclesiasticus 1:25; Ecclesiastes 4:2; 6:12; 9:4–6; 12:9–11; 3 John 1:2; see also *Explicatio Epistola Beati Joannis Apostoli Tertia* (*Historia et Monumenta,* 2:361): "*Perfecti autem viri justitiam, vocat ingressum, ad significandum, quod homo, quantumcunque sit bonus, semper se debet cogitare ingressum in inchoatione, et nunquam inconsummatione.*"

22. A heller (*haléř*) was the smallest monetary unit and valued at one hundredth of a crown (*koruna*). It derived its name from the imperial mint in Schwäbisch Hall, Germany.

23. Ecclesiasticus 4:1–10; 29:8–13; See Proverbs 3:9–10; Matthew 10:42; 1 Timothy 6:17–19. Cf. *Super Quattuor Sententiarum,* 4.45.6.

24. See Proverbs 2:12; 11:9; Matthew 5:11–12; 1 Peter 2:19; 3:13–17; 4:14. Cf. *Česká nedělní postila* (*MIHOO,* 2:172): "When he says, 'I honor my Father,' he is giving his faithful the instruction that if they suffer reproach for the Lord God, they will greatly honor God their Father, for having been taught by each member of the Holy Trinity, the disciples of Christ know that the more they suffer the more they will

Chapter 2

honor God, and they will receive a greater reward because they have gratefully and humbly suffered reproach."

25. See Ecclesiasticus 3:17–24; Proverbs 15:33; Luke 14:11; James 4:10; 1 Peter 5:6–7. Cf. *Sermones de sanctis*, 24.6.

26. Or *attributes every single thing that he is and has to God*. See Romans 12:1–2; 1 Corinthians 15:10.

27. Hus intended to communicate the figurative meaning of "standing something on its head" as when someone makes a complete nonsense of a particular proposition or when someone irrationally places the effect before the cause. That is, here he wanted the reader to focus on doing what God has commanded (i.e., surrender everything to him and wholeheartedly trust in him) rather than doing something which God has not commanded at all. People consider surrendering all they have to God to be impossible, yet they somehow imagine that they could earn God's favor by walking around the whole world while standing on their heads—which is impossible.

28. See Psalms 56:8; 119:136; 126:5; Ecclesiastes 3:4; Joel 2:12; Matthew 13:36–43; James 4:8–9.

29. Or *commits his whole being*.

30. See Exodus 20:3; Proverbs 3:5–6; Ecclesiasticus 11:21; Matthew 6:19–21.

31. See Proverbs 20:25; Ecclesiastes 4:6; Matthew 5:21–26; 7:1–5; Luke 6:37; 1 Corinthians 13:3. Cf. *Super Quattuor Sententiarum*, 4.20.3. Saint Lawrence (ca. 225–258) was an early Christian martyr who according to legend said, "Look, wretch, you have me well done on one side, turn me over and eat!" (453). See Jacobus de Voragine, *The Golden Legend: Readings on the Saints*, trans. William Granger Ryan (Princeton: Princeton University Press, 2013), 449–460.

32. Proverbs 12:10; See Micah 6:8; Zechariah 7:8–10; Matthew 5:7; Luke 6:36–37; James 2:12–13.

33. See 2 Corinthians 12:1–10.

34. Cf. *Dcerka* (*MIHOO*, 4:184–185).

35. For more details on Zbyněk's character, see František Kavka, "Dvorská komora Karla IV. a její nejvyšší mistr Zbyněk Zajíc z Házmburka," in *Pocta Josefu Petráňovi: Sborník prací z českých dějin k 60. narozeninám prof. dr. Josefa Petráně*, compiled by Zdeněk Beneš, Eduard Maur, and Jaroslav Pánek (Praha: Historický ústav Československé akademie věd, 1991), 23–36.

36. The University of Prague was founded in 1348 by Charles IV in order to promote education in the Czech kingdom. The university (*studium generale*) was divided into four "student nations" (*natio*) which represented the geographical areas from which the students came: Bavarian, Bohemian, Polish, and Saxon. See R.R. Betts, "The University of Prague: 1348," and "The University of Prague: The First Sixty Years," in *Essays in Czech History* (London: Athlone Press, 1969), 1–28; see also Sir Maurice Powicke, "The Three *Studia Generale*," in *Prague Ess*ays. *Presented by a Group of British Historians to the Caroline University of Prague on the Occasion of Its Six-Hundredth Anniversary*, ed. R.W. Seton-Watson (Oxford: Clarendon Press, 1949), 29–52.

37. For a recent comprehensive study, see Martin Nodl, *Dekret kutnohorský* (Praha: Nakladatelství Lidové noviny, 2010).

38. See Michal Svatoš, "Das Kuttenberger Dekret und das Wirken von Magister Jan Hus an der Prager Universität," in *Die Prager Universität Karls IV: Von der europäischen Gründung bis zur nationalen Spaltung* (Potsdam: Deutsches Kulturforum östliches Europa, 2010), 45–70.

39. Leipzig University was founded on December 2, 1409. For more details concerning its founding in relation to the Decree of Kutná Hora, see Enno Bünz, "Die Leipziger Universitätsgründung: Eine Folge des Kuttenberger Dekrets," *Acta Universitatis Carolinae: Historia Universitatis Carolinae Pragensis: Příspěvky k dějinám Univerzity Karlovy* 49, no. 2 (2009): 55–64; see also Ivana Čornejová, "Das Kuttenberger Dekret und die Interpretation der Universitätsautonomie im Wandel der Geschichte," ibid., 257–262; see also Karl Adolf Konstantin Höfler, *Magister Johannes Hus und der Abzug der deutschen Professoren und Studenten aus Prag, 1409* (Prague: Tempský, 1864).

40. For Hus's activities within the administration of the University of Prague, see Blanka Zilynská, "Mistr Jan Hus a pražská univerzita: Několik zamyšlení nad možnostmi poznání jejich vzájemného vztahu a Husovy pedagogické činnosti," *Acta Universitatis Carolinae: Historia Universitatis Carolinae Pragensis: Příspěvky k dějinám Univerzity Karlovy* 58, no. 1 (2018): 209–221.

41. Wyclif's condemned works are mentioned in *Zbynco archiepiscopus Pragensis, mandatum Alexandri V (dd. 20 Dec. 1409) exsequens, libros Wiclef a se condemnatos sibi tradi jubet, eos, qui non obedient, excommunicationis poena se affecturum esse minatur, interdicit, ne verbum dei in locis privatis civitatis Pragensis praedicetur* (*Documenta*, 380): *Dialogus, Trialogus, De incarnatione verbi divini, De corpore Christi, De trinitate, De ideis, De materia et forma, De hypotheticis, De individuatione temporis, De probatione propositionum, De universalibus realibus, Super evangelia sermones per circulum anni, De dominio civili, Decalogus, De simonia, De attributis, De fratribus discolis et malis*. Hus and his friends also mentioned some of these books in the *Notarial Instrument of Appeal on June 25, 1410* (*Korespondence*, 61).

42. *De libris hereticorum legendis* (*MIHOO*, 22:19–37). For an excellent Czech translation and interpretation, see Jan Hus, *Knihy kacířů se mají číst*, trans. Martin Wernisch (Praha: Kalich, 2015).

43. *Letter to Pope John XXIII* (*Korespondence*, 82).

44. *Defensio Libri de Trinitate* (*MIHOO*, 22:46): *"Malum dico conbustionem librorum, que conbustio nullum peccatum de cordibus hominum, nisi condempnatores probaverint, sustulit, sed veritates multas et sentencias pulchras et subtiles in scripto destruxit, et in populo disturbia, invidias, diffamaciones, odia multiplicavit et homicidia, et cristianissimum regnum Bohemie in suspicionem malam regionibus aliis stulte et inprovide deputavit."* The same problems were mentioned in the *Notarial Instrument of Appeal on June 25, 1410 (Korespondence,* 59) and in Hus's *Letter to Pope John XXIII (Korespondence, 82)*. Many of these certain vices are found in 1 Tim 6:4–5.

45. See *Declaratio, qua M. J. Hus aliique magistri universit. Prag. Profitentur, se quosdam libros J. Wiclef publice defensuros esse* (*Documenta*, 399–400).

46. See *Magistri Iohannis Hus Opera Omnia*, 22:8–11, 39–107.

47. *Questio de indulgentis (de cruciata)* in *Corpus Christianorum Continuatio Mediaevalis 205* (Turnhout: Brepols, 2004), 67–155; *Historia et Monumenta,* 1:215–235.

48. *Defensio articulorum Wyclif* (*MIHOO*, 22:141–232).

49. *Responsiones ad Articulos Páleč* (*MIHOO,* 24:270–271); *Letter to Archbishop Zbyněk* (*Korespondence,* 29).

50. For a recent interpretation of those fateful events, see Pavel Soukup, *11.7.1412: poprava tří mládenců: Odpustkové bouře v Praze* (Praha: Havran, 2018).

51. See Ephesians 5:25–27. Hus cited this same passage in his treatise on the church numerous times. See *Tractatus de Ecclesia* (7, 9, 23–24, 34, 36, 45, 47, 170).

52. Václav Novotný, *M. Jan Hus: Život a učení,* 1–2:115–119.

53. For relevant research on Hus's appeal, see František Michálek Bartoš, *Čechy v době Husově (1378–1415)* (Praha: Jan Laichter, 1947), 361–363; Jiří Kejř, "Husovo odvolání ke Kristu," in *Dialog Evropa XXI* 5/2 (1994): 15–18; idem, *Husovo odvolání od soudu papežova k soudu Kristovu* (Ústí nad Labem: Albis International, 1999); idem, *Z počátků české reformace* (Brno: L. Marek, 2006), 100–105; Kybal, *M. Jan Hus: Život a Učení,* 2–1:386–390; Jan Lášek, "Aktuální Husův apel na svědomí," in *Jan Hus: 600 let od smrti,* ed. Marek Loužek (Václav Klaus Institute, 2015), 19–22; Václav Flajšhans, "Husovo odvolání ke Kristu," in *Český časopis historický* 39, no. 2 (1933): 237–258; idem, *Mistr Jan Řečený Hus z Husince* (Prague: Josef R. Vilímek, 1904), 301–303; Amedeo Molnár, "Husovo odvolání ke Kristu," in *Husův sborník: Soubor prací k 500. výročí M. Jana Husa,* ed. Rudolf Říčan and Michal Flegl (Prague: Komenského evangelická fakulta bohoslovecká, 1966), 73–83; Molnár, "Hus et son appel à Jesus Christ," *Communio Viatorum* 8 (1965): 95–104 (previous article in French). Hus's appeal is also briefly discussed in major biographies and monographs. See Thomas A. Fudge, *Jan Hus: Religious Reform and Social Revolution in Bohemia* (London: I. B. Tauris, 2010), 129–132; idem, *The Trial of Jan Hus: Medieval Heresy and Criminal Procedure* (Oxford: Oxford University Press, 2013), 188–214. Matthew Spinka, *John Hus: A Biography* (Princeton: Princeton University Press, 1968), 162–164; idem, *John Hus at the Council of Constance* (New York: Columbia University Press, 1965), 43, 68, 175, 196–197, 227–228, 267, 297; Jan Sedlák, *M. Jan Hus* (Prague: Dědictví sv. Prokopa, 1915), 257–263; Václav Novotný, *M. Jan Hus: Život a Učení,* 1–2:172–176; František Šmahel, *Jan Hus: Život a dílo,* 131–141, 211; David S. Schaff, *John Huss: His Life, Teachings and Death after Five Hundred Years* (New York: Charles Scribner's Sons, 1915), 138–139; Paul de Vooght, *L'hérésie de Jean Huss,* 2nd ed. (Louvain: Publications Universitaires de Louvain, 1975), 1:251–252; Jiří Spěváček, *Václav IV (1361–1419): K předpokladům husitské revoluce* (Praha: Svoboda, 1986), 448–449; Marcela K. Perett, *Preachers, Partisans, and Rebellious Religion: Vernacular Writing and the Hussite Movement* (Philadelphia: University of Pennsylvania Press, 2018), 47–50.

54. This famous event has, of course, been disputed by several historians, with different views ranging from "very unlikely" to even those expressing a "near certainty" that it never happened at all. See, for example, Herman Selderhuis, *Martin Luther: A Spiritual Biography* (Wheaton: Crossway, 2017), 98–104. For an excellent overview of the various sources representing opposing viewpoints, see Volker Leppin and

Timothy J. Wengert, "Sources for and against the Posting of the Ninety-Five Theses," *Lutheran Quarterly* 29 (2015): 373–398.

55. *Sentencia Diffinitiva Contra Iohannem Hus* in *Fontes Rerum Bohemicarum*, 8:503: ". . . *Christi fideles per suam pertinaciam nimium scandalizans, cum appella-cionem ad Dominum Jesum Christum tanquam ad supremum iudicem, omissis mediis, interposuerit . . .*"

3

Appeal to Jesus Christ the Supreme Judge (*Appellacio ad Jesus Christum Supremum Judicem*)

By Jan Hus
Translated from Latin and with explanatory
notes by Angelo Shaun Franklin

APPEAL TO JESUS CHRIST THE SUPREME
JUDGE (OCTOBER 18, 1412)[1]

Since God Almighty himself—one in essence and three in person—is the first
and last "refuge[2] for the oppressed" (Ps 9:9) and the Lord who "guards the
truth forever" (Is 26:2), "executing justice and mercy upon those who willingly suffer injustice" (Ps 146:7), he "is near to all who call upon him in truth"
(Ps 145:18), he "sets the prisoners free" (Ps 146:7), he "fulfills the desire of
those who fear him" (Ps 145:19), and he "preserves all who love him, but
all of the incorrigible sinners he will destroy" (Ps 145:20).[3] And even Christ
Jesus—who is true God and true man—was in dire distress when he was sur-
rounded and besieged by the high priests, scribes, Pharisees, priests, unjust
judges, and hostile witnesses;[4] yet he desired by his most agonizing and most
ignominious death to redeem from eternal damnation those who have been
chosen "before the foundation of the world to be sons of God" (Eph 1:4–5);
in memory of this most excellent example which he has bequeathed to his
followers, they should commit their cause to the omnipotent, omniscient, and
omnibenevolent Lord.[5] Thus, he pleaded, "See, O Lord, my affliction, for the
enemy has arisen" (Lam 1:9), because "You are my helper and my protector"
(Ps 119:114). "The Lord made it known to me and I knew; then you showed
me their deeds. But I was like a gentle lamb led to the slaughter. I did not

23

know it was against me they devised schemes, saying, 'Let us destroy the tree with its fruit,[6] let us cut him off from the land of the living, that his name be remembered no more.' But, O Lord of hosts, who judges righteously, who tests the heart and the mind, let me see your vengeance upon them, for to you have I committed my cause" (Jer 11:18–20), because indeed, "My adversaries have increased" (Ps 3:1), and "they conspire together, saying, 'God has abandoned him. Pursue him and seize him, for there is no one to rescue him'" (Ps 71:10–11). Therefore, "See, O Lord, and consider" (Lam 1:11), because "You are my confidence" (Ps 71:5). "Deliver me from my enemies" (Ps 59:1), for "You have been my God . . . do not desert me, for trouble is near, and no one else can help me" (Ps 22:10–11). "O God, my God, look upon me. Why have you forsaken me?" (Ps 22:1). "My enemies surround me like a pack of dogs; a company of maliciously contriving men has besieged me" (Ps 22:16). "They have spoken against me with deceitful tongues, and they surround me with hateful words; they attack me without cause. In return for my love they accuse me. They repay me evil for good, and hatred for my love" (Ps 109:2–5).

Being supported here[7] by this most holy and most valuable precedent[8] of the Redeemer, I appeal to God: "committing my cause[9] to him" (Job 5:8) against the harsh oppression,[10] the unjust sentence,[11] and the alleged[12] excommunication by the high priests, the scribes, the Pharisees, and the judges "sitting in the seat of Moses" (Matt 23:2)[13] and following in the footsteps of the Savior Jesus Christ in the same way as the holy and bold Patriarch of Constantinople John Chrysostom did against the two synods of bishops and priests.[14] Similarly, when they were unjustly oppressed, the blessed in hope Bishop Andreas of Prague[15] and Bishop Robert of Lincoln[16] humbly and wholesomely[17] appealed against the pope to the supreme and most righteous Judge who is neither intimidated by fear, nor swayed by sentiment,[18] nor influenced by bribes,[19] nor deceived by false witnesses.[20]

Therefore, I desire for all of Christ's faithful ones—and especially the princes, barons, knights, vassals, and all of the other inhabitants of our kingdom of Bohemia to understand and to have compassion on me—as one so grievously oppressed[21] due to the alleged excommunication acquired specifically by its instigator and my adversary, Michael de Causis[22] (formerly the parish priest of the Church of Saint Vojtěch in the New Town of Prague) through a consensual agreement[23] and with the assistance of the canons of the Prague Cathedral. {The excommunication} was issued and solemnly declared[24] by Pietro, the Cardinal-Deacon of the Roman Church Sant'Angelo,[25] who was deputed as my judge by the Roman Pope John XXIII,[26] whereby for nearly two years he was not willing to grant a hearing[27] to my advocates and procurators[28]—which should by no means be denied even to a Jew, a pagan, or a heretic.[29] Nor was he willing to acquiesce to any reasonable excuse[30] for my personal non-appearance.[31] Nor did he gently and kindly receive with a paternal sense of duty the testimony[32] of the University of Prague with the pendent seal and the attestation of the public notaries summonsed to testify to {its authenticity}.[33] As a consequence of which, it is obviously evident that the charge of contumacy[34] has not incurred, since[35] it is not out of contempt[36] but due to reasonable cause[37] that I did not appear at the Roman curia when summonsed. Moreover, {it is} because a treacherous ambush[38] had been plotted and set up against me from every place along the journey,[39] and because I was made cautious and wary by the perilous trials of others—namely, by the robbing and imprisonment of Master Stanislav and Master Štěpán Páleč, who were willing to comply with the citation, yet were robbed of their money and other possessions in Bologna and were disgrace-fully imprisoned and treated as nefarious criminals {there} without {receiv-ing} a full preliminary hearing.[40] Furthermore, {it is} because my procurators were willing to put themselves under obligation at the Roman curia to undergo the punishment of being burned by fire along with anyone wishing to stand against me as the opposing party.[41] And yet even in spite of that, my lawful representative[42] was imprisoned at the aforementioned curia without (as I appraise it) any actual guilt being ascertained.[43] In addition to this, {it is} because by the goodwill[44] of the lord king,[45] I was reconciled with the Archbishop of Prague, Lord Zbyněk of holy memory;[46] the princes and lords and the royal council officially announced[47] between Lord Zbyněk and me and other masters as well,[48]—even appending their seals to it—that the lord archbishop should write to the lord pope that he was unaware of any heretical errors within the kingdom of Bohemia,[49] within the city of Prague, and within the Margraviate of Moravia, that no one had been convicted of heresy,[50] and that he was in full agreement[51] with me and with the other masters. Besides, he also should have written[52] to the apostolic lord[53] in order to absolve[54] me from my personal appearance,[55] citations, and excommunication.

Therefore, since all of the ancient laws,[56] both the divine {laws} of the Old and the New Testament[57] and even those in the canons,[58] contain an existing[59] arrangement[60] which requires for judges to visit the place where the alleged offense[61] has been committed and in that place[62] to investigate the charge[63] concerning the one being accused or defamed from those people who live among {him} and are familiar with the defendant's way of life and who are not malevolent,[64] rivals, or enemies[65] of the one being slandered or accused, but rather honorable men,[66] not slanderers,[67] but those who are fervent and zealous lovers of the law of Jesus Christ[68]—finally, it is required that the person cited or accused have appropriate, safe and secure, and open access to the place and that neither the judge nor the witnesses are his enemies.[69] It is obviously evident that these terms and conditions[70] warranting my appear-ance have not been sufficiently met. Therefore, being in favor of preserving

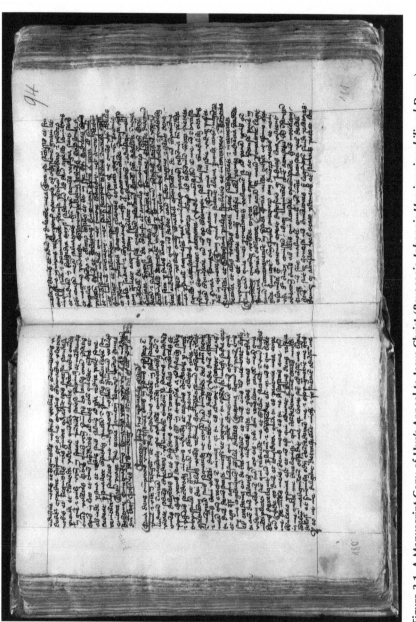

Figure 3.1. A Manuscript Copy of Hus's Appeal to Jesus Christ (*Revocacio Johannis Hus irracionabilis ad Deum*).

Source: State Regional Archives in Třeboň, MS A 16, fol. 93b–94b.

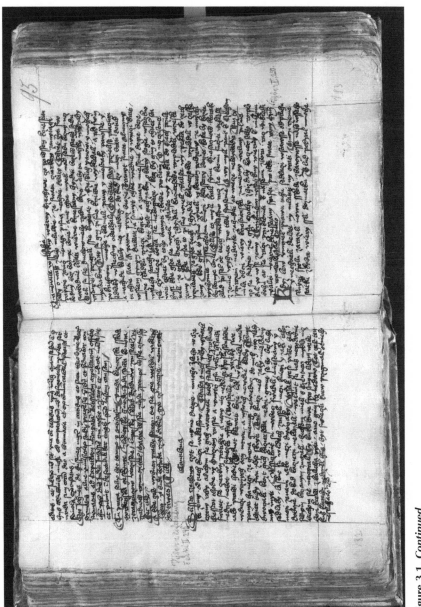

Figure 3.1. *Continued.*

my own life,[71] before the face of God I am exempt[72] from contumacy and also from the alleged and frivolous[73] excommunication.[74]

I—Jan Hus of Husinec, a master of arts and a formed bachelor[75] of sacred theology of the University of Prague, the confirmed[76] priest and preacher at the chapel called Bethlehem—present this appeal to Jesus Christ,[77] the most righteous Judge[78] who unfailingly examines, defends and judges, and discloses and "upholds the just cause" (Ps 9:4) of every man.[79]

NOTES

1. The source texts for this translation are: *Mistra Jana Husi korespondence a dokumenty*, ed. Václav Novotný (Praha: Nákladem komise pro vydávání pramenů náboženského hnutí českého, 1920), 129–133; *Appellatio M. Joannis Hus a sententiis pontificis Romani ad Jesum Christum supremum judicem* in *Documenta Mag. Joannis Hus vitam, doctrinam, causam in constantiensi Concilio actam et controversias de religione in Bohemia annis 1403–1418 motas illustrantia*, ed. František Palacký (Praha: F. Tempský, 1869), 464–466; *Appelatio Joannis Hus à Papa Joan. XXIII. ad Christum* (*Historia et Monumenta*, 1:22–23). As noted by Novotný in *Korespondence* (133), different headings exist within the various manuscripts: *Revocacio Johannis Hus irracionabilis ad Deum* (State Regional Archives Třeboň, MS A 16, fol. 93b–94b); *Protestacio et appellacio Magisti Johannis Hus a concilio Constanciensi ad deum supremum iudicem* (Vienna, Österreichische Nationalbibliothek, cod. 4902, fol. 59r–59v); *Appellacio contra papam perversa* (Library of the Metropolitan Chapter of Prague, MS O 13 fol. 38); *Appellacio Magisti Johannis Hus a papa ad supremum iudicem* (Stará Boleslav, Kapitulni knihovna, MS C 132, fol. 151–153) (National Library of Prague, MS Cim D 79); *Appellacio Jo Husa papa Joanne XXIII ad Christum* (Bautzen, Stadt-und Kreisbibliothek, MS IV 24, fol. 4); *Appellacio M. Jo publica in die Luce* (Bautzen, Stadt-und Kreisbibliothek, MS VIII 7, fol. 98–99). Hus's appeal is also found in two manuscripts which are not included in Novotný's *Korespondence*: Bestand Alte Kapelle 1884, fol. 330ra–330vb, Bischöfliche Zentralbibliothek Regensburg, and MS 2148, fol. 40r–41r, Jagiellonian Library in Kraków. Cf. Václav Flajšhans, *Literární činnost mistra Jana Husi* (Prague: Česká akademie císaře Františka Josefa pro vědy, slovesnost a umění, 1900), 114–115.

Concerning the title of Hus's appeal, it is significant to note that he ascribed the adjective "supreme" to Christ in a variety of contexts. See: *Sermo de Pace* (*MIHOO*, 24:3–4): ". . . *pontifex summus* . . ."; *De Sufficiencia Legis Cristi* (*MIHOO*, 24:57): "*Cristus Iesus est summus anime humane medicus*"; "*Cristus enim est magister optimus et iudex supremus* . . ." (*MIHOO*, 24:57); "*Quaestio de supremo rectore* (*MIHOO*, 19A:171–175): "*supremus rector*"; in *Korespondence: Letter to King Władysław* (86): "*summi regis pacifici*"; *Letter to Archbishop Zbyněk*: ". . . *sed committo ipsam potentissimo, scientissimo et optimo iudici* . . ." (41). Thus, for Hus, all three distinctions of the law—the divine law *(supremus rector)*, the civil law *(summi regis pacifici)*, and the ecclesiastical law *(pontifex summus)*—were interconnected with Christ's threefold ministry as prophet, priest, and king: "... *simul est rex, sacerdos et propheta*" (*De Sufficiencia Legis Cristi* in *MIHOO,* 24:44–45, 52). The appeal itself is a reflection of Hus's pervading conviction that appealing to God rather than to the pope is a proper course of action for true believers. He had earlier appealed directly to God against the ban on preaching in a sermon in June of 1410: "... *ab huiusmodi mandato iniquo appelo primo ad deum, cuius est principaliter dare auctoritatem predicandi . . .*" (Sedlak, *Jan Hus: Appendix XII,* 159–160). Shortly after leaving Prague, within the context of expressing his disdain for the current practices of the priests, Hus began composing *On Simony,* wherein he spoke about believers appealing to God instead of the pope: "And this is how it has happened this year in our own archiepiscopal diocese, since they have first of all made a contribution with the intention of extirpating those who preach the word of God and castigate others for their sins. Second, people have contributed out of fear that they would be strangled, for a fine was imposed on them for entering the church unless they would commit simony by 'depositing money to Simon.' And third, there are those who were moved by the Holy Spirit yet perhaps being afraid that they would also be subjugated and oppressed afterwards, appealed to the pope, because they were unwilling to make a contribution. But it would have been better if they had courageously appealed to God himself and willingly refused to participate in committing simony" (*Knížky o svatokupectví* in *MIHOO,* 4:258).

2. *Refugium.* Or *recourse* as: (1) a source of help in very difficult circumstances (e.g., a court of last resort), (2) the last possible course of action, or (3) the means and actions in solving a legal dispute. *Refugium* has both a personal and a legal connotation, depending on the context. While in prison in Constance, Hus wrote a few letters where he identified his own *refugium* in contrast to the refuge of Pope John XXIII, who was deposed on May 29, 1415. The first letter was written to Václav of Duba and Jan of Chlum (c. June 18–21, 1415) and included a sarcastic rhetorical question concerning certain statements of Stanislav of Znojmo, Štěpán Páleč, and other doctors about the pope: "What, then, are we to make of the viewpoint of the late Master Stanislav of blessed memory (may God have mercy upon him) and of Páleč and his other fellow-teachers which they had reiterated through Stanislav: that the pope is the head of the church, who himself rules it most sufficiently, the heart of the church who himself gives it life, the unfailing fountain full of authority, the channel through which all authority flows to the inferiors, and indeed the unfailing and all-sufficient refuge (*refugium*) of every Christian, to whom every Christian should flee for refuge?" (*Korespondence,* 288). The second letter was written to his friends in Bohemia on June 24, 1415, wherein he critiqued the jurists who called the pope "the all-sufficient refuge (*útočiště*) to whom every Christian should flee . . ." (*Korespondence,* 306). For their view concerning the pope, see Stanislav of Znojmo, *Alma et venerabilis facultas,* Johann Loserth (ed.), in: *Beiträge zur Geschichte der husitischen Bewegung 4. Die Streitschriften und Unionsverhandlungen zwischen den Katholiken und Husiten in den Jahren 1412 und 1413, Archiv für österreichische Geschichte* 75 (1889): 361–413, esp. 370–373: "... *papa, in quo est fontalis et capitalis plenitudo ecclesiastice auctoritatis et potestatis in terris . . . generandi, reformandi, nutriendi, pascendi, perficiendi, protegendi, regendi, conservandi in vita mistica et ecclesiastica universitatem ovium Christi super terram*" (370); Stanislav of Znojmo, *Tractatus de Romana*

Ecclesia (312–322), and Štěpán Páleč, *Antihus* (366–514), in *Miscellanea husitica Ioannis Sedlák*, eds. Jaroslav V. Polc and Stanislav Přibyl (Praha: Karolinum, 1996). Hus critiqued this specific way of thinking of the pope as the most sufficient refuge or recourse in: *Contra Octo Doctores* (22:424); *Tractatus de Ecclesia, 50*: "*. . . nec tercio, ut credatur, quod ad ipsum oportet omnen christianum recurrere*"; 131. In his critical response to Stanislav of Znojmo (*Contra Stanislaum de Znoyma*), Hus referred to each member of the Trinity as *refugium*. First, he wrote: "*Sed benedictus sit Cristus, qui existens solus ecclesie sue certum, securum et indeficiens, sed omnino sufficiens refugium regendi et illuminandi ipsam ecclesiam . . .*" (*MIHOO,* 22:316). Next, he cited Gregory the Great's homily on John 16:23–31 (2.30.8 in *Patrologia Latina*, 76:1225–1226) and affirmed that "*. . . sanctus Spiritus, qui est sancte ecclesie sufficientissimum et securissimum refugium . . .*" (*MIHOO,* 22:337). Then, he reiterated that "*. . . Cristus ut Deus . . . Sanctus ergo Spiritus est ecclesie sancte securissimum refugium principalissimum et humanitas Cristi secundarium in eternum permanens*" (22:339 *et passim*). Only two weeks before his death, Hus wrote a letter to Petr of Mladoňovice and Jan Kardinál of Rejštejn acknowledging the omnipotent God as his refuge while citing Psalm 144:2: "*. . . misericordia mea et refugium meum, susceptor meus et liberator meus et in ipso speravi*" (*Korespondence*, 311).

In the Vulgate, God is also described as being a *refugium* in Psalms 9:10; 17:3; 30:3–4; 31:7; 45:2; 58:17; 70:3; 89:1; 90:2, 9; 93:22; 143:2 (in English Bibles: Psalms 9:9; 18:2; 31:2–4; 32:7; 46:1; 59:16; 71:3; 90:1; 91:2, 9; 94:22; 144:2), Jeremiah 16:19, and 2 Samuel 22:3.

3. Throughout his appeal Hus used the common Latin conjunction *quia* as an explanatory link to provide specific evidence undergirding his defense. In the first section, he used *quia* in a parallel structure to contrast God's righteous character with the deeds of his adversaries:

The righteous character of the supreme judge: (129–130)

(1) "*Quia deus omnipotens, unus in essentia, trinus in personis, oppressorum est primum et ultimum refugium . . .*"

(2) "*. . . quia tu es adiutor et susceptor meus . . .*"

(3) "*. . . quia tu es paciencia mea . . .*"

The wicked deeds of his enemies: (130)

(1) "*. . . quia super me cogitaverunt consilia dicentes: Mittagum lignum in panem eius . . .*"

(2) "*. . . quia multiplicati sunt, qui tribulant me . . .*"

(3) "*. . . quia locuti sunt adversum me lingwa dolosa . . .*"

In the third section, he offered a brief rejoinder consisting of six main reasons (*tum quia; tum eciam, quia; eciam*) to bolster his affirmative defense why he should not be held in contempt of court: (132)

(1) "*. . . tum quia insidie undique posite sunt michi in itinere . . .*"

(2) "*. . . tum quia me aliena fecerunt pericula cautum, magistrorum Stanislai et Stephani Palecz spoliacio et incarceracio, qui in Bononia peccuniis et aliis rebus, volentes citati parere, sunt spoliati et incarcerati turpiter et tractati tamquam malefici, nulla penitus audiencia precedene . . .*"

(3) "... *tum eciam, quia mei procuratores voluerunt se ad penam ignis cum quocumque volente contra me opponere ac partem se ponere in Romana curia obligare* ..."

(4) "... *tum eciam, quia meum procuratorem legittimum incarceraverunt in prefata curia, nulla culpa, ut estimo, exigente* ..."

(5) "... *tum eciam quia concordatus eram sancte memorie cum domino Sbincone Pragensi archiepiscopo per graciam domini regis, inter quem dominum Sbinconem et me aliosque magistris pronuncciaverunt principes et domini consiliumque domini regis et sua apposuerunt sigilla, quod dominus archiepiscopus scriberet domino pape, quod errores hereticos in regno Boemie, in civitate Pragensi et in marchionatu Moravie nescit, quodque nullus de heresi est convictus, et quod mecum et cum aliisque magistris plenarie concordatus.*"

(6) "*Eciam debebat scribere, quod dominus apostolicus me a comparicione, citacionibus et excomunicacione absolveret.*"

4. Persecution of Jesus and his disciples by the "Pharisees" is a dominant theme recounted by Hus frequently throughout his *Treatise on the Church* and in his letters. See *Tractatus de Ecclesia*, 16, 40, 90, 133–139, 159–164, 187–189, 209–210, 226–227, 231, 236; see in his letters *(Korespondence)*: *Letter to Archbishop Zbyněk* (39–41); *Letter to a Certain Nobleman* (69–70); *Letter to the Praguers* (146–151); *Letter to the Praguers* (158–160). See also Hus's preface in *Česká nedělní postila* (*MIHOO*, 2:59–60). Cf. *Enarratio psalmorum (Ps. 109–118)* (*MIHOO*, 17: 311).

5. Cf. *Letter to Jan of Chlum (Korespondence, 246)*: "*Ego commisi me domino Jesu Christo, ut ipse procuret et advocet et iudicet causam meam*"; *Letter to Petr of Mladoňovice (Korespondence, 252–253)*: "*Dominus Jesus meus advocatus sit et procurator, qui vos omnes brevi iudicabit: illi commisi causam meam, sicut et ipse commisit deo patri causam suam.*" On the final day of his life, Hus responded to the council's condemnation of his appeal to God as being an error with the same conviction: "*O domine deus! Ecce jam hoc concilium tua facta et legem damnat ut errorem, qui cum ab inimicis tuis gravatus opprimereris, deo patri tuo justissimo judici causam tuam commisisti, in hoc nobis miseris dans exemplum ut gravati quomodolibet ad te justissimum judicem recurramus, suffragia humiliter postulantes*" (*Relatio de Magistri Joannis Hus* in *Documenta*, 319).

6. The biblical citation here from the Latin Vulgate is literally rendered as "Let us put wood into his bread." This verse was used often in discussions concerning the meanings of the words "body" and "bread" in relation to the Eucharist. See: Tertullian, *Adversus Marcionem*, 3.19; 5.8 (*PL*, 2:347–349; 488–491); Jerome, *Commentariorum In Jeremiam Prophetam* 2.11 (*PL*, 24:756–757). See also Josef Miklík, "*Mittamus lignum in panem eius. Jer. 11, 19,*" *Časopis katolického duchovenstva* 9 (1923): 488–490.

7. Or *resting here and now upon this most holy and most persuasive precedent.*

8. *Exemplum*. Or *useful example. Cf. Tractatus de Ecclesia* (200): "*Et patet quod oportet fidelem Christi discipulum respicere ad primum exemplar Christum* ..." Hus never failed to depict Christ as the highest example in all matters of obedience, and even claimed in a letter written to King Sigismund that it was his commitment to *imitatio Christi* which caused him to be hated by the clergy who opposed the Lord

himself with their sinful lifestyles (*Korespondence*, 198). In his *Exposition of the Decalogue*, he wrote that "Jesus—our Savior, King, and Bishop at the same time—is the primary and the best mirror in which we should seek for wisdom, for each one of his deeds is an instructive lesson for us" (*MIHOO*, 1:221–222; cf. *Zrcadlo hřiešníka větší* in *MIHOO*, 4:132; *Speculum Peccatoris* in *PL*, 40:985); he then quoted Cyprian to support his assertion that following Christ's example takes priority over all other obligations: "For this reason, if Christ alone is to be obeyed, we are not under obligation to pay attention to what anyone else before us thought should be done, but that which Christ, who is superior to all, did first" (*Výklad delší na desatero přikázanie* in *MIHOO*, 1:222). Hus also cited the same passage from Cyprian in *Tractatus de Ecclesia*: "*Si solus Christus audiendus est, non debemus attendere, quid aliquis ante nos faciendum putauerit, sed quid, qui ante omnes est, Christus prior fecerit*" (200). The original source is Cyprian's letter to Cecil and was included in *Decretum* D.8 c.9 (*Corpus Iuris Canonici*, 1:15). See Cyprian, *Epistola 63 (PL*, 4:385).

Hus specifically mentioned two other biblical instances of following Christ's example which were pertinent to his case: (1) "And since our Savior, often withdrawing from being put to death, did not appear before the Sanhedrin and Caiaphas, who was the greatest Jewish high priest at that time, until he was brought there before him" (*Knížky proti knězi kuchmistrovi* in *MIHOO*, 4:322); (2) "The question remains as to the manner in which Christ himself was excused according to the law by not going to Passover due to a presentiment of danger. Here is the answer: because those who experienced malicious and perilous adversity were excused before God for not appearing. By this very same observance, I hope and trust in God that I am excused because I did not appear before the pope in Rome when I was cited" (*Česká nedělní postila* in *MIHOO*, 2:164).

For Hus's constant calls to pursue *imitatio Christi*, see (in *Korespondence*): *Letter to Archbishop Zbyněk* (30); *Letter to a Certain Noblewoman* (70); *Letter to Master Křišťan* (153); *Letter to the Praguers* (223); see also: *Dcerka* (*MIHOO*, 4:177–179); *Tractatus de Ecclesia*, 30, 42, 90–93, 129–130, 222, 227, 253–254; *Česká nedělní postila* (*MIHOO*, 2:86, 149–150, 179, 201–204, 215–216, 245, 270–271, 310–311, 436, 446, 452–453); *Sermo Synodalis Joannis Hus* (*Historia et Monumenta*, 47–56); *Sermones de tempore qui Collecta dicuntur* (*MIHOO*, 7:586–592).

9. *Causa*. Or *present my case to him; make my plea before God. Causa* has multiple meanings including cause, plea, lawsuit, trial, or case (e.g., *causa fidei*). Hus appears here to be linking Job 5:8 ("*Quam ob rem ego deprecabor Dominum, et ad Deum ponam eloquium meum*" or "*Profecto ego requirerem Deum fortem, et in Deo reponerem causam meam*") with Psalm 9:5 ("*Quoniam fecisti iudicium meum et causam meam sedisti super thronum qui iudicas iustitiam*" or "*. . . sedisti super solium iudex iustitiae*") and Jeremiah 20:12 ("*Et tu, Domine exercituum, probator iusti, qui vides renes et cor, videam, quæso, ultionem tuam ex eis: tibi enim revelavi causam meam*"). His understanding of those verses coincides with the *glossa interlinearis* for Psalm 9:5: "*quando iudicatus est Christus . . . quam egit contra impios accusatus*," the *glossa marginalis* from Augustine: "*Vel Christus in fine iuste iudicabit cui Pater omne iudicium dedit*" (adapted from *In Iohannis Evangelium Tractatus* 19.5, *Enarrationes in Psalmos*, 9.6, and *De Civitate Dei*, 20.30), and the glossa marginalis for Jeremiah

20:12: "*Solus Deus est qui probat iustitiam sicut solus est qui cordis videt conscientiam. Unde Hiesus sciens cogitationes hominum non ex profectu tu quidam putant sed natura Deus est. Cui simile non iustificabitur in conspectu tuo omnis vivens. In virtutibus scilicet multo minus ergo in peccatis mortuus.*" Based on the Old Testament verses which he had just cited, Hus was likely drawing from other similar passages which emphasize presenting one's *causa* to God and receiving God's vindication: Psalms 9:5; 16:1; 34:23; 42:1; 73:22; 118:154; 139:13 (in English Bibles: 9:4; 17:1; 35:23; 43:1; 74:22; 119:154; 140:12); Job 13:18; 29:16; 35:13; 36:17; Jeremiah 11:20; 20:12; 50:34; 51:10, 36; Lamentations 3:31–36, 58–59.

10. *Oppressio*. On September 1, 1411, Hus wrote a letter to the cardinals in which he reminded them of their responsibilities related to their position, one of which included coming to the aid of the oppressed: "*Patres in Christo reverendissimi, qui apostolorum typum geritis, cum sitis positi velud precipua luminaria, que debent singula mundi illustrare climata, cumque sitis positi in potestate, ut possitis mundi tollere crimina, de faucibus sathane animas erripere, oppressisque in Christi nomine subvenire*" (*Korespondence*, 101). It is important to note that in his *Letter to the Lords Gathered at the Provincial Court of the Kingdom of Bohemia*, Hus stated that "The oppression and deprivation of the rights of princes, lords, knights, squires, and the community of poor people and summoning them outside of the kingdom are against the law of God, against the constitution of ecclesiastical laws, and against the imperial laws" (*Korespondence*, 157).

The imperial laws to which Hus was referring were probably either: (1) a reference to *privilegia de non evocando* in chapter 8 of the Golden Bull of 1356 issued by Charles IV, where inhabitants of the Kingdom of Bohemia were given immunity from being summonsed outside of the realm to any other tribunal (*De regis Boemie et regnicolarum eius immunitate*). See Wolfgang D. Fritz, ed., *Die Goldene Bulle Kaiser Karls IV. vom Jahre 1356: Text* in *Monumenta Germaniae Historica. Fontes Iuris Germanici in Usum Scholarum Separatim Editi, vol. 11: Bulla Aurea Karoli IV. Imperatoris Anno MCCCLVI Promulgata* (Weimar: H. Böhlau, 1972), 62–64; or (2) a pronouncement of the Provincial Court on June 5, 1411: "*Barones communiter invenerunt, et consilium dominorum exportauerunt Zdeslaus de Siermberg et Boczko de Podiebrad ac Vlricus de Noua domo, quod quicunque o zemskú věc (about provincial issues) aliquem by pohnal (would be cited) ad ius spirituale,* because the lords have established and determined that this should not happen, and the royal officials along with the burgrave of Prague should put an end to it by the means of royal power. And whoever sues another person or whoever is seeking to resolve the claim in court is to have his income and property seized by the royal officials and the burgrave, and they are to be held as long as necessary to compensate for the damages and costs to the one who was summonsed. If the one who prosecutes another person owns nothing, the burgrave of Prague and the royal officials are to arrest and keep him in prison until his royal grace and the lords render their judgment upon the matter. And the same is to be done to the one to whom the case was delegated, since this is what his royal grace and the lords desire—that the provincial issues be judged before them and the spiritual matters be judged before the archbishop, as it has been since ancient times. And this is proclaimed both up in the castle and down in the town. *Act. coram baronibus predictis a. d. MCCCCXI fer. VI quat. temp. Penthecostes.*" This text is cited from Josef Emler, ed., *Reliquiae tabularum terrae regni Bohemiae anno MDXLI igne consuptarum—Pozůstatky desk zemských království českého r. 1541 pohořelých, vol. 2* (Praha: Otto, 1872), 80. There was also a future adjudgment of the Provincial Court on June 9, 1418, where a legal prohibition was pronounced by King Václav IV concerning the citation of inhabitants of Bohemia to foreign ecclesiastical courts. See: Jaromír Čelakovský, *Codex juris municipalis Regni Bohemiae – Sbírka pramenů práva městského království Českého, vol. 1: Privilegia měst pražských. Privilegia civitatum Pragensium* (Praha: Eduard Grégr, 1886), 214–216; Václav Vladivoj Tomek, *Dějepis města Prahy, vol. 3* (W Praze: W komissí u Františka Řiwnáče, 1875), 622–626.

Hus mentioned the impropriety of such citations in: *Conditiones Concordiae* (*Documenta*, 491: first term of agreement); *Výklad delší na desatero přikázanie* (*MIHOO*, 1:203): "There are many priests nowadays . . . who value their own contrived regulations more than God's commandments, especially those such as the jurists, bishops, masters, and Pharisees who wish for their own rules to be followed more diligently than God's commandments. Therefore, when the faithful disciples of Christ violate their orders (which are at times evil), then they unfurl and fling around interdicts, citations, and accusations of heresy"; *Výklad na páteř* (*MIHOO*, 1:374–375); *Česká nedělní postila* (*MIHOO*, 2:67–68); (*MIHOO*, 2:165): "It is not commanded in the law of God for people to be summonsed so far as Rome on account of nothing"; *Letter to His Friends in Constance* (*Korespondence*, 238); *Letter to the Praguers* (*Korespondence*, 149–150). For more on Hus's understanding of oppression, see (in *Korespondence*): *Letter to a Nobleman* (25); *Letter to the Lords and Masters in Prague* (139–141); *Notarial Instrument of Appeal on June 25, 1410* (56–69); *De Ecclesia*, 56, 167, 197; *Documenta*, 177–178. For using appeals as a remedy against oppression, see *Extravagantes Communes* 5.8.1 (*Corpus Iuris Canonici*, 2:1302–1303): ". . . *contra oppressiones debuerat esse appellatio ipsa remedium* . . ."

11. *Sentencia.* When listing the Latin words in parentheses, I have followed Hus's original spelling where the letter *c* is often used instead of the letter *t* in several words, which was common practice for Czech medieval Latin. See Anežka Vidmanová, *Laborintus: Latinská literatura středověkých Čech* (Praha: KLP, 1994), 34.

12. *Pretensa.* In the legal sense of something being under the pretense of appearing true (i.e., alleged) but not actually representing the state of affairs under current consideration (i.e., the *status quo*). For Hus's earlier interpretation of excommunication, see *Super Quattur Sententiarum,* 4.18.4–5. Hus, of course, distinguished between an alleged excommunication issued by ecclesiastical authorities but not according to the truth of the divine law and a legitimate excommunication due to mortal sin. See (in *Korespondence)*: *Letter to Jan Bradatý and the People of Český Krumlov* (89–92); *Letter to the Praguers* (155–156); *Letter to the Lords Gathered at the Provincial Court of the Kingdom of Bohemia* (157–158); *Tractatus de Ecclesia,* 190–191.

13. For Hus's interpretations of this particular verse within the wider Matthean pericope and especially in the context of ecclesiastical authority, see: *Česká nedělní postila* (*MIHOO*, 2:371); *Výklad delší na desatero přikázanie* (*MIHOO*, 1:148–152); *O šesti bludiech* (*MIHOO*, 4:281); *Knížky o svatokupectví* (*MIHOO*, 4:250–251);

Contra Octo Doctores, (*MIHOO*, 22:384–385, 439–446, 486–487); *Responsiones ad Articulos Wyclef* (*MIHOO*, 24:250); *Responsiones ad Articulos Páleč* (*MIHOO*, 24: 277–279, 283); *Letter to Jan Bradatý and the People of Český Krumlov* (*Korespondence*, 89–92); *Tractatus de Ecclesia*, 32, 36, 90–91, 148–150, 155; 159: "*Sedes vero maiestatis Christi intelligitur eterni regni collacio, a quo non poterit removeri, et illa sedes Christi est eius sedes intrinseca. Sedes autem eius extrinseca, in qua quiescit, habitat vel residet per graciam, sunt omnes sancti . . .*"; 160–164, 176–178, 183–193.

14. John Chrysostom (349–407) was tried *in absentia* on multiple false charges and deposed at the Synod of Oak in July 403, then later deposed a second time and exiled on June 24, 404. See Photius I of Constantinople, *Synodus ad Quercum illegitima, contra B. Joannem Chrysostomum* in *Patrologia Graeca*, 103:105–114. See also Karl Joseph von Hefele, *Conciliengeschichte* (Freiburg im Breisgau: Herder, 1856), 2:76–84. See also J. N. D. Kelly, *Golden Mouth: The Story of John Chrysostom—Ascetic, Preacher, Bishop* (Ithaca: Cornell University Press, 1995), 211–227. (The charges against Chrysostom are in Appendix C: 299–301.) In a letter written to his friends in Bohemia on June 24, 1415, Hus reminded them that "Saint John Chrysostom was twice humiliated as a heretic by the ecclesiastical synod; however, the Lord God exposed their lies after the death of Saint John" (*Korespondence*, 305). He also referred to Chrysostom's case in his polemical works: *De Libris Hereticorum Legendis* (*MIHOO*, 22:21, 53); *Contra Iohannem Stokes* (*MIHOO*, 22:64, 70); *Defensio Articulorum Wyclif* (*MIHOO*, 22:152–153, 211–212); and in *Ordo Procedendi* (*Korespondence*, 233). Cf. *De Ecclesia*, 196: "*Sic sanctus Johannes Os Aureum, concilii contra se congregati renuit intrare collegium.*" Chrysostom's case at the synod is recorded in both parts one and two of *Decretum Gratiani.* See (*Decretum* in *Corpus Iuris Canonici*): D.50 c.13 (1:181); C.3 q.5 c.15 (1:519). Hus's other source of knowledge about Chrysostom was *Legenda aurea* by Jacobus de Voragine, which he cited in *Enarratio psalmorum* (Ps. 109–118) (*MIHOO*, 17: 311): "*Et quia persecutio respicit tria, scilicet causam, personam et ecclesiam, ideo fraus persequentium persecutionem ingerit multis modis. Aliquando enim simulant se persequi causam, non personam, sicut fecit Eudoxia imperatrix in persecutione Ioannis Chrysostomi et sicut faciunt continue clerici avari, qui se dicunt esse inimicos causarum, et tamen sunt odiosi inimici personarum.*"

15. Hus was undoubtedly drawing his understanding of Bishop Andreas von Guttenstein (d. 1224) from older Bohemian chronicles and legends. See: Jiří Daňhelka et al., eds., *Staročeská kronika tak řečeného Dalimila: Vydání textu a veškerého textového materiálu* (Praha: Academia, 1988), 2:228–229; *Pokračovatelé Kosmovi*, trans. Karel Hrdina, V. V. Tomek, and Marie Bláhová (Praha: Svoboda, 1974), 94, 97–98; see also the references to *Codex Diplomaticus et Epistolaris Regni Bohemiae* in Jaroslav V. Polc, *Tisíc let pražského biskupství: 973–1973* (Rome: Křesťanská akademie, 1973), 164–186. For the historical context of Andreas and his struggles with the church in Bohemia, see Václav Novotný, *České dějiny, vol. 1, part 3: Čechy královské za Přemysla I. a Václava I* (Praha: Jan Laichter, 1928), 323–325; 449–534. František Pondělík, "Ondřej, biskup pražský," *Časopis katolického duchovenstva* 7 (1862): 481–491; Peter Hilsch, "Der Kampf um die Libertas ecclesiae

im Bistum Prag," in *Bohemia Sacra: Das Christentum in Böhmen 973–1973*, ed. Ferdinand Seibt (Düsseldorf: Schwann, 1974), 295–306; Josef Žemlička, *Přemysl Otakar I. Panovník, stát a česká společnost na prahu vrcholného feudalismu* (Praha: Svoboda, 1990), 225–239; idem, *Počátky Čech královských 1198–1253: Proměna státu a společnosti* (Praha: Lidové noviny, 2002), 118–125; idem, *Století posledních Přemyslovců: Český stát a společnost ve 13. století* (Praha: Panorama, 1986), 45–57; idem, "Spor Přemysla Otakara I. s pražským biskupem Ondřejem," *Československý časopis historický* 29, no. 5 (1981): 704–730; Robert Antonín, "The Bishop Andrew of Prague and Church in Bohemia after the Fourth Lateran Council," *Zeitschrift für Ostmitteleuropa-Forschung* 69, no. 4 (2020): 453–469; idem, "S kým se přel biskup Ondřej?: K meandrům v právní krajině Čech na počátku 13. století na základě 'známého' příběhu," in *Právní kultura středověku (Colloquia mediaevalia Pragensia 17)* (Praha: Filosofia, 2016), 45–63. Kamil Krofta, "Kurie a církevní správa zemí českých v době předhusitské," in *Český časopis historický* 10 (1904): 15–36, 125–152, 249–175, and especially 373–391 ("Proměna staré ústavy církevní ve stol. 13.—Boj biskupa Ondřeje za svobodu církve"); Richard Mahel, "'První česko-moravský konkordát': Fragment Dudíkova textu ke sporu pražského biskupa Ondřeje II. s králem Přemyslem I. (Příspěvek k poznání pozůstalosti II.)," *Archivní sborník* 13 (2007): 18–35. See also Matthew Spinka's brief comment in *The Letters of John Hus*, 217 fn. 18.

Jiří Kejř made specific reference to a manuscript (V E 89, fol. 218r in the National Library of Prague) which includes the following fragment about Andreas: "Concerning Bishop Ondřej of Prague: In the year of our Lord 1207, the priest Ondřej, Bishop of Prague, when he had suffered many adversities and injustices from the Czech lords and yeomen, he then summonsed them to go to Rome. When he was unable to obtain any measure of justice from the pope, he appealed to the highest bishop, Christ the Lord, and asked that after his death the bishops would appear on the third day before Christ—the highest bishop. And that is the way in which it happened, because the bishop Ondřej died eight days later. And when the pope heard the death-knell, he asked for whom it was ringing. They told him that it was for Bishop Ondřej; upon hearing it, he became very grieved and fell ill, and on the third day the pope died. Then the other Roman bishops beheld the miracle, they became greatly afraid, and they have since rendered only righteous verdicts at the papal court" (my translation). The cited text is in Jiří Kejř, *Husovo odvolání od soudu papežova k soudu Kristovu* (Ústí nad Labem: Albis International, 1999), 27.

16. In 1253 Robert Grosseteste (1168–1253) wrote an impassioned letter to Stephen de Montival and Master Innocenzo in order to explain and defend his unwillingness to allow Frederick of Lavagna (the nephew of Pope Innocent IV) to be granted an ecclesiastical position in Lincoln Cathedral. Details are provided in Francis Seymour Stevenson, *Robert Grosseteste, Bishop of Lincoln: A Contribution to the Religious, Political and Intellectual History of the Thirteenth Century* (London: Macmillan & Co., 1899), 306–318. For the actual letter, see *Roberti Grosseteste Episcopi Quondam Lincolniensis Epistolae*, ed. Henry Richards Luard (Cambridge: Cambridge University Press, 2012), 432–437 (*Letter 128*). For an English translation, see *The Letters of Robert Grosseteste, Bishop of Lincoln*, trans. F.A.C. Mantello and Joseph Goering (Toronto: University of Toronto Press, 2010), 441–446.

Although Grosseteste's letter is not to be construed as a legal appeal, Hus certainly found inspiration from the main argument and defense found in it, especially concerning the relation of apostolic commands, papal authority, and personal obedience: "*Apostolica enim mandata non sunt nec possunt esse alia quam Apostolorum doctrinae et Ipsius Domini Jesu Christi, Apostolorum Magistri et Domini, cujus typum et personam maxime gerit in ecclesiastica hierarchia dominus Papa, consona et conformia. Ait enim Ipse Dominus noster Jesus Christus, Qui non est mecum, contra me est; contra Ipsum autem nec est nec esse potest Apostolicae sedis sanctitas divinissima*" (433–434). And in Grosseteste's sermon which Hus cited in *Sermo de Pace*, the Bishop of Lincoln used an intriguing phrase which Hus likely interpreted as a sort of appeal to the divine court of justice: ". . . *Deo et curie celesti* . . ." (*MIHOO*, 24:24).

It is interesting to note that in his letter, Grosseteste restated the papal rescript of Pope Innocent IV which mentioned Canon 37 of the Fourth Lateran Council (1215): *De litteris non impetrandis ultra duas diœtas et sine speciali mandato*. See *Decrees of the Ecumenical Councils*, 2 vols., ed. N.P. Tanner (London: Sheed & Ward, 1990), 1:251–252: "Some people, abusing the favour of the apostolic see, try to obtain letters from it summoning people to distant judges, so that the defendant, wearied by the labour and expense of the action, is forced to give in or to buy off the importunate bringer of the action. A trial should not open the way to injustices that are forbidden by respect for the law. We therefore decree that nobody may be summoned by apostolic letters to a trial that is more than two days' journey outside his diocese, unless the letters were procured with the agreement of both parties or expressly mention this constitution. There are other people who, turning to a new kind of trade, in order to revive complaints that are dormant or to introduce new questions, make up suits for which they procure letters from the apostolic see without authorization from their superiors. They then offer the letters for sale either to the defendant, in return for his not being vexed with trouble and expense on account of them, or to the plaintiff, in order that by means of them he may wear out his adversary with undue distress. Lawsuits should be limited rather than encouraged. We therefore decree by this general constitution that if anyone henceforth presumes to seek apostolic letters on any matter without a special mandate from his superior, then the letters are invalid and he is to be punished as a forger, unless by chance persons are involved for whom a mandate should not in law be demanded."

Hus also referred to Grosseteste's letter, death, or sermon in: *De Ecclesia*, 164–168; *Contra Octo Doctores* (*MIHOO*, 22:375); *Sermo de Pace* (*MIHOO*, 24:23–25); *Responsiones ad Articulos Páleč* (*MIHOO*, 24:283–284); Cf. John Wyclif: *Tractatus de Civili Dominio, vol. 1*, ed. Reginald Lane Poole (London: Trübner & Co., 1885), 384–394; *De Ordine Christiano* in *Opera Minora*, ed. Johann Loserth (London: C.K. Paul & Co., 1913), 138; *Tractatus de Potestate Pape*, ed. Johann Loserth (London: Trübner & Co., 1907), 190: "*Item, simile narrat Cestrensis libro suo VII MCCVI ad papam Innocencium misit Robertus Lynconiensis epistolam invectivam satis et tonantem, pro eo quod ecclesias Anglie indebitis exaccionibus vexare videretur; hac de causa ad curiam vocatus est, et cum ibi molestaretur, appellavit constanter a curia Innocencii ad tribunal Christi; unde contigit, quod Roberto in Anglia obeunte audita est vox in curia pape: Veni miser ad iudicium; repertusque est in crastino papa exanimis, quasi cuspide baculi in latere percussus. Qui licet perspicacius effulserit miraculis, transferri tamen in sanctorum cathalogo a curia non est permissus.*" The original source acknowledged by Wyclif is Ranulf Higden's famous *Polychronicon.* See Joseph Rawson Lumby, ed., *Polychronicon Ranulphi Higden Monachi Cestrensis, vol. 8* (Cambridge: Cambridge University Press, 2012), 238–243. Although in a different context, Workman claimed that Hus would have been introduced to the *Polychronicon* through the works of Wyclif but added that Hus "appears to have actually read this for himself." See Herbert B. Workman and R. Martin Pope, *The Letters of John Hus* (London: Hodder and Stoughton, 1904), 125 fn. 2; 131 fn. 4.

Jan of Jesenice used the same legend in his *Repetitio pro defensione causae Magistri Joannis Hus (Historia et monumenta,* 1:418): "*Et Dominus Robertus Linconiensis Archiepiscopus, a Curia Innocentii quarti appellavit ad tribunal Christi. Unde contigit, ut Anglicanae referunt Historiae, quod Roberto in Anglia obeunte, audita est vox in Curia Papae: Veni miser ad judicium, repertusque est in crastino Papa mortuus, tanquam cuspide baculi in latere percussus.*" The legend of Grosseteste was also included in a short biographical introduction to his works in *Catalogus Scriptorum Ecclesiae.* See S. Harrison Thomson, *The Writings of Robert Grosseteste, Bishop of Lincoln 1235–1253* (Cambridge: Cambridge University Press, 2013), 4–5. His legend was also spread through the *Chronica Majora* written by Matthew of Paris. *Matthæi Parisiensis, Monachi Sancti Albani, Chronica Majora, vol. 5,* ed., Henry Richards Luard (London: Longman & Co., 1880), 389–393, 429–430 *(De ira et impetu quodam domini Papae).* See also *Roberti Lincolniensis episcopi Scriptum Innocentio papae IV a. 1250 apud Lugdunum traditum praecedente nota historica* (Prague, National Library of the Czech Republic, MS IV.G.31 (Y. I. 1. n. 77.), fols. 79b–87a).

17. Or *in an advantageous or beneficial way.*

18. Cf. *Tractatus de Ecclesia,* 82: "*Item deus est, qui non potest ignorare, cui remittendum sit peccatum, et solus ipse est, qui non potest moveri affecione perversa et iudicare iniuste.*"

19. See Deuteronomy 16:19.

20. Cf. Hus's response to the council's condemnation of his appeal to God as being an error in *Mag. Petri de Mladenowic relatio de mag. Joannis Hus causa in Constantiensi concilio acta (Documenta,* 319): "*Et ego dico constanter, quod non est tutior appellatio, quam ad Jesum Christum dominum, qui non flectitur pravo munere, nec fallitur falsa attestatione, unicuique quod meruit tribuendo.*" See also *Letter to the Praguers:* ". . . *qui nec munere, nec timore, nec favore declinatur . . .*" (*Korespondence,* 181).

21. Or *deeply overwhelmed; bearing an excessive and oppressive burden.*

22. Hus also mentioned Michael de Causis when explaining certain events which transpired in his case. See: *Česká nedělní postila (MIHOO,* 2:166): ". . . Michael, parochial priest of Saint Vojtěch in the New Town assumes that all faithful Christians who are in the Kingdom of Bohemia consider me to be a heretic, that I am preaching errors and heresy every day at Bethlehem, and that I am a heretical priest and the chief of heretics"; *Tractatus de Ecclesia,* 231; and in his letters (in *Korespondence*): *Letter to the Lords Gathered at the Provincial Court of the Kingdom of Bohemia* (157); *Letter to Friends in Bohemia on November 4, 1414* (218); *Letter to Friends*

in Bohemia on November 6, 1414 (220); *Letter to Petr of Mladoňovice (*244–245);
Letter to Friends in Constance (261); *Letter to Jan of Chlum* (300). For a helpful
evaluation of his overall involvement in Hus's case, see Thomas A.
Fudge, "The Role
of Michael de Causis in the Prosecution of Jan Hus," in *The Bohemian Reformation
and Religious Practice*, vol. 10, ed. Zdeněk V. David and David R. Holeton (Prague:
Filosofia, 2015), 123–143.

23. *De consensu.*

24. *Fulminatum.* Or *solemnly declared and publicly imposed* by formally denouncing or issuing a formal censure. The distinction is made in *Liber Sextus* 5.11.1
(*Corpus Iuris Canonici* (1093–1094). One gloss adds "*Ec haec est differentia inter
fulminare excommunicationem et proferre*" in *Liber Sextus Decretalium Bonifacii
Papae VIII. Suae integritati una cum Clementinis et Extravagantibus, earumque
Glossis restitutus. Ad exemplar Romanum. Editio ultima* (Paris: 1612), 633. Cf. *Letter
to Master Křišťan of Prachatice* (*Korespondence*, 167).

25. On July 29, 1412, Cardinal Pietro degli Stefaneschi (d. 1417) reaffirmed
the previous interdict of Odo de Colonna (later Pope Martin V) and then issued a
formal order of major excommunication on September 4, 1412. See *Documenta*,
461–464; "Tak zvaná kronika University pražské," ed. Jaroslav Goll, in *Fontes
Rerum Bohemicarum, vol. 5* (Prague: Nákladem nadání Františka Palackého,
1893), 573–574; *Korespondence, 125–128.* For helpful biographical information on
Stefaneschi, see Cristina De Benedictis, "*La Vita del Cardinale Pietro Stefaneschi
di Sebastiano Vannini,*" in *Annali della scuola normale superiore di Pisa: Classe di
lettere e filosofia (series 3, volume 6, fascicle 3)* (Pisa: Scuola Normale Superiore di
Pisa, 1976), 955–1016.

26. A Pisan antipope, Baldassare Cossa (c. 1370–1419) studied law at the University
of Bologna, served as pope from 1410 to 1415 during the Great Western Schism, and
eventually was deposed in the twelfth session at the Council of Constance on May
29, 1415. For details of his life, see Mandell Creighton, *A History of the Papacy
During the Period of the Reformation*, vol. 1 (London: Longmans, Green, and Co.,
1882), 234–299.

27. Hus mentioned this again later in *Tractatus de Ecclesia*, 165: ". . . *anno domini
1410 ad papam Johannem XXIII appellavi, qui per duos annos nullam meis advocatis
et procuratoribus prestitit audienciam, et tempore medio sum amplius processibus
aggravatus.*" Contrary to this claim, Štěpán Páleč denied that Hus's delegates were
not granted a hearing in his treatise against Hus's *Tractatus de Ecclesia*. See Jan
Sedlák, "Pálčův spis proti Husovu traktátu 'de ecclesia,'" in *Miscellanea husitica,*
171. However, Hus affirmed it again before the council on July 6, 1415: ". . . *et
quamvis duplicatos procuratores ad curiam Romanum destinavi, causas de non
comparitione personali rationabiles allegando, numquam tamen potui audientiam
obtinere . . .*" (*Documenta,* 319).

28. *Advocati* and *procuratores.* Only a few months before his death (shortly
after March 5), Hus would refer to Jesus Christ himself as his advocate, procurator,
and judge. See *Letter to Jan of Chlum (Korespondence, 246)*: ". . . *dominus Jesus
Christus, meus procurator et advocatus et iudex graciosissimus . . .*"; *Letter to Petr
of Mladoňovice* (*Korespondence,* 252–253): "*Cogitacionem de obiciendis commisi*

domino deo, ad quem appellavi, quem iudicem, procuratorem et advocatum mihi elegi, coram commissariis expresse dicens: Dominus Jesus meus advocatus sit et procurator, qui vos omnes brevi iudicabit: illi commisi causam meam, sicut et ipse commisit deo patri causam suam." For the important distinction between *advocatus* and *procurator,* see: Donald E. Queller, *The Office of the Ambassador in the Middle Ages* (Princeton: Princeton University Press, 1967), 26–59; James A. Brundage, "The Medieval Advocate's Profession," in *Law and History Review* 6, no. 2 (1988): 439–464; idem, "The Advocates Dilemma: What Can You Tell the Client? A Problem in Legal Ethics," in *Medieval Church Law and the Origins of the Western Legal Tradition: A Tribute to Kenneth Pennington,* ed. Wolfgang P. Müller and Mary E. Sommar (Washington, D.C.: The Catholic University of America Press, 2006), 201–210; Anton-Hermann Chroust, "Legal Profession during the Middle Ages: The Emergence of the English Lawyer Prior to 1400," *Notre Dame Law Review* 31, no. 4 (1956): 537–601, especially 553–559.

29. Cf. *Knížky proti knězi kuchmistrovi* (*MIHOO,* 4:321), where Hus stated that pagans, Jews, heretics, and even the devil himself should be granted a hearing if requested. This medieval depiction of the devil being involved in a lawsuit against humanity was expressed vividly in a work written by renowned Italian jurist Bartolo da Sassoferrato which later became widely known as *Processus Sathanae.* See *Tractatus Quaestionis Ventilatae Coram Domino Jesu Christo. Inter Virginem Mariam ex una parte et diabolum ex alia parte* in *Bartoli a Saxoferrato Omnium Iuris Interpretum Antesignani Consilia, Quaestiones, et Tractatus, vol. 10* (Venice: Luca Antonio Giunta, 1590), 127–129. See also the Latin copy of *Consistorium diaboli* (National Library of the Czech Republic, MS VI.A.5, fol. 1r–5v) as well as the Czech translation *Súd Astarothóv proti lidskému pokolení* (Library of the National Museum in Prague, MS III E 43, fol. 138a–150a). For the references to canon law which served as the basis for Bartolo's composition, see Beatrice Pasciuta, *Il diavolo in Paradiso: Diritto, teologia e letteratura nel Processus Satane* (sec. XIV) (Rome: Viella, 2015), 187–221, especially 188–189. This legal principle of granting a hearing even to the devil himself was also stated succinctly by Guillaume Durand in his procedural treatise *Speculum Iudiciale:* "*Defensio non est excommunicato, nec etiam diabolo, si in iudicio adesset, deneganda . . . Et si proprium non habeat, abbas non privabit eum defensione, quae excommunicato, et etiam diabolo, si in iudicio adesset, non negaretur.*" Cited from *Speculi clarissimi viri Gulielmi Durandi pars tertia et quarta, vna cum Io. Andreae, ac Baldi, Doctorum in vtroque Iure longè praestantißimorum theorematibus, quàm diligentißimè excusa,* vol. 2 (Basel: Frobenius et Episcopius, 1563), 3.1 (p. 40). See also *Wilhelmus Durandus. Speculum iudiciale* (Library of the National Museum in Prague MS XII A 11).

30. *Racionabili excusacioni.* Or *justifiable reason* (i.e., an excusation). Hus's usage of the term was intended to communicate both the act of presenting any reasonable excuse and the actual justification itself, as expressed in similar terms in *Ordo Procedendi* (*Korespondence,* 228–230).

31. In the legal sense of a failure to appear in person at court. Hus mentioned in a letter to the Carthusian monks in Dolany that he was advised not to appear by both his own procurators and those from the other party. See *Letter to the Carthusian*

Monks (*Korespondence,* 121): "*Quod autem citatus ad curiam non parui, multe cause sunt. Volebam enim in principio citatus exire, sed procuratores tam mei quam partis adverse scripserunt michi, quod non parerem, quia gratis vitam consumerem.*" Cf. *Decretum* C.3 q.9 cc.2–6 (*Corpus Iuris Canonici,* 1:530).

32. *Testimonia.* Or *deposition* (i.e., a formal statement given by witnesses to be used as evidence).

33. Or *called forth as witnesses.*

34. *Contumacia.* Cf. *Ordo Procedendi* (*Korespondence,* 230–231) where the canon law concerning contumacy was cited: *Liber Sextus* 5.2.7 (*Corpus Iuris Canonici,* 2:1071); For Hus's earlier interpretation of contumacy, see *Super Quattur Sententiarum,* 4:18.5: "*Ex isto patet, quod notorium et grave delictum oportet esse, pro quo sit excommunicacio inferenda. Unde Magister dicit in litera, quod »emendacionem manifesti delicti et satisfacere vilipendens« excommunicacione ligatur, et Archidiaconus in 6° de excepcionibus ca° 'Paria,' super verbo contumacie declarat, quod maior excommunicacio propter solam contumaciam est ferenda, et fundat hoc lege multiplici.*" Hus's most precise definition of heresy in relation to contumacy is found in *Super Quattur Sententiarum,* 4.13.5. Following Augustine's *De Utilitate Credendi* 1.30–31 (*PL,* 42:86–88), Hus also offered similar definitions of heresy in *De Libris Hereticorum Legendis* (*MIHOO,* 22:35–37), *Contra Iohannem Stokes* (*MIHOO,* 22:64–67), *Knížky proti knězi kuchmistrovi* (*MIHOO,* 4:313–314), and *Knížky o svatokupectví* (*MIHOO,* 4:192–193): "Heresy is an obstinate adherence to an error contrary to the Holy Scripture . . . Therefore, every faithful Christian should resolve in his mind that he is not willing to adhere to anything at all which is contrary to the Holy Scripture . . . thus, it is pertinaciously continuing in error which constitutes heresy. And considering that some adhere to an error against the Holy Scripture in deed, while others do so in word, not only is the one who would adhere to an error in word a heretic, but also even the one who adheres to it in deed . . . Furthermore, you should know from these words that if the Holy Scriptures did not exist, then there would be no heresy, just as there would be no night unless it were preceded by the day." See also *Responsiones ad Deposiciones Testium* (24:239). For the definition of heresy and heretics according to canon law, see *Decretum* C.24 q.3 cc.26–39 (*Corpus Iuris Canonici,* 1:997–1006).

35. Or *whereas; taking into consideration the fact that . . .*

36. *Ex contemptu.*

37. *Ex causis racionabilibus.*

38. Or *they set up traps and were lying in wait to attack.* Cf. Jeremiah 9:8 in the Vulgate: "*Sagitta vulnerans lingua eorum dolum locuta est in ore suo pacem cum amico suo loquitur et occulte ponit ei insidias.*"

39. Cf. *Česká nedělní postila* (*MIHOO,* 2:166): "And finally, I did not appear at the papal court so that I would not consequently lose my life for nothing; for every place was full of enemies (even Czechs and Germans) who were intent on my death—the pope as judge and also the cardinals—all are my enemies, as I have found in their letters, who write that I am heretic without ever having even heard me or seen me at all. For even the pope and the cardinals are implicated when censured against pride, against avarice, and especially against simony. And especially because I found false

witnesses and their false testimony by which they incriminated me in Prague by sending their witnesses to Rome."

40. *Audiencia.* Charges had been laid against Stanislav of Znojmo claiming that he espoused the heresy of remanence (expressed particularly in his treatise *De Corpore Christi)*, even though he had made significant changes to the actual text to align it with the doctrine of transubstantiation. Later charges of heresy were extended to Štěpán Páleč as well. In 1408 both were summonsed to the papal court by Pope Gregory XII to respond to the charges of Wycliffite heresy, but while they were on their journey to Rome, they were imprisoned in Bologna for almost a year by the order of Cardinal Baldassare Cossa (the future antipope John XXIII) under suspicion of maintaining a political mission. For more details on the charges of heresy and the papal decree, see František M. Bartoš, "V předvečer Kutnohorského dekretu," *Časopis Národního Musea* 102 (1928): 92–123.

Hus explained this scenario involving these masters in more detail in *Knížky proti knězi kuchmistrovi (MIHOO,* 4:320–322), and he later used their experiences in Rome as an explanation for their "change of heart" against the truth, against their own conscience, and against him personally. See *Letter to Jan Kardinál of Rejštejn*: ". . . duos aversos a veritate . . . Cognovi enim ambos, quod prius vere fatebantur secundum legem Christi veritatem, sed timore percussi in adulacionem pape et in mendacium sunt conversi . . . Quomodo ergo possum eis credere, quod non libenter facerent contra conscienciam?"* (*Korespondence,* 170–171). And in his *Public Instrument Against the Theological Faculty,* he wrote that both of them had previously adhered to and defended many of the forty-five articles of Wyclif until they surrendered to worldly fear (*Korespondence,* 162).

41. For the identification of Hus's legal representatives, see: *Ordo Procedendi (Korespondence,* 228); *Documenta,* 190; *Contra Stephanum Palecz (MIHOO,* 22:237 fn. 23). This is a reference to retaliatory punishment *(pena talionis)* which Hus wrote about earlier in his letter to Pope John XXIII on September 1, 1411. *"Nam offerebam me ad respondendum omnibus et singulis obiciendis eciam referens me ad totum auditorium, quod, si quid contra me deduceretur, vellem eciam ignis incendio, nisi cederem, emendari. Paratusque sum hodie coram universitate Pragensi et omnium prelatorum multitudine de obiciendis, si quis ex adverso consurget, reddere racionem. Sed nec usque huc quisquam wlt se ponere partem, qui se ad pene talionem astringeret iuxta canonicas sancciones"* (*Korespondence,* 98). He also mentioned it in the third term of agreement in *Conditiones Concordiae* (*Documenta,* 491–192): *". . . et ibi quicunque voluerit sibi errorem vel haeresim objicere, objiciat, obligando se ad poenam talionis, si non probaverit"* (491). Cf. *Decretum* C.2 q.2 c.3 (*Corpus Iuris Canonici,* 1:450): *"Nullus episcoporum, dum suis fuerit rebus expoliatus, debet accusari, priusquam omnia, que ei ablata sunt quocumque ingenio, legibus redintegrentur ita ut omnes possessiones, atque omnes fructus ante acceptam accusationem primates et sinodus episcopo, de quo agitur, funditus restituant."* See also *Liber Extra* 5.1.1–16, 24 (*Corpus Iuris Canonici,* 2:733–738, 745–747).

Later in December 1412 he wrote a letter in Czech to the Bohemian Provincial Court expressing the same sentiments: "I did not face the papal court, because my appointed delegates were thrown into prison without being guilty, though they were committed to undergoing death by fire versus anyone who would bring any charge of error against me. As well, I did not appear in person because traps had been set for me everywhere so that I would not be able to return to Bohemia" (*Korespondence*, 158). Hus later proclaimed his own willingness on numerous occasions to hear any charge against him and to answer it in the presence of masters, priests, officials, prelates, and lords on the condition that the accuser would stand forth. See, for example (in *Korespondence*): *Letter to Pope John XXIII* (98); *Letter to the Lords Gathered at the Provincial Court of the Kingdom of Bohemia* (157–158); *Public Notice on August 26, 1414* (192–195: in Latin, Czech, and German): "I, Master Jan of Husinec, publicly announce to the entire kingdom of Bohemia that I am ready and willing to appear before the court of the priest archbishop at the forthcoming synod of the clergy concerning all of the accusations of which I am falsely accused and charged . . . Therefore, you good people who love justice, prudently consider whether or not I am making any improper demand in this public notice which is contrary to divine or human rights. If I am not hereby granted a hearing, then let it be solemnly known and announced to the entire kingdom of Bohemia that it will occur through no fault of my own" (194: translated from the Czech version).

In *Tractatus de Ecclesia* (196), Hus also cited Pope Fabian's judgment concerning *pena talionis* in *Decretum* C. 3 q. 6 c. 1 (*Corpus Iuris Canonici*, 1:519); cf. *Contra Stephanum Palecz* (*MIHOO*, 22:237): "*Secundo, ostendetur fictori, quod nostra pars, preter ipsos duos aversos, fuit in curia Romana per aliquot annos, per se et per procuratores et per advocatos postulans iusticiam et offerens se eciam ad penam ignis, quod nullus heresim de aliquo nostrum poterit comprobare.*"; *Knížky proti knězi kuchmistrovi* (*MIHOO*, 4:321).

42. *Legittimus procurator.* Or *legitimate attorney (i.e., in accordance with the law)*.

43. *Nulla culpa.* Or *without examining, weighing, or discerning any actual guilt*. This is an affirmation of Hus's conviction of the legal principle of *nulla poena sine culpa*, which he expressed in: *Výklad delší na desatero přikázanie* (*MIHOO*, 1:239); *Tractatus de Ecclesia*, 213; *Letter to an Unnamed Prelate of the Council* (*Korespondence*, 282–283); *Relatio de Magistri Joannis Hus*: ". . . *nec denegare petenti rite justitiam, nec potest hominem sua lege supposita sin demerito condemnare* . . ." (*Documenta*, 295). This principle was stated by Boniface VIII in Rule 9 of *De Regulis Iuris* in *Liber Sextus* 5.12.5 (*Corpus Iuris Canonici*, 2:1122): "*Sine culpa, nisi subsit causa, non est aliquis puniendus.*" *Liber Extra* 2.23.16 (2:358–359) also seems to mention the notion of presumption of guilt related to due process.

Hus referred to the events involving his legal representatives in: *Contra Octo Doctores* (*MIHOO*, 22:446): ". . . *post incarceracionem meorum procuratorum* . . ."; *Česká nedělní postila* (*MIHOO*, 2:164–165).

According to Kejř (*Husitský právník M. Jan z Jesenice,* 60–61), Jesenice was imprisoned probably sometime around March 1412, although he later escaped and went to Bologna before returning to Prague. In *Tractatus de Ecclesia* (209–212), Hus claimed that Jesenice had shown that the legal trial fulminated against him was aberrant and worthless, which was probably a reference to the *Repetitio* presented at the disputation at the University of Prague on December 18, 1412. For more details surrounding Jesenice's arguments, see Václav Novotný, *M. Jan Hus: Život a učení* (Praha: Jan Laichter, 1921), 1–2:222–231. For the standard monograph on Jesenice, see Jiří Kejř, *Husitský právník M. Jan z Jesenice* (Praha: Československé akademie věd, 1965). For the actual text of Jesenice's defense, see *Repetitio Magistri Joannis Jessinetz, Doctoris Juris Canonici, pro defensione causae Magistri Joannis Hus* (*Historia et monumenta*, 1:408–419). Unfortunately, Jesenice's *Summaria de Iusticia et Nullitate Sentenciarum Contra Hus* is no longer extant (as noted by Kejř in *Husitský právník M. Jan z Jesenice*, 163).

44. Or *favorable kindness and friendship.*

45. Václav IV (1361–1419), who reigned as King of Bohemia from 1378 to 1419. On February 2, 1412, he convened a synod at the palace of the archbishops (originally planned to be held at Český Brod) in the attempt to reconcile the opposing parties. For Hus's personal explanation of the king's role throughout his case, see (in *Korespondence*): *Letter to Pope John XXIII* (98); *Letter to the Lords Gathered at the Provincial Court of the Kingdom of Bohemia* (157–158); *Ordo Procedendi* (227–228, 231); *Letter to King Václav, Queen Žofie, and Their Court* (195–196); *Letter to Friends in Constance* (293).

46. Cf. The first term of agreement in *Conditiones Concordiae* (*Documenta*, 491). Zbyněk Zajíc of Hazmburk died on September 28, 1411, in Pozsony, the Kingdom of Hungary (present-day Bratislava, Slovakia).

47. *Pronuncciaverunt.* In the legal sense of "pronouncing" a judgment or decision. In canon law this term is normally used with the same meaning in reference to both ecclesiastical laws and secular laws. See (*Decretum* in *Corpus Iuris Canonici*): C.2 q.3 d.p.c.7 (1:452–453); C.2 q.3 a.p.c.8 (1:453–454); C.2 q.6 c.29 (1:475–477); C.2 q.6 c.41 (1:481–483); C.3 q.7 c.4 (1:527); C.6 q.4 c.1 (1:563). Based on his numerous future references to this event, it seems that Hus viewed the arbitration as an exoneration or at least some kind of partial legal settlement of his dispute.

48. Hus also mentioned this reconciliation in his *Letter to Pope John XXIII* (*Korespondence*, 98) and in his *Letter to the Lords Gathered at the Provincial Court of the Kingdom of Bohemia* (*Korespondence*, 157). For details of that particular judicial discretion on July 6, 1411, see *Arbitrium Arbitrorum in Causa M. Joannis Hus atque Archiepiscopi et Cleri Pragensis Allegatorum* (*Documenta*, 437–439).

49. This fact was mentioned by Hus and his supporters in the *Notarial Instrument of Appeal on June 25, 1410* (*Korespondence*, 63): "*Nam ipse dominus Sbinco prefatus in sinodo generali . . . neminem erroneum vel hereticum reperit, nec potuit reperire.*" Cf. Hus's second response to the second article in *Responsio M. Hus ad Articulos* (*Documenta*, 161–162); see also *Ordo Procedendi* (*Korespondence*, 230). Jan of Jesenice also mentioned this fact in his *Repetitio pro defensione causae Magistri Joannis Hus*: "*Nescio causam, rationem vel obstaculum, cum in Regno Bohemiae nullus fidei erroneus, vel Haereticus hucusque sit compertus vel convictus, prout pronunciatio Principum et Baronum inter Dominum Sbynkonem pie memoriae Archiepiscopum olim Pragensem, et partem adversam, approbat*" (*Historia et monumenta*, 1:419).

50. In 1410 Hus wrote in the introduction of his polemical tractate defending Wyclif's *De Trinitate* that no true Czech had been condemned for heresy up until that time. See *Defensio Libri de Trinitate* (*MIHOO*, 22:41): "*Ceterum ad fulciendum*

famam laudabilem cristianissimi regni Bohemie, que semper retroactis temporibus firmitate orthodoxe fidei in veris Bohemis germinavit continue ad tantum, quod numquam verus Bohemus pertinax hereticus est repertus." See also the later testimonies of Hus's orthodoxy by Bishop Mikuláš of Nezero (*Mag. Petri de Mladenovic Relatio de Mag. Joannis Hus causa in Constantiensl concilio acta* in *Documenta*, 239–243, 266–272) and Archbishop Konrád and others (*Documenta*, 531–537).

51. *Plenarie concordatus.* Or *full reconciliation.* Cf. *Ordo Procedendi* (*Korespondence*, 231–232): "*Item prefatus Magister Johannes Hus, concordatus fuit plenarie per dictos principes et regis consilium cum prefato domino Sbincone, qui ex edicto ipsius consilii et dictorum principum, debuit literas suas domino pape scribere, quarum forma habetur sive copia, in qua confitetur prefatus dominus Sbinco, quod nullam heresim vel errorem aliquem scit de prefato Magistro Johanne Hus, et quod petit, ut dominus papa det relaxacionem citacionis personalis et absolucionem Magistro Johanni; sed morte cita preventus, legacionem huiusmodi non perfecit.*"

52. Cf. *Exemplar literarum, quas Zbynco archiepiscopus Pragensis ex arbitrio consiliariorum regis Wenceslai ad Romanum pontificem dare debebat, (nec tamen dedit)* (*Documenta*, 441–442).

53. *Dominus apostolicus.* This is an epithet or designation which was ascribed to popes (mainly between the sixth and eleventh centuries), since the pope is a human ruler or lord (*dominus*) and since he occupies the apostolic see (*apostolicus*). For its particular usage during the Middle Ages, see: Michael Wilks, "The *Apostolicus* and the Bishop of Rome, I," *The Journal of Theological Studies NS* 13 (1962): 290–317; idem, "The *Apostolicus* and the Bishop of Rome, II," *The Journal of Theological Studies NS* 14 (1963): 311–354; idem, "Legislator divinus-humanus: The Medieval Pope as Sovereign," in Pierre Guichard et al., *Papauté, monachisme et théories politiques, vol. 1: Le pouvoir et l'institution ecclésiale* (Lyon: Presses universitaires de Lyon, 1994), 181–195; idem, *The Problem of Sovereignty in the Later Middle Ages: The Papal Monarchy with Augustinus Triumphus and the Publicists* (Cambridge: Cambridge University Press, 1963), 254–410.

54. Of course, the important distinction between jurisdictional absolution and sacramental absolution needs to be kept in mind here. Hus explained this distinction in: *Super Quattur Sententiarum*, 4.18.1–5; *Tractatus de Ecclesia*, 73–89; *Quaestio de Indulgentiis* (*MIHOO*, 19A:76–77). See also *Repetitio pro defensione causae Magistri Joannis Hus* (*Historia et Monumenta*, 1:412): "*Et excommunicare cum non sit Sacramentum, nec ordinis, sed jurisdictionis, non solum Sacerdotes, sed et Laici virtute Ecclesiae possunt excommunicare et absolvere.*"

55. Hus later questioned the overall advantage or benefit of his appearance at the Roman curia in *Tractatus de Ecclesia*, 196: "*Et quis fructus comparicionis?*" See also *Česká nedělní postila* (*MIHOO*, 2:164–165).

56. *Iurium antiquorum.* Or *rights of ancient legal systems.* This is probably a reference to particular ancient Roman laws from the jurisprudence during the period of *ius antiquum*, especially those derived from *Corpus Iuris Civilis* and incorporated into canon law. In this instance, he was likely referring to (*Corpus Iuris Canonici*): *Decretum* C.3 q.5 c.15 (1:518); *Decretum* C.3 q.6 c.16 (1:523–524); see also: *De Sufficiencia Legis Cristi* (*MIHOO*, 53: from *Codex Justinianus* 1.1.8); *Responsiones*

ad Articulos Páleč (*MIHOO*, 24:268; *Decretum* D.96 c.14). (Recall footnote 10 on the imperial laws concerning being summonsed outside of Bohemia in reference to ecclesiastical cases; cf. *Korespondence, 157.*)

In his defense of the third article of Wyclif, Hus differentiated between divine, canon, and civil law in relation to rights and justice. See *Defensio Articulorum Wyclif (MIHOO,* 22:206*)*: ". . . *quod aliquod est ius divinum, aliquod est ius canonicum et aliquod ius civile.*" In the *Notarial Instrument of Appeal* to Pope John XXIII against the burning of Wyclif's books, specific reference was made to natural reason (*racio naturalis*), the provisions of common law (*iuris comunis provisio*), the sacred canons (*sacri canones*), the rules of natural law (*leges iuris naturalis*), and the equity of reason (i.e., natural equity) (*racionis equitate*) (*Korespondence,* 57–58). For the concept of *rationis equitate* found in canon law, see *Corpus Iuris Canonici*: D.2 c.5 (1:4); D.40 c.10 (1:164–165); C.4 q.4 c.1 (1:541); C.25 q.1 d.p.c.16 (1010–1012); C.25 q.2 d.p.c.21 (1:1017–1018).

Hus mentioned some of these same distinctions of law in: *Leccionarium Bipartitum Pars Hiemalis* (*MIHOO,* 9: 339); *Quaestio de lege divina* (*MIHOO,* 19A:17): "*Triplex est lex: divina, naturalis et humana seu positive*"; *Quaestio de supremo rectore* (*MIHOO,* 19A:169–175); *Responsiones ad Desposiciones Testium* (*MIHOO,* 24:217–218): ". . . *Boemi in regno Boemie secundum leges, ymmo secundum legem Dei et secundum instinctum naturalem . . .*"; *De Sufficiencia Legis Cristi* (*MIHOO,* 24:41, 61): "*iudicio racionis . . . iura humana . . . iura divino . . . ius canonicum . . . ius civile . . . ius divinum . . . ius evangelicum*"; and in *Tractatus de Ecclesia,* where he thrice distinguished the threefold nature of obedience: (1) ". . . *maioris ad minorem . . . equalis ad equalem . . . minoris ad maiorem . . .*" (152); (2) ". . . *sufficiens, perfecta, indiscreta . . .*" (153); (3) ". . . *spiritualis, secularis et ecclesiastica . . .*" (156). Citing Thomas Aquinas (*Summa Theologiae,* 2–2.104.5), Hus related sufficient obedience with respect to natural law and positive law: "*Sufficiens obediencia est illa, que in hiis tantum obedit ad que obligatur de iure naturali atque positivo fines suos non excedens*" (153); and thus he affirmed that neither the pope nor the emperor possessed the right to act contrary to natural law: "*quod papa . . . potest dispensare contra Apostolum, contra iuramentum, contra votum, contra ius naturale, et quod nemo habet sibi dicere: 'Cur hoc facis?'*" (142); "*Nec defensionis, que a iure naturali provenit, facultas adimi debet, cum illa eciam imperatori tollere non licet, que iuris naturalis existunt*" (195). "*Utrum aliquid lege divina prohibitum possit in aliquo casu homini esse licitum*" (*MIHOO,* 19A:19). This understanding of obedience was based on Hus's association of the *lege nature* with the Golden Rule (Matthew 7:12) in *Super Quattur Sententiarum,* 4.21.6. See *Decretum* D.1 d.a.c.1 (*Corpus Iuris Canonici,* 1:1): "*Humanum genus duobus regitur, naturali videlicet iure et moribus. Ius naturae est, quod in lege et evangelio continetur, quo quisque iubetur alii facere, quod sibi vult fieri, et prohibetur alii inferre, quod sibi nolit fieri.*" Thus, Hus's overall understanding of the divine law in terms of obedience and justice is succinctly summarized in his conclusion of *Quaestio de lege divina* (*MIHOO,* 19A:17–22): "*Omnes leges humane debent regulari lege divina . . . Omnis lex dissonans legi divine est prohibenda*" (22).

For other important disputations of that time concerning the law of God in relation to civil law, see the *quodlibet* of Nicolaus Cacabus from 1411 (*Utrum expedicius sit comunitatem regi secundum legem Dei a iudicibus quam secundum legem civilem a regibus vel e contra*) and the *quodlibet* of Iohannes de Werona (*Utrum lex pure humana canonica legi ewangelice in aliquo quoad direccionem hominis sit adversa*) in Bohumil Ryba, ed., *Iohannis Hus Quodlibet: Disputationis de Quolibet Pragae in Facultate artium mense Ianuario Anni 1411 habitae enchiridion* (Prague: Orbis, 1948), 40–41, 171.

57. *Cf. Tractatus de Ecclesia* (136–137, 192–208), where Hus cited either directly or indirectly several biblical verses from both the Old and the New Testaments to explain his underlying rationale concerning obedience (both in general and particularly in relation to the circumstance of *place*): Genesis 2:15–17; 18:16, 21; Isaiah 1:16–18; Daniel 11:31–34; Micah 6:3; Matthew 7:12; 9:35–36; 10:16–17; 16:21–23; 18:15; 23:2–3; 24:15, 23, 25–26; 25:[31–46]; Mark 13:14; Luke 6:42; 10:16; 19:10; John 5:39; 7:47–51; 8:7; Acts 5:29; 13:27–28; 1 Corinthians 16:14; Colossians 3:17; Galatians 2:11–14; 1 Timothy 6:17.

58. *Cf. (Corpus Iuris Canonici): Decretum* C.3 q.5 c.15 (1:518); *Decretum* C.3 q.6 d.a.c.1 (1:519); *Decretum* C.3 q.6 c.16 (1:523–524); *Decretum* C.3 q.9 c.20 (1:533:534); *Liber Extra* 2.6.4 (2:261–263); *Liber Extra* 2.28.47 (2:428); *Liber Extra* 5.1.24 (*Corpus Iuris Canonici,* 2:745–747). See also *Knížky proti knězi kuchmistrovi* (*MIHOO,* 4:321–322): ". . . having the Holy Scripture and even ecclesiastical and papal laws which protect a person from appearing before a judge . . ."; see also Canon 8 of the Fourth Lateran Council (*De inquisitionibus*), which sets forth the procedures for making inquiries.

For Hus's understanding of canon law, law in general, and his legal sources, see Jiří Kejř, "Johannes Hus als Rechtsdenker," in *Jan Hus—Zwischen Zeiten, Völkern, Konfessionen: Vorträge des internationalen Symposions in Bayreuth vom 22. bis 26. September 1993*, Ferdinand Seibt et al., eds. (Munich: R. Oldenbourg, 1997), 213–226; idem, *Z počátků české reformace* (Brno: L. Marek, 2006), 85–94, 132–145; idem, "M. Jan Hus o právnictví," *Právněhistorické studie* 1 (1955):83–100; idem, "Právnické otázky Husova quodlibetu," *Právněhistorické studie* 5 (1959): 33–47; idem, *Stát, církev a společnost v disputacích na pražské universitě v době Husově a husitské* (Praha: ČSAV, 1964), 3–15; idem, *Husovo odvolání od soudu papežova k soudu Kristovu* (Ústí nad Labem: Albis International, 1999); *Žil jsem ve středověku* (Praha: Academia, 2012), 212–213.

59. In the legal sense of something "being on record and serving as a directive." This word is important since canon law stated that even popes should not exercise arbitrary power over existing laws. See in *Decretum* in *Corpus Iuris Canonici*: D.25 q.1 c.16 (1:1010–1012); D.25 q.2 cc.3–4 (1:1013); D.25 q.2 cc.7–9 (1:1013–1014); D.25 q.2 c.21 (1:1017–1018). Hus explained this idea in more detail within the context of obedience to God in his *Letter to Jan Bradatý and the People of Český Krumlov* (89–92), where he quoted several verses from Scripture and then supported his argument by citing *Decretum Gratiani*: D.95 c.6 (1:333–334); C.11 q.3 c.93 (1:669); C.11 q.3 c.97 (1:670); C.11 q.3 c.99 (1:671); C.11 q.3 c.101 (1:671–672).

60. *Disposicio. Dispositio* has multiple meanings, including a principle, an ordinance, or even a conclusive legal verdict. In his *Quaestio de Lege Divina,* Hus used the same term in defining the uncreated divine law as objective law, since it is the eternal disposition and preordination of God's intentions and plans: *"Divina duplex: increata, hoc est disposicio eterna et preordinacio mentis divine, et illa est divina essencia et vocatur lex obiectiva"* (*MIHOO,* 19A:19). Here, it certainly refers to existing legal regulations or stipulations found in all three divisions of the law, but especially in relation to *iuris comunis* (*Notarial Instrument of Appeal* in *Korespondence,* 63).

61. *Crimen.* Or *criminal offense.* Hus made a "legal-theological" distinction between *crimen* and *peccatum* in Sermones de tempore qui Collecta dicuntur (*MIHOO,* 7:518): *"Crimen enim secundum Augustinum et Crisostomum peccatum sic, quod omne crimen est peccatum, sed non omne peccatum est crimen, cum veniale peccatum non sit crimen."* See also *Responsiones ad Articulos Páleč* (*MIHOO,* 24: 274): *". . . crimen dicitur sive mortale peccatum . . .";* see also *Tractatus de Ecclesia,* 176. Following Augustine and canon law, Hus affirmed that *"nunquam aliquis iudex debet aliquem excomunicare nisi propter crimen sive propter peccatum mortale"* (*Tractus de Ecclesia,* 213; see also 183). See *Decretum* C.11 q.3 c.41 (*Corpus Iuris Canonici,* 1:655). Cf. *Decretum* C.2 q.1 c.18 (1:446–447). See also Wyclif, *Tractatus de Civili Dominio,* 1:31–32. Cf. Isidore of Seville, *Etymologiarum* 5.26.1–26, where *crimina* and *peccatum* are virtually synonymous in the section *De criminibus in lege conscriptis* (*PL* 82:209–211).

62. In his *quaestio* concerning the divine law, Hus reached the conclusion concerning the circumstance of *place* in relation to the divine law that *"aliquid lege divina preceptum potest mutari secundum necessitatem temporibus aut locum aut epykeiam"* (*MIHOO,* 19A:21). In chapter twenty-one of his *Tractatus de Ecclesia* (195–198), after citing the comments of Bernard of Clairvaux concerning the category of *opus medium* (i.e., things neither absolutely good or evil) and the circumstances of those deeds (i.e., time, manner, and person), Hus developed his argument related to the circumstance of *place* especially in relation to citations to go to Rome: *"Similiter pensanda est loci circumstancia. Nam si prelatus preciperet subdito comparere in loco inimicorum subdito mortem machinancium, non tenetur subditus obedire"* (195); (202): *"Ubi, quia in uno loco competit in actu bono de genere vel neutro obedire et non sic in alio vel quolibet."* He then cited canon law to support his argument, mentioning five specific examples:

(1) John Chrysostom's refusal to attend a synod full of his enemies (*Decretum* C.3 q.5 c.15);

(2) Gratian's conclusion that "no one who is charged with being guilty is under any circumstances to be summonsed outside of his own province" (*Extra provinciam autem reus nullatenus est producendus*) (*Decretum* C.3 q.6 d.a.c.1);

(3) Pope Fabian, who stated that cases should be tried where the offense has occurred (*Decretum* C.3 q.6 c.1);

(4) Pope Stephen I, who spoke against making accusations outside of provincial boundaries and stated that charges should be heard within the province itself (*Decretum* C.3 q.6 c.4);

(5) A decision of the Roman synod (*Super appellationem alterius provinciae iudices adire non oportet*) in *Decretum* C.3 q.6 c.16; see Pope Felix I, *Epistola II. De Auctoritate Judicis Sedis Apostolicae, Et De Episcopis Accustatis* (*PL*, 5:148–152), where the pope cited a passage on appeals from the imperial constitutions of *Theodosii Imperatoris Codex* (2.1.1–2.1.5) which was also included in *Corpus Iuris Germanici.* See Ferdinand Walter, ed., *Corpus Iuris Germanici Antiqui, vol. 2* (Berolini: Impensis G. Reimeri, 1824), 831–832.

Earlier in chapter sixteen of *Tractatus de Ecclesia*, within the context of legal jurisdiction, Hus critiqued the opinion of the doctors who conjectured that "the Roman church is the place which the Lord has chosen and the place where the Lord has placed the primacy of the whole church" (. . . *romanam ecclesiam esse locum quem elegit dominus, ubi dominus ecclesie tocius posuit principatum . . .*) (131). He then used a slightly sarcastic argument of refutation (*reductio ad absurdum*) to demonstrate that his opponents were virtually admitting that Christ was justly condemned merely because the judgment against him occurred in "the place which the Lord had chosen" ("*in loco sancto, quem elegit dominus*") (136). Hus denied that their meaning of the word "place" in relation to the Roman church as "the place where the Lord has chosen" (139) was valid at all, since he affirmed that "Christ is the Great High Priest who presides over that place" (. . . *in qua ecclesia non iste papa, sed Christus est summus sacerdos, qui preest loco* . . .) (140). Cf. *Liber Extra* 1.3.28 (*Corpus Iuris Canonici*, 2:31).

In the *Ordo Procedendi* the same previous references to canon law were made in relation to the circumstance of *place* (*Korespondence*, 233–234). Overall, Hus's explanation of the qualifying circumstance of *place* in relation to both temporal and final judgment is consistent with his previous interpretation in *Super Quattur Sententiarum* (4.48.1), his response against the assertions of Štěpán Páleč in *Antihus* (*Miscellanea husitica,* 458–459), and his comment in *Tractatus de Ecclesia* (51): "*Tercia causa est, ut notetur, quod non locus sive antiquitas sed fides formata fundet Christi ecclesiam.*"

63. See (in *Corpus Iuris Canonici*): *Liber Extra* 1.31.1 (2:186); *Liber Extra* 5.1.24 (2:745–747): "*debet coram Ecclesiæ senioribus veritatem diligentius perscrutari . . .*"; see also Canon 8 of the Fourth Lateran Council (*De inquisitionibus*).

64. Or *ill-disposed.* See (in *Corpus Iuris Canonici*): *Liber Extra* 5.1.21 (2:741–742); *Liber Extra* 5.1.24 (2:745–747): "*. . . non quidem a malevolis et maledicis . . .*"

65. See *Tractatus de Ecclesia* (195–196), where Hus mentioned Pope Clement V, Pope Nicholas, Canon 6 of the Council of Constantinople (381), the emperor Justinian, and John Chrysostom to support his point. See (in *Corpus Iuris Canonici*): *Clementines* 2.11.2 (2:1151–1153); *Decretum* C.3 q.5 cc.2–3 (1:514–515); *Decretum* C.3 q.5 c.15 (1:518–519). Cf. *Česká nedělní postila* (*MIHOO*, 2:164–165).

66. See (in *Corpus Iuris Canonici*): *Decretum* C.2 q.1 c.2 (1:438); *Decretum* C.3 q.5 c.4 (1:515); *Decretum* C.4 q.2–3 c.3 (1:538–541); *Liber Sextus* 1.3.11 (2:941–942); *Liber Extra* 5.1.24 (2:745–747): "*. . . sed a providis et honestis . . .*"

67. See *Liber Extra* 5.1.21 (*Corpus Iuris Canonici*, 2:741–742). Throughout his letters Hus protested against the slander, lies, defamation, and rumors of his opponents. See in *Korespondence*: *Letter to Pope John XXIII* (96); *Public Instrument Against the*

Theological Faculty (161–162); *Letter to Jan Kardinál of Rejštejn* (169–171: against the lies of Stanislav of Znojmo and Štěpán Páleč); he also wrote a letter to a theology professor at the University of Vienna and protested the mendacious and defamatory speech against Jerome of Prague and other members of the University of Prague (174–175). Cf. *Tractus de Ecclesia*, 132–134 (against the lies of Štěpán Páleč); 142, 148–149 (against the lies of the theological faculty). See also "Vyhláška proti pomluván (1409)," in M. Jan Hus, *Obrany v praze: (r. 1408–1412). Obran Husových*, vol. 1, trans. Václav Flajšhans (Praha: J. Otto, 1916), 31–33.

68. *Legis Ihesu Christi. Cf. Tractatus de Ecclesia*, 181: ". . . *cordati amatores legis Christi* . . ." Hus applied the *legis Christi* as the standard for his critique of papal citations: "*Si enim pape perpenderent illam Christi legem . . . estimo, quod non racionabiliter vellent, quod homines citarent et necessitarent illos ad talem viam periculosam et incognitam peragendum*" (197). And he expressed the following as the first and second of the four primary intentions of those within his party: ". . . *quod populus sit unus a lege Christi concorditer regulatus . . . Secundo . . . quod regnet sincere lex Christi cum conswetudine populi ex lege domini approbata*" (148–149). For Hus's overall understanding of *legis Christi*, see: *Sermones de sanctis*, 3.3; 9.3; 37.4; 45.1–2; *Super Quattur Sententiarum*, 4.18.3–5; 4.38.4; and mainly *De Sufficiencia Legis Cristi (MIHOO*, 24:39–79). Hus asserted in *De Ecclesia* that "*Ideo nemo debet obedire homini in aliquo eciam minimo, quod divino obviat mandato . . .*" (177); and in *De Fidei Sue Elucidacione* (*MIHOO*, 24:84): "*Ulterius admitto omnes sanctorum doctorum sentencias ipsam legem fideliter declarantes, veneror eciam omnia concilia generalia et specialia, decreta et decretales et omnes leges, canones et constituciones, dequanto consonant explicite vel implicite illi legi.*"

69. Hus was referring to canon law, of course, where the same requirements are noted. See *Liber Extra* 2.6.4 (*Corpus Iuris Canonici*, 2:261–263); *Liber Extra* 2.28.47 (*Corpus Iuris Canonici*, 2:428).

70. *Condiciones.* In relationship to personal obedience to the ecclesiastical commands of superiors, Hus cited Bernard of Clairvaux's five conditions which regulate obedience: ". . . *quinque condiciones rectificantes obedienciam* . . ." (*Tractatus de Ecclesia*, 179). He also borrowed from Thomas Aquinas's *Summa Theologiae* (2–1.7.3) and identified eight circumstances which regulate virtuous acts: "*quis, quid, ubi, quantum, quot, cur, quomodo, quando*" (*Tractatus de Ecclesia*, 201). Cf. Canon law on due process: *Decretum* C.2 q.1 d.p.c.14 (*Corpus Iuris Canonici*, 1:445); *Clementines* 5.11.2 (*Corpus Iuris Canonici*, 2:1200).

71. Hus often referred to the preservation of his own life as a spiritual matter of discerning and obeying God's will. On July 11, 1412, only a few months before Hus wrote his appeal, three young journeymen were beheaded for their participation in public protests during Sunday services against the sale of indulgences. Hus tried to intervene on their behalf and appeared before the town councillors and pleaded for the release of the young men by admitting that they had been roused by his own preaching against indulgences. He accepted personal responsibility and asked for whatever judgment they were to receive to first be given to him since he was the cause. These events are recorded in *Fontes Rerum Bohemicarum (Series Nova)*, 3:54, 288; see also Jaroslav Porák & Jaroslav Kašpar, *Ze starých letopisů českých* (Praha:

Svoboda, 1980), 35. Hus also mentioned these three young men again in his *Tractatus de Ecclesia* (201), *Česká nedělní postila* (*MIHOO*, 2:115), and *Knížky o svatokupectví* (*MIHOO*, 4:201). Later, on September 29, 1412, still just a few weeks before he wrote his appeal, Hus preached: *"Ergo et ego, ex quo citatus sum personaliter ad Romanum curiam propter evangelium, cu (si voluntas Dei fuerit) non essem paratus non solum comparere, sed alligari et mori cum auxilio D. Jesu Christi?"* (*Mag. Io. Hus Sermones in Capella Bethlehem*, 5:138). He reiterated the same sentiments in *Tractatus de Ecclesia* (198) and in his *Letter to the Carthusian Monks*: *"Unde si possem habere coniecturam probabilem, quod possem per comparicionem et per mortem meam aliquibus ad salutem proficere, libenter auxiliante Ihesu Christo domino comparerem"* (*Korespondence*, 121). Earlier, on September 1, 1411, Hus had written to Pope John XXIII and described his reason for not personally appearing at the Roman curia as a matter of sinning, since he would be tempting God by exposing his life to death (Matthew 4:7): *". . . iudicavi, quod foret deum temptare vitam morti tradere profectu ecclesie non urgente"* (*Korespondence*, 98).

72. *Excusatus.* Though they are semantically related, "excused" and "exempt" are distinct legal concepts and should not be equated as terms. See Miranda del Corral, "Excuses and Exemptions," in *Tópicos, Revista de Filosofía* 49 (2015): 231–256. The terms may be seen as relating (albeit very broadly) to the distinction between *fas* and *jus* in canon law: *"Fas lex divina est: ius lex humana. Transire per agrum alienum, fas est, ius non est."* Here, the motive to perform right actions (*fas*) is distinguished from the performance of the action (*ius*). See *Decretum* D.1 c.1 (*Corpus Iuris Canonici*, 1:1). Using the Passover and Christ as his example (see footnote 8), Hus presented seven specific reasons why he was excused from appearing in Rome in *Česká nedělní postila* (*MIHOO*, 2:164–165); see also *Knížky proti knězi kuchmistrovi* (*MIHOO*, 4:321–322) and *Ordo Procedendi* (*Korespondence*, 228–232) for Hus's explanation of these same reasons.

(1) "First of all, because my delegates represented me in Rome for three years, and they were never given a hearing; and they were arrested and imprisoned, because they appealed to the truth.

(2) Second, because the distance from Prague to Rome is farther than the distance from Jerusalem to the Sea of Galilee—the place to which Christ traveled from Jerusalem.

(3) Third, because it is not commanded in the law of God for people to be summonsed so far as Rome on account of nothing.

(4) Fourth, because there is hardly any truth to be found at the papal court by which they would be led according to the law of God.

(5) Fifth, because the people would be deprived of the word of God, and what good would I myself be able to accomplish along the journey? And even if I were to arrive at the papal court, what kind of holiness would I gain there? I would find only conflict and strife and they would want me to commit simony.

(6) Sixth, because I would waste many alms for nothing by collecting them from the people.

(7) Seventh, because this lawsuit of which I am at the forefront is against the pope's customs and lifestyle and against his power, which is not derived from God but fabricated by the devil."

73. Or *worthless*. In a letter written to Hus on September 8, 1410, Richard Wyche described the censures and fulminations of the Antichrist with the same term: frivolous. See *Korespondence*, 78: ". . . *ad viam revoca veritatis, quia non propter censuras frivolas et fulminaciones Antichristianas est veritas ewangelica subticenda.*"

74. *Excomunicacio*. Cf. *Responsiones Breves ad Articulos Ultimos* (*MIHOO*, 24:296–298: *articulos 14–19)*; *Tractatus de Ecclesia*, 209–217.

75. *Baccalarius formatus*. The title "formed bachelor" (*baccalarius formatus*) meant that a student had completed his required lectures on Peter Lombard's *Libri Quattuor Sententiarum* (*The Four Books of Sentences*), a medieval textbook of theology which was widely used in universities throughout Europe. See Monika Asztalos, "The Faculty of Theology," in *A History of the University in Europe, Volume 1: Universities in the Middle Ages*, ed. Hilde de Ridder-Symoens (Cambridge: Cambridge University Press, 1992), 418–419.

76. *Confirmatus*. Or *appointed*. Hus mentioned on several occasions that Pope Alexander V issued a bull which sought to forbid preaching the word of God, even in chapels which had already been confirmed (*stvrzeny*) by the pope. See: *Knížky proti knězi kuchmistrovi* (*MIHOO*, 4:320–321); *Česká nedělní postila* (*MIHOO*, 2:166): ". . . and the priest Jan, the Archbishop of Prague, established and confirmed Bethlehem Chapel with his own hand."; 2:320. In a similar brief narrative of pertinent events, Hus wrote: "*Quia predicavi in Bethleem, capella erecta in beneficium ecclesiasticum pro verbo dei predicando ad populum, confirmata a sede apostolica, et conveniente multo populo, plebani Pragenses invidentes, pecierunt a domino Zbinkone Pragensi archiepiscopo, ut predictam capellam destrueret*" (*Korespondence*, 123). He also reminded Pope John XXIII in a letter that Bethlehem Chapel had been confirmed by the ordinary: "*False denique suggesserunt, quod capella Bethleem foret locus privatus, cum ipsa sit ab ordinario locus in beneficium ecclesiasticum confirmatus . . .*" (*Korespondence*, 97). *Defensio Libri de Trinitate* (MIHOO, 22:48–49): "*Cum ergo in causa simili prohibetur nobis non loqui in nomine Iesu in locis, consecratis ad ewangelisandum a dyocesano et a sede apostolica confirmatis . . .*"; This fact seemed important to Hus, since an ordinary (e.g., a bishop within a diocese) possessed immediate jurisdiction in cases concerning ecclesiastical law. Cf. *Documenta*, 422–425: ". . . *capellanus noster fidelis devotus dilectus, ad eandem capellam confirmatus, pacifice praedicet verbum dei.*" For Hus's similar critique of closing chapels confirmed by diocesans (*confirmatarum*) for preaching the word of God, see *De Ecclesia*, 164–165.

77. *Cf. De Ecclesia*, 164–165: "*Unde confidens in domino et in Christo Ihesu . . . Unde ab illo mandato ad ipsum Allexandrum pro meliori ipsius informacione appellavi . . . anno domini 1410 ad papam Johannem XXIII appellavi . . . Cum ergo appellacio ab uno papa ad successorum suum michi non profuit, et a papa ad concilium appellare est in longum et in incertum auxilium in gravamine postulare, ideo ad caput ecclesie dominum Ihesum Christum ultimo appellavi.*"; *Letter to an Unnamed Prelate at the Council*: "*Et quia ad Christum Ihesum potentissimum et*

iustissimum iudicem appellavi, sibi comittens causam meam: ideo sto sue diffinicioni et sentencie sanctisime, sciens, quia non iuxta falsa testimonia, nec iuxta erronea consilia, sed iuxta veritatem et merita unumquemque hominem iudicabit et premiabit" (*Korespondence*, 282). Hus explained the events surrounding his appeal in more detail in *Česká nedělní postila*: "For Alexander V issued a bull in exchange for money in which it was decreed that the word of God should not be preached to the people anywhere in chapels, even though they had been established and confirmed by the papacy. And in this bull it was also insisted that the word of God could be not preached anywhere else except in parish churches and in monasteries. And the priest Zbyněk, Archbishop of Prague (of blessed memory), solicited for this bull with the other prelates. And the monk Jaroslav, a disingenuous bishop, traveled on a mission for the bull, in which it is also alleged that the hearts of many had become greatly defiled with heresy in the Kingdom of Bohemia, in Prague, and in the Moravian Margravate, and that inspection and punishment were necessary. And so this bull demonstrates that even the pope and Zbyněk the priest acted against the law of God: the pope by issuing it and Zbyněk by enforcing it, in order that the word of God would not be preached freely . . . How, then is this bull in agreement with Scripture and the deeds of Christ. In no way whatsoever! Therefore, I first of all appealed to the pope against the bull, since [the matter] was also concerning the pope himself, and because the truth was unfounded. And so the second part of the bull might actually be true in this sense: that the hearts of many in Prague have been defiled with heresy—namely, those who have obtained, consented to, and enforced bulls which are against the Scriptures and against the salvation of the people . . . And then the recently deceased Zbyněk, Archbishop or Prague, being advised and led by the canons, Prague priests, and monks who directed? with the priests concerning Bethlehem, wanted to invalidate the word of God {being preached} in the chapel and thus force me to stop preaching . . . Therefore, taking the merciful Savior as my refuge, I protested" (*MIHOO,* 2:165–166).

"And against this {i.e., Jesus' example of preaching openly and freely in Luke 5:1–11} the priest Zbyněk, the Archbishop of Prague, along with the canons purchased from Pope Alexander V a bull in which it was forbidden for the word of God to be preached, not even in the chapels confirmed by the papacy, except for parish churches and monasteries and in collegiate churches. And with God's help, I appealed against this bull to the pope, and immediately after he had issued the bull, he died along with the chancellor as well. Then, I appealed to his vicar John XXIII, and not finding any support from him for the liberation of the word of God, I appealed to the Lord God—to Jesus, the venerable and righteous bishop—for him to judge me (*MIHOO,* 2:320)." See also Hus's similar remarks concerning Alexander V in: *Contra Octo Doctores* (*MIHOO,* 22:373–376; 446: ". . . *ad supremum iudicem appelavi.*"); *Contra Stanislaum de Znoyma* (*MIHOO,* 22:359); *Defensio Articulorum Wyclif* (*MIHOO,* 22:150); *Ordo Procedendi* (*Korespondence,* 226): "*Et dominus Allexander, sinistre et mendose iniormatus, mandavit per rescriptum suum dicto domino Sbinconi, ut diligenciam apponeret, et si qui sunt errores vel hereses, extirparet; et mandavit, quod nullibi predicaretur verbum dei ad populum, nisi in ecclesiis kathedralibus, collegiatis, monasteriis et parrochialibus, sed non in capellis eciam ad hoc a sede apostolica confirmatis et privilegiatis.*"; *Responsiones Breves ad Articulos Ultimos* (*MIHOO,* 24:300–301).

78. Hus preached that the holy attributes of God's character are especially evidenced in his just judgments as the righteous Judge in *Česká nedělní postila* (*MIHOO,* 2:59, 64–65, 320, 342, 349, 425, 432). In the introduction of his appeal, Hus began by emphasizing his *cause* to God *(Quoniam fecisti iudicium meum et causam meam)*, while in his conclusion he emphasized not the *causa* itself, but the expectation of God rendering a righteous judgment (*sedisti super thronum qui iudicas iustitiam*), since "God himself is judge" (Psalm 50:6). Based on the Old Testament verses which he had previously cited in the first section of his appeal, Hus was likely drawing from the Psalms and other similar passages which portray God as a righteous judge who judges righteously. See: Job 21:22; 23:7; Psalms 5:9; 7:9–12; 9:9; 10:8; 17: 21–25; 30:2; 34:24; 35:11; 36:6–7, 28; 39:10–11; 44:5; 49:6; 57:12; 70:15–16, 19, 24; 71:2–3; 74:3, 8; 75:9–10; 84:11–14; 95:10–13; 96:2, 6; 97:2, 9; 98:4; 110:3, 7–8; 118:84, 121, 137, 142, 149, 154–156; 139:13; 142:1–2; 145:7 (in English Bibles: 5:8; 7:8–11; 9:8; 11:7; 18:20–24; 31:1; 35:24; 36:10; 37:6–7, 28; 40:9–10; 45:6; 50:6; 58:11; 71:15–16, 19, 24; 72:1–3; 75:2, 7; 76:8–9; 85:10–13; 89:14–16; 94:15; 96:11–13; 97:2, 6; 98:2, 9; 99:4; 103:6; 111:3, 7–8; 119:84, 121, 137, 142, 149, 154–156; 140:12; 143:1–2; 146:7); Jeremiah 9:23–24; 23:5.

"The most righteous Judge" is a biblical description which Hus used to refer to Jesus Christ frequently in his letters. See (in *Korespondence*): *Letter to a Priest-Judge* (1); *Letter to the Praguers* (181); *Letter to King Zikmund* (198); *Letter to an Unnamed Prelate at the Council* (282–283); *Letter to Václav of Duba and Jan of Chlum* (289); *Knížky proti knězi kuchmistrovi* (*MIHOO,* 4:321); see also: *De Ecclesia*, 137: "*Ecce doctores nostri in dictis suis pro inconvenienti iudicant, quod nostra pars wlt habere legem iudicem, qui iudex iustissime iudicat, qui non aliter iudicat quam deus iustissimus iudex.*"; 192: "*Sed veniet magister, episcopus et iudex iustissimus . . .*"; 213; *Relatio de Magistri Joannis Hus* (*Documenta*, 319); *Responsiones ad Articulos Páleč* (*MIHOO,* 24:288).

79. These five specific actions of "the most righteous Judge" which Hus enlisted here in concluding his appeal are also mainly drawn from the Psalms in the Vulgate: *examines* (Psalms 7:10; 16:3; 17:31; 25:2; 65:10; 118:129; 138:1), *defends* (Psalms 16:8; 17:3, 19, 31, 36; 19:2; 21:20; 26:1; 27:7–8; 30:3–5; 32:20; 36:39; 39:18; 53:6; 58:12; 60:5; 63:3; 70:3, 6; 83:10; 90:1, 14; 113:17–19; 120:5; 140:9), *judges* (Job 6:29; Psalms 7:9; 9:5, 9; 25:1; 34:1, 24; 36:32–33; Jeremiah 11:18–20), *discloses* (Psalms 24:14; 49:3; 50:8; 97:2; 147:8–9), and *upholds* (Psalms 17:21, 25; 27:4; 36:17, 24; 57:12; 62:9; 144:14; Jeremiah 32:17–19).

Hus's conclusion may be viewed as a distinction between personal jurisdiction and subject-matter jurisdiction. In any case where an alleged miscarriage of justice occurred, the predominant question immediately arose: *Et iudicem quis iudicavit?* Hus was definitely concerned about this, since he wrote that it would surely lead to his death if he were to be judged by the same judges whose public sins he preached against. See: *Knížky proti knězi kuchmistrovi* (*MIHOO,* 4:321–322): "I also did not appear because I am handling a lawsuit against the pope, and I know that the pope is not going to convict himself; and especially because I determined to work against his charlatans, who had come with their bulls only in order to plunder the people; *Letter to the Carthusian Monks* (*Korespondence*, 121): "... *quia iudicari a iudice illum, qui manifesta iudicis impungnat peccata, est in mortem se dare.*" Canon law expressed the virtual impossibility of appealing against papal verdicts: *Decretum* C.9 q.3 c.16—c.17 (1:611). Hus, however, denied in principle that the pope should be the judge of all causes since he did not possess universal jurisdiction. See: *Tractatus de Ecclesia*, 76–77; 138: "... *quod papa debet esse iudex omnium causarum* ..." *Contra Stanislaum de Znoyma* (*MIHOO*, 22:314): "*Sed estimo, quod non faciet nec Stanislaus ad illa prestabit sibi consilium, qui determinat omnes causas civiles per ipsum papam de plenitudine potestatis esse iudicandas*"; *Letter to Master Křišťan of Prachatice* (*Korespondence*, 164–168). He also distinguished between *mandata apostolica* and *mandata papalia* and made it clear that the pope must render any judicial decisions in accordance with the law of God (*Contra Octo Doctores* in *MIHOO*, 22:375–376). Cf. *Tractatus de Ecclesia*, 112–118, 164–169, 176–177. Thus, for Hus the highest form of justice is to be righteous before God (*Sermones de Sanctis*, 8.2).

Ultimately, Hus's appeal to Jesus Christ as the supreme judge on October 18, 1412, may be summarized by his own explanation written in his treatise on the church, his bold declarations in Constance, and the accompanying explanation recorded by his dear friend Petr of Mladoňovice in his *Relatio de Magistri Joannis Hus*. Hus had earlier explained, "I ultimately appealed to head of the church, the Lord Jesus Christ, since he himself is superior to any pope at all in deciding a case: he cannot err nor can he deny justice to the one solemnly and duly pleading for justice ..." (*Tractatus de Ecclesia*, 165–166). Then on June 8, 1415, Hus repeated his previous conviction and declared that the Lord Jesus Christ is superior to any pope in judging cases, since Christ is the infallible head of the church: "*Ideo ad caput ecclesiae dominum Jesum Christum ultimo appellavi; ipse enim est quolibet papa in decidendo causam praestantior, cum non potest errare* ..."); Petr of Mladoňovice wrote that Hus confessed that where the final ground or essential element of a legal action is unjust, there is no more effective appeal than to Jesus Christ himself: "*Confessus igitur est M. Joannes, quod in finali gravamine non est efficacior appellatio, quam ad Christum*" (*Documenta*, 295). Even on the very last day of his life, on July 6, 1415, Hus declared his unwavering conviction: "I resolutely continue to declare that there is no safer appeal than to the Lord Jesus Christ" (*Documenta*, 319: "*Et ego dico constanter, quod nonest tutior appellatio, quam ad Jesum Christum dominum* ...").

4

Hus in Exile and in Constance

After making his appeal to Jesus Christ, Hus struggled exceedingly in his own soul; he was deeply troubled with deciding whether he should leave or stay in Prague. He mentioned his own conflicting thoughts and emotions in a letter written to the preachers and other believers in Bethlehem Chapel sometime in the autumn of 1412.

> I have contemplated in my soul that word from the gospel of our Savior in John 10: "The good shepherd lays down his life for the sheep. He who is a hired hand, and not a shepherd, who is not the owner of the sheep, sees the wolf coming, and leaves the sheep and flees; and the wolf snatches them and scatters the flock." I have also contemplated the other passage in Matthew 10: "When they persecute you in one town, flee to the next." Behold Christ's precept or his permission: I do not know which of these two opposite choices to make.[1]

Hus chose to leave Prague for the sake of the salvation of his flock and sojourned in the countryside, at first with Lord Jan of Ústí at Kozí Hrádek (the Goat Castle), located southeast of Tábor. Nevertheless, he secretly visited Prague during Christmas in 1412, at some point after the New Year in 1413, and during Easter in 1413. Hus was persistently preaching to the common people in rural areas. I do not want to romanticize here what has already been elaborated in Czech literature, especially many times in *belles-lettres*, but the content, significance, and consequences of the sermons which he preached during this time cannot in any way be overestimated. He was preparing peasants who would come to realize and appreciate quite clearly those truths for which they were fighting when they were later forced to take up arms and fight against those who were crushing their freedom with unlawful demands. Although these sermons have not been preserved, we can still adequately surmise what their original content might have been. This quiet period of seclusion was also beneficial for Hus from one important perspective. Towards the end of 1412 and in 1413 he composed a series of texts which are crucial for understanding his overall thought and the underlying motivation of his reformatory activities: *An Exposition of the Creed,*[2] *An Exposition of the Decalogue,*[3] *An Exposition of the Lord's Prayer,*[4] *The Three-Stranded Cord,*[5] *On Simony,*[6] *The Mirror of a Sinner,*[7] *The Little Daughter: On Knowing the True Path to Salvation,*[8] *On the Six Errors,*[9] and his Czech *Postil.*[10] These writings became the prized and shared possession of the common Czech people. Hus also wrote a few Latin treatises in order to defend himself against the attacks made by his opponents. These polemical tractates include *Contra Stephanum de Palecz* [*Against Štěpán Paleč*],[11] *Contra Stanislaum de Znoyma* [*Against Stanislav of Znojmo*],[12] and one of his most important writings—titled *Tractatus de Ecclesia* [*A Treatise on the Church*],[13] which was read publicly and copied by scribes in Bethlehem Chapel from the beginning of June until the final dictation was finished on June 8, 1413.[14]

This latter text, which has been called the "magnum opus of the Bohemian Reformation,"[15] became one of the most widely read of all of Hus's writings.[16] The fact that it was originally composed in Latin, a language which was understandable to the educated population of all countries at that time, greatly contributed to its wide readership. Hus's theological treatise on ecclesiology consists of two main parts. The first part is comprised of ten chapters in which Hus explained and argued for his theological interpretation of the church as the congregation or flock of people who are predestined unto salvation:

> These above-mentioned writings of the saints elicit the conclusion that the holy universal church is the number of all those who have been predestined and the mystical body of Christ (of whom Christ himself is the head) and the bride of Christ whom he redeemed through his own blood out of his abundant love so that he would ultimately have and hold her in glorious splendor, not having any wrinkle of mortal sin or spot of venial sin or any other blemish which defiles her, but being holy and blameless she would embrace Christ her bridegroom forever.[17]

In the second part (chapters 11–23) he provided a more personal rationale in order to show what specifically had led him to stand against the existing church order.[18] He publicly spoke out against the papacy, which had compromised its spiritual calling (i.e., declaring that the pope was derelict in his pastoral duties), against indulgences, and against the papal summons to come to Rome. Although there are marked differences in numerous areas, in many ways Hus understood spiritual authority in a way similar to its expression by earlier Bohemian reformers and John Wyclif:

> Just as every pilgrim should faithfully believe the holy catholic church, he should also love Jesus Christ (the Lord and the bridegroom of his church) and

the church herself, which is his own bride. But he only loves his spiritual mother as much as he comes to know her through faith; therefore, he should seek to know her through faith and to honor and cherish her as his own precious mother.

In the nineteenth century, Austrian historian Johann Loserth (1846–1936), in his book *Huss und Wiclif: Zur Genesis einer Lehre,* made an audacious effort attempting to prove that Hus's *Tractatus de Ecclesia* was actually plagiarized from Wyclif.[19] His spurious claims, however, can be easily dismissed as an inaccurate portrayal. Hus was working with multiple sources (which of course included Wyclif's writings in this case) completely according to the typical medieval method. For instance, he copied entire paragraphs from Wyclif, but Hus's work also conveyed an utterly new meaning—a meaning conditioned by an unmistakably different social situation and personal context than that experienced some forty years prior during the time of Wyclif. Hus's sharing of personal details of his own life in the second half, in addition to theological formulations found throughout his work, leaves no doubt that in a certain sense Hus's *Tractatus de Ecclesia* served as "the basis of charges in the most famous formal trial of a single individual in the history of the Christian church."[20]

In 1414, a general council whose aim was to bring an end to the chaotic schism and to reestablish order by eradicating heresies and reforming the corrupt morals in the church was convened in Constance, Germany.[21] It was here that Hus as a reformer and one who diligently sought renewal in the church would stand trial and, ironically, be declared as a heretic and burned at the stake by the very council promoting church renewal and reformation in its head and its members (*reformatio in capite et in membris*). Hus was hoping to defend himself in a public hearing, while it seems to some historians that his enemies were looking forward to getting rid of him once and for all.[22]

In the summer of 1414, Hus relocated from Kozí Hrádek to a castle in Krakovec near Rakovník owned by Master Jindřich Lefl of Lažany. He began preaching there again and focused on preparing a speech which he wanted to deliver at the Council of Constance.[23] He entitled it *Sermo de Pace [A Sermon on Peace]*.[24] The fundamental idea which he expressed in this sermon or discourse was that all of the disorders, deformities, and dissensions within the church arise from sinful strife and a lack of godly peace. He concluded *Sermo de Pace* with these memorable words:

> Since, therefore, according to the divine proclamation of the prophets and the testimonies of other saints, the withering and atrophying of the church are caused by the sins of the shepherds and the other priests—confusion and disorder are being increased, peace is in exile, leading to the damnation of souls—let us who exercise the office of the priesthood humbly bow our souls before the

most gracious and merciful Lord and with a broken and contrite spirit of devotion proclaim, "Most gracious and most powerful Lord, may peace be found in your strength" (Psalm 122:7). *Peace be to this household* in order for sin to be extinguished. *Peace be to this household* in order to overcome the persecuting enemy. *Peace be to this household* in order to end the hostile schism. And *peace be to this household* in order to live in glory with God the Father, the Son, and the Holy Spirit—blessed forever and ever![25]

Regrettably, the assembly which Hus wanted to address with these peaceful words not only did not accept him in *peace,* but they also handed him over to the secular arm (*bracchium saeculare*) in order to be burned at the stake. Without delving into the complexity of the historical era and its related circumstances, it is worth noting that even several centuries later the complicated moral ramifications of the council's actions still pose a problem for Rome, as Roman Catholic theologian Karel Skalický expressed in a letter written to Pope John Paul II (1920–2005):

The real problem, your Holiness, is not whether or not Hus was a heretic, but rather this: the fact that Hus taught something displeasing to the Council and something which he was unwilling to recant for reasons of conscience—does it justify his death sentence or not? For here, your Holiness, is it necessary to let your statement be "Yes, yes" or "No, no." If *yes*, then we must retract the Second Vatican Council's declaration on the freedom of conscience and many other declarations of popes and especially your own, your Holiness, on the freedom of conscience and on religious freedom. In that case, Monsieur Lefebvre is right, and in that case the only way into the kingdom of God is [through] clerical totalitarianism. If *no*, then the Council of Constance behaved evilly. *Tertium non datur.*[26]

Just before his departure from the Kingdom of Bohemia to Constance, Hus visited Prague and it was publicly confirmed that no one openly indicted him of any of the charges brought against him.[27] King Sigismund promised to offer protection for Hus and later confirmed it in a letter of safe conduct (*salvus conductus*) on October 18, 1414.[28] Hus had already begun his journey on October 11, 1414, accompanied by Jan of Chlum, Václav of Dubá, and Jindřich Lacembok, and he traveled through Sulzbach, Nuremberg, and Ulm on his way toward Constance, where he finally arrived on November 3, 1414. He was initially free and allowed to visit the city, yet after a provocation when his enemies spread the rumor that he had sought to flee and escape, Hus was arrested and imprisoned on November 28, 1414. At first he was imprisoned in the Dominican monastery, then from March 1415 in Gottlieben Castle on Lake Constance. Thanks to the fact that the Czech lords managed to pay his guards, even while in prison Hus was able to work diligently on composing some minor tracts such as *De penitencia* [*On Repentance*],[29] *De peccato mortali* [*On Mortal Sin*],[30] and mainly *De sanguine Cristi sub specie vini a laicis sumendo* [*Concerning the Partaking of the Blood of Christ under Both Species by the Laity*][31] and *De sacramento corporis et sanguinis Christi* [*On the Sacrament of the Body and Blood of Christ*].[32]

Meanwhile in Prague, Hus's friend and successor to the pulpit Jakoubek of Stříbra (1372–1429) came to the conclusion that a visible sign of the reform of the church should be communion under both kinds (*communio sub utraque specie*—that is, partaking of both the consecrated bread and the wine in the chalice). Jakoubek started serving the chalice to the laity and inquired about Hus's viewpoint concerning the matter. At first, Hus cautioned his friend not to implement the practice too hastily. Hus's treatise *De sumpcione sangwinis Iesu Cristi sub specie vini* begins with this question: *Utrum expediat laicis fidelibus sumere sanguinem Cristi sub specie vini* [*Whether it is expedient for the blood of Christ is to be served to the faithful laymen under both kinds*].[33] His answer was an expression of support for the participation in communion under both kinds for the laity, even though the Council rejected and condemned it.[34] Although Hus insisted on the legitimacy of utraquism, he also advised Jakoubek to wait until his return to Prague before implementing the practice. On June 21, 1415, Hus composed a letter to Havlík (his substitute preacher at Bethlehem), offering the following biblical counsel:

Dearly, beloved brother, Master Havlík—preacher of the word of God!

Do not continue opposing the sacrament of the cup of the Lord which Christ instituted by himself and also through his apostles, for there is no Scripture which is opposed to it, but only a custom which I suppose has arisen and become engrained due to negligence. We should not follow custom, but the example of Christ and the truth.[35] Now the Council, alleging custom [as its reason], has passed judgment and condemned communion of the cup by the laity as an error, and that whoever partakes of it shall be punished exactly the same as a heretic . . . unless he comes to his senses! Behold! Spiteful malice now even condemns the very institution of Christ himself as an error!

I urgently beg you for the sake of God, do not argue and dispute with Magister Jakoubek anymore, so that no division would arise among the faithful in which the devil would take delight. Also, dearly beloved, prepare yourself for suffering on account of partaking in the communion of the cup. And stand courageously in the truth of Christ—putting aside unwarranted fear and comforting the other brethren in the gospel of the Lord Jesus Christ. I have given you an account of the arguments [supporting] the communion of the cup in what I have written in Constance. Greet the faithful ones in Christ.[36]

For a long time, Hus believed that he would be able to be released from prison (or escape from the clutches of the Council, depending on one's interpretation). Although he was not given a public hearing, he did appear before the deliberations of the Council on the fifth, seventh, and eighth of June; however, the Council unambiguously demanded that he recant. But his opponents (some have even gone as far as to say "devious torturers") failed to achieve their goal. He was brought before the Council again on the first day of July, where he made the following famous final declaration to the Council:

Final Declaration to the Council (July 1, 1415)

I—Jan Hus, in hope a priest of Jesus Christ, fearing that I would offend God and fall into perjury—am not willing to abjure any and all of those articles which have been brought forward against me by the testimonies of false witnesses. For God himself is my witness that I have neither preached, nor asserted, nor defended them in the same manner which they are claiming that I have defended, preached, and asserted them, etc.

Moreover, concerning the articles extracted from my books, at least those articles which have been extracted correctly, my plea is this: I denounce[37] any single one of them which includes a false interpretation. However, fearing that I should sin against the truth and speak against the teachings of the saints, I am not willing to abjure any single one of them.

And if it were somehow possible for my voice to be heard throughout the whole world right now, just as every lie and each one of my sins will be revealed on the day of judgment, I would most gladly in front of the whole world rescind every falsehood and every error which I have ever even imagined saying or have actually asserted.

I declare and write this freely and voluntarily,
Written with my own hand on the first day of July.[38]

HUS'S LETTERS

Another profoundly important chapter concerning Hus's personal struggles can be discerned from the many poignant and emotional letters which he wrote during the latter years of his life.[39] In the preface to his English translation of Hus's letters, Matthew Spinka (1890–1972) aptly noted that "as is usually the case, letters, written spontaneously to personal friends and not intended for publication, reveal the writer's intimate feelings and personal characteristics not to be found in his formal writing."[40] Since his letters have already been translated into several languages, we encourage readers to peruse these "heartfelt treasures" and gain a deeper understanding of Hus's personality, which appears easier to discern in his letters than in his polemical texts.[41] Perhaps the most beautiful letters are those penned when Hus was in prison in Constance, especially the ones which were written to the university, to individual masters or Czech nobles, to all faithful Czechs, and to his friends in Bohemia. In a letter written in November 1414, perhaps to his successor at Bethlehem Chapel, Hus admonished the priest with these words:

> Be diligent in "preaching the gospel" and "do the work of a good evangelist" (2 Timothy 4:2–5). Do not neglect your calling: "labor as a good soldier of Christ" (2 Timothy 2:3). First, live a devout and holy life, and then teach faithfully and truly. "Be an example to others in good works" (Titus 2:7) so as not to be reprehended in conversations. Chastise sins and praise virtues. Threaten those who live wickedly with eternal punishment, but declare eternal joy to those who are faithful and live uprightly. Preach assiduously, but briefly and profitably, with a discerning knowledge of the Holy Scriptures. Never affirm uncertain and dubious [issues], so that you would not be reprehended by adversaries who delight in disparaging their neighbors and treating the ministers of God with reproach. Exhort them to the confession of faith and to communion of the body and the blood of Christ in both kinds, in order that those who have truly repented of their sins would often draw near to communion.[42]

In another very touching letter written to his friends in Bohemia, we encounter the following well-known phrase: "I also pray that you would love one another, would not allow good men to be oppressed by violence, and would desire for everyone [to know] the truth."[43] Finally, here is an excerpt from one of his last letters which was written to his friends in Bohemia on July 5, 1415, the day before Hus was martyred for his faith:

> May God be with you, and may it please him to grant you an eternal reward on account of the many good things you that have done for me . . . I also pray that you would live a virtuous life and obey God, just as you have heard from me.
> And to the Queen, my gracious consort, give thanks to her on my behalf for all of the good that she has done for me. Greet your household and the other faithful friends of whom it is impossible to give an account.
> I also implore all of you to pray to the Lord God for me that we will soon be reunited together in his holy grace by his holy help. Amen. This letter is written in prison and in chains with the expectation of a sentence of death—which I hope that I am suffering for the law of God. For the sake of the Lord God, do not allow the good priests to be rooted out and completely destroyed.
> Master Hus, in hope a servant of God.[44]

The very next day, on July 6, 1415, Hus was condemned, defrocked, and put to death by being burned at the stake. One of Hus's close friends, Petr of Mladoňovice, compiled a detailed description of Hus's stay in Constance titled *Relatio de magistri Joannis Hus causa in Constantiensi consilio acta* [*A*

Narrative Account of Master Jan Hus in Constance].[45] All of the documents
and a detailed description of the course of events related to Hus's trial are
captured in his report. The account itself contains five main sections:[46]

1. Events Prior to Hus's Journey to Constance
2. The Trial to the Beginning of Hus's Imprisonment
3. Hus's "Hearings" (Inappropriately Named Hearings since in Truth They Involved Derision and Abuse)
4. Hus's Hearing on the Eighth Day of June in 1415
5. The End of the Holy and Honorable Master Jan Hus, a Zealous Lover of the Truth of Jesus Christ (and the Agony which He Patiently Suffered)

Utraquist churches later commemorated the memory of Hus's martyrdom by
using this fifth section as their liturgical reading instead of a reading from
the lives of saints.[47] Petr of Mladoňovice's eyewitness account may sound
emotionally appalling to modern ears, but let us now humbly remind ourselves of the very last moment of Hus's life according to what his dear friend
witnessed:

> And having come to the place of execution, he, bending his knees and stretch-
> ing his hands and turning his eyes toward heaven, most devoutly sang songs,
> and particularly, "Have mercy on me, God" and "In Thee, Lord, I have trusted,"
> repeating the verse "In Thy hand, Lord." His own [friends] who stood about
> then heard him praying joyfully and with a glad countenance.
>
> And rising at the order of the executioner from the place where he was pray-
> ing, he said in a loud and clear voice, so that his [friends] could plainly hear
> him, "Lord Jesus Christ, I am willing to bear most patiently and humbly this
> dreadful, ignominious, and cruel death for Thy gospel and for the preaching of
> Thy Word." Then they decided to take him among the bystanders. He urged
> and begged them not to believe that he in any way held, preached, or taught the
> articles with which he had been charged by false witnesses. Then having been
> divested of his clothing, he was tied to a stake with ropes, his hands tied behind
> his back. And when he was turned facing east, some of the bystanders said: "Let
> him not be turned toward the east, because he is a heretic; but turn him toward
> the west." So that was done. When he was bound by the neck with a sooty chain,
> he looked at it and, smiling, said to the executioners: "The Lord Jesus Christ,
> my Redeemer and Savior, was bound by a harder and heavier chain. And I, a
> miserable wretch, am not ashamed to bear being bound for His name by this
> one." The stake was like a thick post half a foot thick; they sharpened one end
> of it and fixed it in the ground of that meadow. They placed two bound bundles
> of wood under the Master's feet. When tied to that stake, he still had his shoes
> on and one shackle on his feet. Indeed, the said bundles of wood, interspersed
> with straw, were piled around his body so that they reached up to his chin. For
> the wood amounted to two wagon- or carloads.

Before it was kindled, the imperial marshal, Hoppe of Poppenheim, approached him along with the son of the late Clem, as it was said, exhorting him to save his life by abjuring and recanting his former preaching and teaching. But he, looking up to heaven, replied in a loud voice: "God is my witness," he exclaimed, "that those things that are falsely ascribed to me and of which the false witnesses accused me, I have never taught or preached. But that the principal intention of my preaching and of all my other acts or writings was solely that I might turn men from sin. And in that truth of the Gospel that I wrote, taught, and preached in accordance with the sayings and expositions of the holy doctors, I am willing gladly to die today." And hearing that, the said marshal with the son of Clem immediately clapped their hands and retreated.

When the executioners at once lit [the fire], the Master immediately began to sing in a loud voice, at first, "Christ, Thou Son of the living God, have mercy upon us," and secondly, "Christ, Thou Son of the living God, have mercy upon me," and in the third place, "Thou Who art born of the Mary the Virgin." And when he began to sing for the third time, the wind blew the flame into his face. And thus praying within himself and moving his lips and the head, he expired in the Lord. While he was silent, he seemed to move before he actually died for about the time one can quickly recite, "Our Father" two or at most three times.

When the wood of those bundles and the ropes were consumed, but the remains of the body still stood in those chains, hanging by the neck, the executioners pulled the charred body along with the stake down to the ground and burned them together by adding wood from the third wagon to the fire. And walking around, they broke the bones with clubs so that they would be incinerated more quickly. And finding the head, they broke it to pieces with the clubs and again threw it into the fire. And when they found his heart among the intestines, they sharpened a club like a spit, and, impaling it on its end, they took particular [care] to roast and consume it, piercing it with spears until finally the whole mass was turned into ashes. And at the order of the said Clem and the marshal, the executioners threw the clothing into the fire along with the shoes, saying: "So that the Czechs would not regard it as relics; we will pay you money for it." Which they did. So they loaded all the ashes in a cart and threw it into the river Rhine flowing nearby.[48]

THE CONTROVERSIAL AFTERMATH

The "roasting of the Bohemian goose" at the stake caused a public uproar in Bohemia and triggered a series of fateful events which would change Bohemia forever. A *Protest Petition* [*Stížný list*] from 452 Czech lords and knights was sent to Constance,[49] but it was already much too late to change the past. The raging storm of events following Hus's tragic death would soon lead to a century of long-lasting division and tumultuous conflict.[50] However, in his death Hus's unwavering commitment to the truth of Jesus Christ as the true head of the church and the preeminent Lord over all proved his dedication to developing true, pure, authentic, and moral lives of both individuals and society as a whole; for it was for that truth which Hus made the ultimate sacrifice of his own life. Hus's ashes were now flowing in the Rhine, and his martyrdom in many regards confirmed the truth of his uncompromising message. The rising tide of truth would soon sweep throughout Bohemia and all of Christendom, and it could not be overcome even by "the gates of hell."[51] Hus's convincing words would not be forgotten: "Truth conquers all."

NOTES

1. *Korespondence*, 137: "*Revolvi in animo illud ewangelicum salvatoris verbum Johannis 10: 'Bonus pastor dat animam suam pro ovibus suis. Mercenarius autem, et qui non est pastor, cuius non sunt oves proprie, videt lupum venientem et dimittit oves, et fugit, et lupus rapit et dispergit oves.' Revolvi ex parte alia illud Mathei X: 'Cum persequentur' vos in una civitate, fugite in aliam.' Ecce preceptum Christi vel permissio; quidque inter duo opposita facere debeam, ignoro.*"

2. *Výklad na vieru* (*MIHOO*, 1:63–106).

3. *Výklad delší na desatero přikázanie* (*MIHOO*, 1:113–326). Hus also composed a shorter Latin exposition of the Decalogue. See *Expositio Decalogi (tom. 1 fasc. 1)* in *Mag. Joannis Hus Opera Omnia: Nach neuentdeckten Handschriften*, vol. 1, ed. Václav Flajšhans (Osnabrück: Biblio-Verlag, 1966), 1–45.

4. *Výklad na páteř* (*MIHOO*, 1:330–391).

5. *Provázek třípramenný* (*MIHOO*, 4:147–162).

6. *Knížky o svatokupectví* (*MIHOO*, 4:187–270).

7. *Zrcadlo hřiešníka (MIHOO*, 4:132–142). Hus also wrote a shorter version of the same work (*MIHOO*, 4:143–146). *The Mirror of a Sinner* is an edited Czech translation of the Pseudo-Augustinian *Speculum Peccatoris*. See *Speculum Peccatoris (PL*, 40:983–992). See also Jiří Daňhelka, "České glosy v textu Pseudo-Augustinova traktátu Speculum peccatoris v mikulovském rukopise Mk 102," *Listy filologické* 114, no. 2/3 (1991): 176–179.

8. *Dcerka: O poznání cěsty pravé k spasení* (*MIHOO*, 4:163–186); Jan Hus, *Dcerka: O poznání cesty pravé k spasení, ed. František Žilka (Praha: Kalich, 1995).*

9. There is a both a Latin and a Czech version of *On the Six Errors*. See Bohumil Ryba, *Betlemské texty* (Praha: Orbis, 1951), 39–63 (Latin); 65–104 (Czech); *O šesti bludiech (MIHOO*, 4:271–296).

10. Jan Hus, *Postilla: Vyloženie svatých čtení nedělních*, ed. J.B. Jeschke (Praha: Komenského evangelické fakulty bohoslovecké, 1952); Jan Hus, *Česká nedělní postila. Vyloženie svatých čtení nedělních*, ed. Jiří Daňhelka (Praha: Academia, 1992) (*Magistri Iohannis Hus Opera Omnia*, vol. 2).

11. *Contra Stephanum de Palecz* (*MIHOO*, 22:233–269).

12. *Contra Stanislaum de Znoyma* (*MIHOO*, 22:271–367).

13. Jan Hus, *Tractatus de Ecclesia*, ed. Samuel Harrison Thomson (Praha: Komenského evangelická fakulta bohoslovecká, 1958); *Tractatus de Ecclesia pronunciatus publice in Civitate Pragensi* (*Historia et Monumenta*, 1:243–318). In English, see *The Church by John Huss*, trans. David S. Schaff (New York: Charles Scribner's Sons, 1915). In Czech, see Mistr Jan Hus, *O církvi*, trans. František M. Dobiáš and Amedeo Molnár (Praha: Nakladatelství Československé akademie věd, 1965). In German, see "Über die Kirche," trans. Michael Beyer and Hans Schneider, in *Johannes Hus Deutsch*, 351–572.

14. Josef Hrabák, "Preface," in *O církvi*, trans. František M. Dobiáš and Amedeo Molnár, 9.

15. Adam W. Darlage, "Bohemian Church," in *Encyclopedia of Martin Luther and the Reformation*, vol. 2, ed. Mark A. Lamport (Lanham: Rowman & Littlefield, 2017), 79.

16. For a constructive evaluation of Hus's ecclesiology, see Matthew Spinka, *John Hus's Concept of the Church* (Princeton: Princeton University Press, 1966); see also František J. Holeček, "Hussens Kirchenverständnis," in *Jan Hus: Zwischen Zeiten, Völkern, Konfessionen*, 183–191.

17. *Tractatus de Ecclesia*, 7: "*Ex iam dictis sanctorum plane elicitur, quod sancta universalis ecclesia est numerus omnium predestinatorum et corpus Christi misticum, cuius ipse est caput, et sponsa Christi, quam ex dilecione maxima redemit suo sangwine, ut possideret eam gloriosam finaliter, non habentem rugam peccati mortalis aut maculam peccati venialis aut aliquid aliud ipsam vilificans, sed ut sit sancta et inmaculata perpetue amplexans Christum sponsum.*"

18. Josef Hrabák, "Preface," in *O církvi*, trans. František M. Dobiáš and Amedeo Molnár, 9.

19. Johann Loserth, *Huss und Wiclif: Zur Genesis der hussitischen Lehre* (München: Oldenbourg, 1925). The first edition has been translated into English. See Johann Loserth, *Wiclif and Hus*, trans. M.J. Evans (London: Hodder & Stoughton, 1884).

20. Schaff, *John Huss*, xxxi.

21. For resources on the council's reforms, see Phillip H. Stump, *The Reforms of the Council of Constance (1414–1418)* (Leiden: Brill, 1994); Christopher M. Bellitto, "The Reform Context of the Great Western Schism," in *A Companion to Great Western Schism (1378–1417)*, eds. Joëlle Rollo-Koster and Thomas M. Izbicki (Leiden: Brill, 2009), 303–331. See also *The Council of Constance: The Unification of the Church*, trans. Louise Ropes Loomis and eds. John Hine Mundy and Kennerly M. Woody (New York: Columbia University Press, 1961).

22. There are of course varying interpretations concerning the legitimacy of the trial and execution of Jan Hus. See Fudge, *The Trial of Jan Hus*, 1–30.

23. Hus mentioned this on January 4, 1415, in his *Letter to Jan of Chlum* (*Korespondence*, 239–240): "*Ego petivi cum protestacione coram notariis, et scripsi supplicacionem toti concilio, quam dedi patriarche, in qua peto, ut respondeam ad quemlibet articulum, sicuti respondi in privato. et manu mea scripsi. Vel si dabitur audiencia, ut respondeam more scholastico. Vel forte dabit deus audienciam, ut faciam sermonem.*" His speech can be viewed as either an academic discourse or a sermon depending on Hus's own legal understanding of the nature of the Council.

24. *Historia et monumenta*, 1:65–71; Jan Hus, *Sermo de Pace/Řeč o míru*, trans. F.M. Dobiáš and Amedeo Molnár (Praha: Česká křesťanská akademie, 1995); *Sermo de Pace* (*MIHOO*, 24:1–38).

25. *Sermo de Pace* (*MIHOO*, 24:25): "*Cum ergo iuxta prophetarum oracula et aliorum sanctorum testimonia ex peccato pastorum et aliorum sacerdotum ecclesie originatur eius coartacio et minucio, perturbacio augetur, exulat pax et animarum provenit dampnacio, nos, qui sacerdocii fungimur officio, humiliemus nostras piissimo Domino animas, in contrito spiritu devote dicentes: Piissime ac potentissime Domine, fiat pax in virtute tua. Fiat pax huic domui a peccato, fiat pax huic domui a persequente inimico, fiat pax huic domui a scismate iniquo et fiat pax domui in gloria cum Deo Patre et Filio et Spiritu sancto, in seculorum secula benedicto.*"

26. Karel Skalický, *Klasma* (České Budějovice: 2015), 10–11. Skalický's reference is to *Dignitatis Humanae*, which was promulgated on December 7, 1965, by Pope Paul VI. Pope John Paul II also delivered several messages on the freedom of conscience and religion: "On the Value and Content of Freedom of Conscience and of Religion" (November 14, 1980), "Religious Freedom: Condition for Peace" (January 1, 1988), "To Serve Peace, Respect Freedom" (January 1, 1981), "If You Want Peace, Respect the Conscience of Every Person" (January 1, 1991). Karol Wojtyla declared his views on religious freedom in his encyclicals *Redemptor hominis* and *Veritatis splendor* and also in his book *Sources of Renewal: The Implementation of Vatican II*, trans. P.S. Falla (San Francisco: Harper & Row, 1980).

27. For example, three barons wrote a letter to Sigismund in which they informed him of Archbishop Konrád's affirmation that he found no heresy in Hus. See *Documenta*, 531–537.

28. For issues surrounding Hus's safe conduct, see Lisa Stith Scott, *"To Go, Stay, Tarry, and Return":* Jan Hus and the Pan-European Authority of the Safe Conduct," *The Bohemian Reformation and Religious Practice* 11 (2018): 18–36.

29. *De penitencia* (*MIHOO*, 24:159).

30. *De peccato mortali* (*MIHOO*, 24:135–140).

31. *De sanguine Cristi sub specie vini a laicis sumendo* (*Historia et Monumenta*, 1:52–54); *De sumpcione sangwinis Iesu Cristi sub specie vini* (*MIHOO*, 24:103–116).

32. *De sacramento corporis et sanguinis Domini* (*MIHOO*, 24:183–210).

33. *De sumpcione sangwinis Iesu Cristi sub specie vini* (*MIHOO*, 24:105).

34. This condemnation occurred on June 15, 1415, during the thirteenth session. See *Enchiridion symbolorum definitionum et declarartionum de rebus fidei et morum (Lateinisch—Deutsch)*, eds. Heinrich Denzinger and Petrus Hünermann (Freiburg im Breisgau: Herder, 1991), 436–438.

35. Cf. Augustine, *De Baptismo Contra Donatistas*, 3.6.9; 3.8.11; 3.9.12; 4.5.8.

36. *Letter to Havlík* (*Korespondence*, 294–295).

37. Or *I call down a solemn curse upon each of them no matter how small they are.*

38. *Sto listů M. Jana Husi*, trans. Bohumil Ryba (Praha: Jan Laichter, 1949), 243; and *Korespondence*, 333:

"*Ego Johannes Hus, in spe sacerdos Ihesu Christi, timens deum offendere et timens incidere periurium, nolo abiurare articulos omnes et quemlibet ex illis, qui per falsos testes in attestacionibus producti sunt contra me, quia deo teste non predicavi nec asserui nec eos defendi, sicut dixerunt me eos defendisse, predicasse vel asseruisse etc.*

Item de articulis extractis de meis libellis, saltem qui sunt debite extracti, dico, quod quicumque ex illis includit aliquem falsum sensum, illum detestor. Sed timendo offendere in veritatem et contra sanctorum sentenciam dicere, non quemlibet eorum volo abiurare. Et si possibile esset, quod toti mundo nunc vox mea pateret, sicut omne mendacium et omne meum peccatum in die indicii patebit, libentissime omnem falsitatem et omnem errorem, quem umquam ad dicendum conceperim vel dixerim, coram toto mundo revocarem.

Ista dico et scribo libere et voluntarie

Scriptum manu mea propria prima die Julii."

39. For an older but still useful article on the chronology of Hus's letters, see Václav Novotný, "Listy Husovy: Poznámky kritické a chronologické," *Věstník Královské České Společnosti Náuk. Třída filosoficko-historicko-jazykozpytná*, no. 4 (1898): 1–89.

40. *The Letters of John Hus*, trans. Matthew Spinka (Manchester: Manchester University Press, 1972), ix.

41. The critical edition for Hus's correspondence is *Mistra Jana Husi korespondence a dokumenty*, ed. Václav Novotný (Praha: Nákladem komise pro vydávání pramenů náboženského hnutí českého, 1920). There are several Czech editions of Hus's letters. See: *Listy z Prahy (do r. 1412): Listy z vyhnanství (1412–1414): Listy z Kostnice (1414–1415)*, trans. Václav Flajšhans (Praha: Otto, 1915); Bohumil Mareš, ed., *Listy Husovy*, 3rd ed. (Prague: Hajn, 1911); Bohumila Ryba, *Sto listů M. Jana Husi* (Praha: Jan Laichter, 1949). Hus's letters have also been translated into several European languages. See, for example: Emile de Bonnechose, *Lettres de Jean Hus, écrites durant son exil et dans sa prison* (Paris: L.R. Delay, 1846); *Die Gefangenschaftsbriefe des Johann Hus*, ed. Constantin von Kügelgen (Leipzig: Richard Wöpke, 1902); Spinka, *The Letters of John Hus*. See also his letters by various translators in *Johannes Hus Deutsch*, v–viii.

42. *Korespondence*, 215: *"Esto diligens in predicacione ewangelii et fac opus boni evangeliste. Vocacionem tuam ne negligas, labora tamquam beatus miles Christi: Prim pie et sancte vive, deinde fideliter et vere doce. Exemplum esto aliis in bono opere, ne in sermone reprehendaris, corrige peccata et virtutes commenda; illis, qui male vivunt, mineris penas eternas, qui vero sunt fideles et pie vivunt, gaudia eterna proponito. Predica assidue, breviter tamen et cum fructu, prudenter intelligendo sacras scripturas. Incerta et dubia numquam affirmes, ne reprehendaris ab adversariis, qui gaudent, ut suis proximis detrahant, quo ministros dei contumelia afficiant. Hortare ad confessionem fidei et communionem utriusque speciei corporis et sanguinis Christi, ut qui de peccatis suis vere penitenciam egerunt, eo sepius ad communionem accedant."*

43. *Korespondence*, 273. An abbreviated version of Hus's sentence appears on the Jan Hus Memorial in the Old Town Square of Prague, which was sculpted by Ladislav Šaloun (1870–1946): *"Milujte se, pravdy každému přejte."* Since the older Czech word *pravda* was related to justice, the last phrase could also be translated as "do not deny the truth to anyone."

44. *Sto listů M. Jana Husi*, 248; *Korespondence*, 336.

45. "Petri de Mladoniowicz relatio de Magistro Johanne Hus," *Fontes rerum Bohemicarum*, ed. Václav Novotný (Praha: Nadání Františka Palackého, 1932), 8:25–120; Matthew Spinka, *John Hus at the Council of Constance*, 87–234; *Hus in Konstanz: Der Bericht des Peter von Mladoniowitz*, trans. Josef Bujnoch (Graz: Verlag Styria, 1963); *Petra z Mladoňovic Zpráva o mistru Janu Husovi v Kostnici*, trans. František Heřmanský (Praha: Univerzita Karlova, 1965), 67–174.

46. *Documenta*, 741; *Petra z Mladoňovic Zpráva o mistru Janu Husovi v Kostnici*, trans. František Heřmanský, 245–246; Spinka, *John Hus at the Council of Constance*, xiii.

47. See David Holeton, "'O felix Bohemia—O felix Constantia': The Liturgical Commemoration of Saint Jan Hus," in *Jan Hus: Zwischen Zeiten, Völkern, Konfessionen: Vorträge des internationalen Symposions in Bayreuth vom 22. bis 26. September 1993* (München: Oldenbourg), 385–403; see also David R. Holeton and Hana Vlhová-Wörner, "A Remarkable Witness to the Feast of Saint Jan Hus," *The Bohemian Reformation and Religious Practice* 7 (2009): 156–184.

48. I have cited here from Spinka, since he already accurately translated this section into English. See Spinka, *John Hus at the Council of Constance*, 231–234. The original Latin is found in *Documenta*, 316–324; see also Petr z Mladoňovic, "Zpráva o Mistru Janu Husovi v Kostnici," *Ze zpráv a kronik doby husitské*, ed. Ivan Hlaváček (Praha: Svoboda, 1981), 156–159.

49. See Petr Čornej, Aleš Knápek, Ladislav Macek, and Pavel Rous, *Stížný list: České a moravské šlechty proti upálení Mistra Jana Husa 1415–2015*, ed. Ladislav Langpaul (Okrouhlice: Spolek Za záchranu rodného domu malíře Jana Zrzavého v Okrouhlici, 2015).

50. For surveys of Hussite history and/or the Hussite wars, see František M. Bartoš, *Husitská revoluce*, 2 vols (Prague: SAV, 1965–1966); idem, *The Hussite Revolution, 1424–1437*, trans. John Martin Klassen (New York: Columbia University Press, 1986); Frederick G. Heymann, *John Žižka and the Hussite Revolution* (Princeton: Princeton University Press, 1955); Howard Kaminsky, *A History of the Hussite Revolution* (Eugene: Wipf and Stock, 1967); Franz Lützow, *The Hussite Wars* (London: J. M. Dent & Sons, 1914); František Šmahel, *Husitská revoluce*, 4 vols. (Prague: Historický ústav, 1993); idem, *Die Hussitische Revolution*, 3 vols., trans. Thomas Krzenck and ed. Alexander Patschovsky (Hannover: Hahnsche Buchhandlung, 2002); Thomas A. Fudge, *The Crusade against Heretics in Bohemia, 1418–1437: Sources and Documents for the Hussite Crusades* (New York: Routledge, 2016); Franz Machilek, ed., *Die hussitische Revolution: Religiöse, politische und regionale Aspekte* (Wien: Böhlau Verlag, 2012).

51. Matthew 16:17–19.

5

Jan Hus as a Reformer: Truth in Word and in Deed

Before we turn to some of Hus's own thoughts and ideas, we must first pose the following questions: What was the actual truth for which Hus so diligently struggled? What was his concept and understanding of truth?[1] What was the actual truth which led him to the very threshold between life and death? What was the truth for which he died at the stake? We do not wish to downplay the turbulent times in which he lived, nor do we want to judge his own motivations nor the charges of heresy against him in relation to his legal case, since others have already evaluated those questions.[2] We must remember that for Hus, truth did not represent a mere acceptance of abstract or rational propositions, or even adherence to Christian doctrine. Hus believed that Jesus Christ is the ultimate embodiment of eternal and personal truth and that the meaning of life is found only in relation to God, in whom all things will finally be revealed and known in the *visio beatifica*.[3] This perspective of truth was founded upon his commitment to following his conscience informed by Holy Scripture.[4]

Throughout his life, Hus assiduously strove to follow his conscience and critiqued others for failing to do so, especially in moments when truth was at stake.[5] Hus differentiated between the individually distinct and hidden discretion in the forum of the human conscience *(in foro consciencie)* and the powerful jurisdiction of ecclesiastical courts.[6] Hus viewed the conscience as "a kind of covenant [that] has been made with each soul so that it would keep its promises to God,"[7] and declared that it is neither safe nor wise to disobey one's conscience.[8]

Due to his passionate commitment to living in the truth and following his own conscience, the main principles of truth to which Hus so faithfully adhered must be seen in the light of his conviction that Jesus Christ himself is the ultimate truth.[9] Hus understood this truth to be eternal, and therefore not as a matter of accommodation to any set of historical circumstances. Yet,

71

as the eternal Truth became incarnate in time in the person of Jesus Christ, living in truth demanded that mankind maintain an unfeigned personal and ethical commitment to pursuing *imitatio Christi* in every unique era of human history.[10] Thus, while Hus was certainly a product of his times, we cannot simply isolate Hus's views on truth to one historical era, but rather we have to interpret him from the perspective of history itself and especially church history—which will include previous, contemporary, and future generations' theological concepts of truth. Since Hus in many ways represents a transitional figure from the late medieval era to the early modern era, his understanding and proclamation of truth will be reflected in his own *terms* but not in entirely different *tones* from other Christian eras. One researcher has aptly noted that "in the Bohemian Reformation, the pre-Reformation, or perhaps the 'First Reformation,' the same ecclesiological, anthropological, and eucharistical tones which are usually considered Lutheran resonated quite deeply, even though their terminology had not yet been fully defined."[11] Therefore, the arduous but vital task placed upon researchers is to seek as much as possible to understand multiple streams of various influences: historical, social, philosophical, theological, personal, etc.[12]

Although historians rightly seek to interpret Hus within his own era and based on his own merits, theologians must aim to be fair to Hus's own theological convictions and to some extent need to share Hus's own mindset in order to understand him fully. In that regard, we need to consider truth from both an historical and what might be called a more eternal perspective (*sub specie aeternitatis*), or else we will misinterpret his aims and actions. However, in seeking to reflect upon selected aspects of his thought in relation to other nations, confessions, and eras, mistakes are simply unavoidable. It is for that reason that Hus has been labeled nearly everything under the sun by a variety of researchers: the greatest of heretics; a rebellious revolutionary; a theological forerunner to the Protestant Reformation; "a patron saint and prophet";[13] a die-hard nationalist; a significant church reformer; and a paragon of a dedicated Christian preacher.[14] The field of Hussite studies is still awaiting a detailed modern monograph specifically investigating the main aspects of Hus's overall theological paradigm and thought.[15] Certainly, Hus's understanding of the law of God and lifelong emphasis on the *legis Dei* and *legis Christi* represent key elements of his thought,[16] and Hus's rightful place within the context and development of the "first reformation" in Bohemia and the European Reformation has been duly noted by both historians and theologians.[17] This brief chapter will not discuss the plethora of debates concerning Hus's alleged Donatism or his supposed divergence from other traditional or medieval ecclesiological formulations.[18] Instead, we will touch upon two of perhaps the most controversial aspects of his theological thought which have been mentioned in most of his biographies.

Although some very reputable scholars have made reasonable claims to the contrary, we believe that there is sufficient evidence in his writings to assert that in anticipation of the later European reformers, Hus was indeed a so-called precursor to the two great Reformation principles: the *formal* principle (*sola Scriptura*) and the *material* principle (*sola fide*). In this regard, it is important to recall that "every major tenet of the Reformation had considerable support in the catholic tradition."[19] One could perhaps claim that Hus even adhered to them more rigorously than some of the other European reformers, since no one can fail to remember that Hus was actually martyred for his beliefs while many other earlier and later church reformers did not suffer a similar fate. In this sense, Hus's actions certainly speak louder than his words (though admittedly there are a host of complicated reasons why Hus was burned at the stake in Constance). At the very least, his own statements at the Council of Constance speak volumes concerning his own commitment to the Lord Jesus Christ and Holy Scripture. Czech church historian Miloslav Kaňák remarked: "Hus established himself in history as a reformer not merely academically, but even in an apostolic way by the fact that he would rather offer up his own body to be burned [as a martyr] than to recant and give offense to those whom he had taught from his firm and holy convictions."[20]

THE FORMAL PRINCIPLE: TRUTH IN WORD[21]

In approaching the formal principle, we must remember that the phrase *sola Scriptura* was coined in order to explain specific doctrinal beliefs, not *vice versa;* the phrase explains or encapsulates the doctrine, but it does not envelop nor exhaust it fully.[22] The phrase is simply a shorthand expression of the doctrine, and doctrinal beliefs throughout church history have shown remarkable unity even in the face of numerous (i.e., seemingly never-ending) heresies, and those beliefs surely include inchoate or implicitly articulated forms of specific doctrines (e.g., a doctrine of Scripture). Some may feel that it is inappropriate to use the phrase at all; but since *sola Scriptura* reflects doctrinal convictions, the doctrine itself must be evaluated in all of its various expressions.[23]

The *formal principle* is clearly evidenced throughout Hus's corpus, and it is virtually impossible to deny Hus's affirmation of the supreme authority of Holy Scripture.[24] Hus understood Scripture to mean the divine Word of truth which became incarnate in Jesus Christ, and the Bible is inspired by the Holy Spirit and is the authoritatively articulated expression of this divine Word of God. Jesus is understood as "the living Lord of the Scripture."[25] Although Hus did not fully elaborate his doctrine of Scripture in an individual treatise on the subject, he did offer several analogies of what Holy Scripture signified in his

Figure 5.1. Jan Hus as depicted on the Luther Monument in Worms.
Source: Wikimedia Commons (public domain)

Commentary on the Sentences of Lombard: "the law of universal Wisdom";
"divinely inspired Wisdom"; "enduring Wisdom"; "the most worthy wisdom
and knowledge of the uncreated Holy Trinity"; "teaching from the light of

the highest knowledge"; "the means of leading [mankind] to blessedness"; "Christ the divine Word"; "everything spoken and revealed through Christ for the salvation of the human race"; "the knowledge of Christ the Word of God"; "the voice or writing or signs signifying Christ the divine Word"; "portraits of Christ depicting his suffering"; "every language in which the truth of Christ is inscribed"; "uncreated Wisdom"; "wisdom from Wisdom"; "the deepest knowledge."[26]

It is important to understand Hus's realist hermeneutic which, much like Wyclif, made frequent use of various analogical definitions for a single word.[27] It is therefore inappropriate to equate each of the complex metaphors Hus provided for *Scriptura*. Neither is it logically consistent to reduce all of the multiple expressions into one by way of strict metonymy, since he used distinct analogies not so much as a simple identity of relation, but as shared attributions related to different modes of predication. Although Hus's understanding of Scripture in relation to *tertium comparationis, res significata*, and *modus significandi* requires a more detailed analysis, we do note that his analogies were adapted from Wyclif's "five degrees of Holy Scripture" (*quinque gradus scripture sacre*) in his *De Veritate Sacra Scripturae*[28] as well as his emphasis on "Christ [being] the subject of theology" (*Christus sit subiectum theologie*) in *De Dominio Divino.*[29] It should be duly noted that in every occurrence of the Czech word for Scripture (*Písmo*) among the more than one hundred usages in his *Česká nedělní postila*, Hus used it only to refer to the written Old and New Testaments (i.e., the Bible). He specifically referred to all the Scriptures concerning Christ in the Old Testament as being "written"[30] and the Scripture in the New Testament as being written by the apostles.[31] "The Law is the divine Scripture which has been written,"[32] and likewise, "the Law is the divine Scripture which is the law above other laws."[33] Hus also followed Wyclif in calling Christ himself "the most Holy Scripture"[34] while also referring to the Bible as "the most Holy Scripture."[35] Thus, for Wyclif and consequently for Hus, since Christ is the true author of Scripture, supreme authority resides in the words of Christ.[36]

Although some have mischaracterized *sola Scriptura* as an anachronism, Richard Muller reverses that inappropriate charge and aptly notes that "it is thus entirely anachronistic to view the *sola scriptura* of Luther and his contemporaries as a declaration that all of theology ought to be construed anew without reference to the church's tradition of interpretation, by the lonely exegete confronting the naked text."[37]

This response might also apply to any previous viewpoints or expressions concerning a theological doctrine of Scripture. Evident in our discussion on Hus's view of Scripture is the need to find realistically viable working definitions.[38] For example, one author proposes: "*Sola Scriptura means that only Scripture, because it is God's inspired Word, is our inerrant, sufficient, and final authority for the church.*"[39] The same author clarifies by noting, "In fact, *sola scriptura* means that the Bible is our chief, supreme, and ultimate authority."[40] Those explicative adjectives are important, since Hus used each one of them to describe Holy Scripture in his corpus, but neither the church nor tradition (not even "holy" tradition) are given those key descriptors.[41] Thus, Scripture legitimately represented the *inerrant, sufficient,* and *final* authority for Hus for establishing Christian doctrine, but not the *only legitimate* authority in life.[42] The following definition is also worth considering in this context:

> Stated positively, *sola scriptura* is meant as a statement that the scriptures are the final, not the sole, authority. All other authorities are to be tested against the norm of scripture, because even tradition and church can err . . . *Sola scriptura* is about authority. *Sola* does not mean, however, that scripture is the sole authority, but that it is the final authority in the Church, to decide what is true and what is not. The question is, not only what is the nature and extent of this authority, but also what is the nature of truth.[43]

Or again, Hus's view is entirely consistent with other appropriate definitions of *sola Scriptura* such as: "*Sola Scriptura* means that the only ultimate norm for theology is the teaching of Scripture. Other norms must justify themselves by their faithfulness to the inspired Word."[44] Was not Hus the very person who declared before the council that even alleged heretics such as himself should be "humbly instructed from the Scriptures and reasons derived from them," following the example of Augustine and others?[45]

In addition, "the slogan *sola Scriptura* is the statement that the church can err."[46] Hus would certainly agree with the assessment that "the church" can err.[47] By contrast, God cannot err,[48] neither can his word err or speak falsehood, since it is "pure truth,"[49] "the inviolable truth,"[50] and the "infallible truth."[51]

Thus, one may say in a certain sense that "the appeal to Scripture alone was in part an appeal to origins, in part—and inseparably—an appeal directly to Christ."[52] Hus would concur with the approach of an "appeal directly to Christ," evidencing it most clearly in four major instances. The first is in his own appeal on October 18, 1412: "I present this appeal to Jesus Christ, the most righteous Judge who unfailingly examines, defends and judges, and discloses and upholds the just cause of every man."[53] Second, in his theological explanation of the power and authority of the church (i.e., "the keys of the kingdom") in discerning, judging, receiving, and excluding declarations of forgiveness, he wrote that "only the Trinity has this kind of authentic sovereign power."[54] Third, his polemical defense aimed to prove that directly appealing to divine authority instead of mediated authority is sometimes necessary in order to secure justice.[55] Fourth, his humble declaration before the Council of Constance showed where his ultimate allegiance was found: "I have never been obstinate, nor am I now, but I have always desired and even to this very day do I desire more effective instruction from the Scripture."[56]

However, for Hus the elevation of Holy Scripture above all other standards did not mean that Scripture was somehow contrary to reason, and this is perhaps slightly different from Luther's particular stance.[57] According to Hus, the tradition of the church bears the role of faithfully interpreting and explaining Scripture, and this is certainly the correct theological perspective. One theologian explained Hus's view as follows:

> Thereby, we arrive at Hus's assessment of church tradition. All of his sermons imply quite clearly that every insight, understanding, and interpretation of the Holy Scripture happened within the context of tradition. Hus was always concerned about and interested in both Scripture and tradition, whereas the function of tradition was to confirm the authority of the God's word, and it did not stand qualitatively on the same level as the Bible itself. Tradition had a rather auxiliary character, but it was not however identical to divine revelation from the perspective of quality. Tradition was in service to the word of God and not vice versa. Hus received the homiletical-exegetical tradition of the past without succumbing to the extreme religious individualism of his time, which despised both the church and tradition while appealing to the Bible, nor did he surrender to the temptation of extreme spiritualism which suspended human reason in favor of faith.[58]

Hus was deeply appreciative of the Christological, Trinitarian, and soteriological dogmas, the early Christian confessions, and the sayings of the church fathers (among whom Augustine, John Chrysostom, Jerome, Gregory, Ambrose, Peter Lombard, and Thomas Aquinas are frequently the most cited in his corpus).[59] Hus accepted the holy tradition of the church, but staunchly denied that canon law and papal bulls or decrees possess the same authority as Holy Scripture. Thus in a certain sense, Hus's conflict with the church was predominately experienced as a crisis between Holy Scripture and the church, not as an antagonistic or indiscriminate separation of Scripture and tradition. On the basis of his view of truth, Hus was morally compelled to distinguish between "corrupt or false traditions" and "true tradition." For him it was evident that the church had adopted false traditions and placed them on par with true tradition. Hus determined to honor true tradition by using Scripture as the norm and arbiter for discerning what should be believed and practiced. For example, Hus saw the pope as a human being and as such a sinner, not *ipso facto* the vicar of God on earth, but indeed a representative of Christ as long as his life reflected the holy morality of Christ expressed in the law of Christ.[60] Hus's overall rationale concerning the relationship of authority for

Scripture, Christians, and the Church is most clearly expressed in the following statement from his *Treatise on the Church*:

> And in this manner, every Christian is obligated to believe explicitly and implic-
> itly all the truth which the Holy Spirit has placed in Scripture; and in the same
> way a man is not bound to believe the sayings of the saints which are contrary
> to Scripture, nor should he believe papal bulls, unless they are affirmed from
> Scripture or to the extent that they are founded implicitly in Scripture . . . Thus,
> no one is permitted to discredit or contradict Holy Scripture, but it is proper at
> any time to disbelieve bulls and even contradict them provided that they either
> praise the unworthy, or place those in authority who smack of avarice, or exalt
> the unrighteous, or oppress the innocent, or implicitly contradict the commands
> and counsels of God.[61]

He had also expressed the same ideas earlier in his life at the university when
he wrote his *Commentary on the Sentences of Lombard*:

> And thus Holy Scripture is Christ the divine Word along with that which was
> spoken and revealed to the human race through him and should be firmly
> adhered to and believed by people in order to obtain eternal blessedness. From
> this it follows that every truth directing a person how he should serve his God
> is [in] Holy Scripture, which whether implicitly or explicitly should be believed
> and adhered to by people, since every such [law] is the necessary law which
> must inevitably be fulfilled by the faith of people according to this oath of the
> Savior in Matthew 5: "Truly I say to you, until heaven and earth pass away, not
> an iota or a dot (i.e., no truth spoken from my mouth) will pass away until all
> is accomplished."[62]

We see this principle being put into practice in his own life, since "in the disputes which transpired between Hus and his opponents, the first and foremost
authority which he framed against the authority of the ecclesiastical officials
was Holy Scripture."[63] Hus's engagement with Scripture and his approach to
interpretation led church historian Matthew Spinka (1890–1972) to claim that
"Hus was a forerunner of Biblical theologians, for he subordinated scholastic
reasoning to the Scriptures. In this he belongs to the Reformation rather than
to the Middle Ages."[64] Furthermore, another church historian fittingly noted
that in relation to his understanding of the infallible and supreme authority of
the Bible "Hus was a true precursor of the Reformation."[65]

Czech-Swiss Protestant theologian Jan Milíč Lochman (1922–2004)
explains why the previous two quotes are justified:

> The later reformational "sola scriptura" is admittedly not so unequivocally and
> familiarly found in Hus, though it emerges all the same in presenting a practi-
> cal emphasis: it is certainly obvious that for Hus the biblical word presents and

envisions the intrinsic standard of Christianity, and he did not hesitate to apply this standard practically and concretely. He also demonstrated this attitude and position before the Council: biblical truth and conscience illumined by the Bible should determine whether or not recanting was even a possibility. Scripture alone corresponded to the final sovereign authority. It was the predominant foundation for deciding arguments in the church.[66]

Therefore, though some would still perceive Hus's views to be more aligned with *prima Scriptura* according to Yves Congar's explanation of "the normative primacy of Scripture,"[67] we feel that ascribing to Hus a position of *sola Scriptura* is warranted for several important reasons:

1. Hus affirmed all of the four main attributes of Scripture commonly expressed in Protestant confessions (i.e., necessity, sufficiency, authority, and perspicuity).[68]

2. Hus distinguished between trusting the authority of "the sacred canon of the Bible" (*sacro canone Bibliae*)[69] and "the holy gospel"[70] versus believing other writings,[71] papal bulls, or sayings of the saints.[72]

3. Hus made a marked distinction between the infallibility of God and his word (". . . *Scriptura sacra, cum sit veritas infallibilis . . .*")[73] in contrast to the tradition of the church which can err and has erred.[74]

4. Hus identified "the voice of Christ" with the "word of Christ"[75] and his voice as "the truth which should be believed and fulfilled."[76]

5. His uncompromising critiques of false traditions of the church and "the commandments of men" imposed by the papacy and other ecclesiastical authorities were based on the greater authority of Scripture.[77]

6. Hus set forth Scripture as the standard for determining how judges (especially ecclesiastical judges) should render judgments,[78] for determining obedience to ecclesiastical commands,[79] for determining what is true,[80] and for determining what should be believed.[81]

7. Hus emphasized hearing "the voice of the Holy Spirit in Scripture,"[82] since Scripture itself is a "thing which is alive" or a "living reality which speaks truthfully by itself" (*"Scriptura sacra eciam est res animata, que per se et vere loquitur . . ."*).[83]

8. Hus maintained a deep commitment to interpreting Scripture as the Holy Spirit intended, where believers are to "yield completely to the meaning which the Holy Spirit demands."[84] He admitted that "with God's own help, we do not intend to expound Scripture other than the way in which the Holy Spirit demands and in the way which it has been expounded by the holy doctors to whom the Holy Spirit gave understanding."[85] At the Council of Constance, he declared that he believed

every single article of the law of Christ "according to the meaning in which the blessed Trinity teaches them to be believed."[86]

9. Hus constantly reiterated that "we must obey God rather than men"[87] in context of following the word of God over against custom or ecclesiastical tradition.

10. Hus expressed the viewpoint that the teaching ministry of the church (i.e., magisterium) should be based on the "authority of Scripture" (*in auctoritate scripture*).[88]

11. Hus professed that Christians should believe the articles of the Nicene Creed[89] as well as the Apostles' Creed (i.e., *regula fidei*) and the Athanasian Creed[90] because each article is founded upon Scripture.

12. Hus affirmed that Scripture is self-attesting and self-authenticating. Scripture "bears witness" or "testifies" to the truth,[91] since "Scripture itself is witness"[92] to the truth of Christ, who himself "bears witness"[93] to the truth of the holy gospel. The gospel bears witness to Christ's own testimony that he was sent into the world by the Father in order to save the world from sin.[94]

Generally speaking, with such a diverse range of analogies employed in the prolegomenon of his longest theological work, Hus's perspective of Scripture is not easily grasped, mainly since medieval words such as "*sacra doctrina, sacra Scriptura, auctoritas* . . . ring differently to the medieval ear than do our modern terms 'theology,' 'Scripture,' and 'authority.'"[95] Nevertheless, we can fully agree with the assessment that "according to Hus, the complete rule of a faithful life (i.e., a life of faith or living by faith) fully expressed in Scripture is the law of the living Christ, the Lord of the Church and of the world."[96]

THE MATERIAL PRINCIPLE: TRUTH IN DEED

Hus also showed evidence of expressing the *material* principle of the Reformation, which is justification by grace alone (*sola gratia*) through faith alone (*sola fide*).[97] Of course, Hus demanded that faith should be the certain kind of living faith which expresses itself through love and the kind of true faith which is evidenced by good works (James 2:14–26; Galatians 5:6).[98] Good works will necessarily flow forth from saving faith; otherwise, that kind of faith is not true faith, since "faith without works is dead" (James 2:26). According to Hus, believing in the sense of only having the correct beliefs or knowing about the truth does not lead someone to salvation.[99] Hus wrote that true faith "is the faith by which we believe and are virtuous. This is the kind of faith by which we act virtuously from love, the kind of faith through which Christ dwells in our hearts, and this kind of faith is imperishable; but the first kind of faith without these is ineffective for salvation."[100] There is no doubt whatsoever that Hus stressed the importance of obedience, but "Hus, with his emphasis on practical following, does not effect a new type of legalism but, rather, stresses that faith must be faith incarnated into the life of the Christian . . ."[101]

Although he still employed the term *fides caritate formata* frequently,[102] Hus was certainly opposed to certain aspects of the scholastic system and appears to have shifted (at least slightly) in principle from the traditional scholastic meaning of the phrase. While Peter Lombard wrote that "love is the mother of all the virtues,"[103] Hus used the term "mother of virtues" in relation to *faith*, since "the movement of faith gives rise to the movement of other virtues."[104] Although not within the same context, it would still be helpful to remember here that Luther in his critique of scholastic theology wrote that "where they speak of love we speak of faith."[105] Not only did Hus affirm that "faith is the foundation of the other virtues,"[106] but he also expressly wrote, "*Ergo sola fides etiam sine opere sufficit ad salutem.*"[107] He critiqued those who thought that it would be better to see signs rather than "only believing" (. . . *credere sola fide*)[108] and affirmed that salvation is given "freely without any of our own merits . . . not because of works which we have done."[109] In his *Commentary on the Epistle of James,* he explained the meaning of true faith by employing several variants of the biblical phrase "faith working through love" from Galatians 5:6.[110]

It is also important to note that the theological content of what Hus wrote in Latin sometimes sounded much different when it was written in Czech; this fact is surely based on his unrelenting desire to reach the common people and help them understand the truth. Hus even personally acknowledged as much in his *Minor Exposition of the Apostles' Creed,* where he encouraged his readers to use different expressions when speaking with the common people and with those who were educated. In his conclusion of his minor exposition of the *Nicean Creed,* he wrote: "It may be said that for the common people it is sufficient unto salvation when they only believe in God and in Jesus Christ."[111] Of course, this belief involved "trusting, fulfilling the commandments of God, and praying to God."[112] Still, unbelief is a causative corollary, since men are damned due to their unbelief, not on account of their lack of sanctifying works performed through love.[113] In fact, in his *Commentary on the Song of Solomon,* he stated that those works are credited (literally "accounted" in Czech) to a person by the grace of God: "She is leaning on her beloved, that is, believing and hoping in Christ alone, and thus all good works are being credited to her by his grace. For she knows and understands that in and of herself she cannot do anything good. Therefore, she says with Saint Paul, 'By the grace of God, I am what I am.'"[114]

When a person truly repents, then his sins are forgiven by God.[115] He quoted Richard of Saint Victor in agreement that "the confession of the heart alone is sufficient unto salvation of the soul for the truly repentant,"[116] although it was perhaps limited to cases of necessity.[117] He also quoted the glossa which mentioned that when *tempus operandi* is lacking, then faith alone is sufficient in cases like the thief on the cross where he believed in his heart and confessed with his mouth (". . . *sufficit sola fides, sicut patet de latrone, cui dictum est propter fidem cordis et confessionem oris* . . .").[118]

For Hus, "faith is the first virtue infused by God upon which every virtue should be founded as the bedrock or foundation."[119] Hus used the phrase "by an enlivening grace" to clarify the manner in which faith saves while at the same time using the traditional distinction made by Augustine to contrast between three kinds of belief or faith.[120] "Each created and rational soul that does not possess true love for the Lord God nor desire him is not living by faith or he is not righteous, concerning which Habakkuk declares, 'The righteous one will live by his faith.'"[121] In his discussion on congruent and condign merit in his *Commentary on the Sentences of Lombard,* his concluding remarks are entirely based on Canons 18–21 of the Second Council of Orange (529), which are clearly against semi-Pelagian doctrine.[122] As well, Hus emphasized the merits of Christ in his letters. In a letter written to the people of Louny, he spoke of trusting in God on account of Christ's merits (*propter merita Iesu Christi*): "Love God with all of your heart and put your confidence in God that on the account of the merits of Jesus Christ he will adorn you in his glory and cause you to participate in his kingdom."[123] And in a letter to the Praguers, he wrote that Jesus "by his agonizing and ignominious death has redeemed us from eternal torment without any merits of our own."[124] Those who are predestined are saved by "the merit of Christ,"[125] and since "Christ himself is the object of our faith and hope,"[126] therefore "faith produces children of God."[127]

At the very least, Hus's view of salvation was reflective of medieval Augustinianism, and wherever Augustine's position falls along the theological spectrum, Hus's view will certainly resonate within that trajectory, since Hus was certainly fond of Augustine's writings—writings which in themselves also present a viewpoint, which is not too easy to determine.[128] Although one should never equivocate the particular meaning of words and phrases of one writer (e.g., *iustificare, fides caritate formata, or sola fide)* with previous or later formulations, the perceptive historian will acknowledge that Protestant reformers like Martin Luther even distinguished between true faith and false faith in terms of virtues such as love and accompanying good works. Luther certainly critiqued the scholastic formulations of *fides caritata formata,*[129] but he also wrote that "faith of course must be sincere. It must be a faith that performs good works through love. If faith lacks love then it is not true faith."[130] Even the *glossa ordinaria* on Romans 3:28 used the phrase "*sola fide*" in relation to salvation contrasted with the works of the law, yet clarified the meaning of saving faith by using Augustine's threefold distinction for the explanation of Romans 4:5.[131] Hus quoted the *glossa ordinaria* in his *Commentary on the Second Epistle of Peter*: "*Non in circumcisione legis, aequati estis antiquae plebi Dei, sed fides, quae sine operibus salvat,*" but surprisingly removed the word *legis* from the original gloss, which read, "*sed fide que sine operibus legis salvat.*"[132]

Some scholars have perceived the similarity of Hus's phrase *simul et semel sit iustus et iniustus, fidelis et infidelis*[133] as a nuanced parallel to Luther's *simul iustus et peccator*,[134] while others have claimed that Hus was in effect actually denying rather than affirming it due to the context of the statement. Hus did, however, ascribe a present righteousness to those who are predestined even when they are living in sin ("*existens in crimine*") based on a "twofold bond" of grace: "*Predestinati vero, licet ad tempus priventur fluente gracia, habent tamen radicalem graciam a qua non possunt excidere. Et sic predestinati iam iusti habentes duplici vinculo sunt ligati.*"[135] Hus also affirmed that a virtuous person is not necessarily deprived of his virtuous disposition even while at the same time being in a state of sin.[136] When speaking of the kind of living faith which saves in contrast to a dead faith which is ineffective for salvation, Hus used several methods and explanations:

1. He linked a "faith formed by love" with "the grace or virtue of perseverance" which is "sufficient for salvation" (*Unde quicunque habuerit fidem caritate formatam in communi sufficit cum virtute perseverancie ad salutem*).[137]

2. He applied a negative qualifier *(non)* to the biblical phrase cited from Galatians 5:6: "*fides, quae per dileccionem non operatur, mortua est, inefficax ad salutem.*"[138] He also explained the meaning of true faith by employing several other variants of the biblical phrase "faith working through love" from Galatians 5:6.[139]

3. He insisted on the necessity of works of mercy in relation to faith: "*Fides sine misericordiae operibus non prodest ad salutem.*"[140]

4. He again linked faith, hope, love, and perseverance together: "*Quicunque credit caritative perseveranter in filium dei habet vitam eternam.*"[141] "I am confident of this, that the Lord will complete what he has begun in you the elect and will grant you perseverance . . ."[142] Hus taught that God opens our hearts by grace and gives us persevering faith.[143] God became incarnate and suffered an agonizing death in order "to destroy sin in his elect and by grace eternally preserve them in joy . . ."[144] God also grants his church "persevering hope,"[145] with "the true church"

being understood as "the congregation of the faithful who have been predestined and justified" (*Ecclesia vero . . . est congregacio fidelium predestinatorum et iustificatorum*).[146]

5. He emphasized an important clarification that the biblical author said "'faith without works' (*fides sine operibus*) but did not say faith without working (*sine opere*), because believing is the accomplishment or work of faith itself . . . (*credere est opus fidei*)."[147]

Overall, Hus's legal-theological view of the law of God influenced his legal-relational view of justification and sanctification, and distinct theological categories sometimes appear to collapse into each other, as well as the Christian virtues of faith, hope, and love seemingly being equivocated at times; yet still, the debate still rages as to whether Hus thought that love develops as a consequence of believing or whether love is somehow a necessary "condition or addition" to faith so as to make faith effective in securing salvation. The former appears more plausible, since Hus taught that a person is not able to attain and enjoy blessedness unless by faith he is engrafted into Christ who himself is love.[148] He wrote: "In so far as we believe, we hope to that extent; and in so far as we believe and hope, we love to that extent; and as much as we work, that is the extent to which we believe, hope, and love."[149] Thus, the faith by which we are saved is always immediately followed by hope and love,[150] since faith, hope, and love are given by grace through union with Christ,[151] but faith alone in Christ can heal our souls.[152] It is on account of faith that one will be saved,[153] because "faith is the foundation of all virtues for salvation."[154] "Christ Jesus himself is the foundation of faith, hope, and love, and thus all good,"[155] and Christ himself is the *charitas* which vivifies faith,[156] seeing that God "loves the predestined more and grants them greater grace and even a greater gift—eternal life . . ."[157] and that the "love of God" is identified with "the grace of predestination."[158] Since "Christ builds the church upon himself by faith, hope, and love,"[159] "the grace of predestination is the bond" of these virtues.[160] Thus, while "unformed faith is a gift infused,"[161] formed faith is a greater gift (i.e., eternal life), because "virtue, grace, and love" are identical.[162]

Drawing from Augustine again, Hus wrote that "to believe in God is to come to him, to be incorporated as a member of his body, and thus to love him above all things."[163] Despite the inconsistencies of expression, it seems that Hus was not teaching that faith *must* have love added to it in order to *become* true saving faith, but that true faith *will* necessarily be united with and accompanied by love because it *is* in fact true faith. He wrote that a dead faith without works is utterly worthless, but the kind of faith which works through love (*quae operatur per charitatem*) is profitable or beneficial.[164] All good works are based on an "inner foundation" which alone can make them profitable.[165] Since there are two acts (*duo actus*) of faith, an "interior" and an "exterior" act,[166] "true faith is shown by your works,"[167] and "faith is increased and proven by works."[168] In fact, "faith is increased, confirmed, manifested, and consummated by works."[169] Believing involves seeing with both the eyes of the heart and with one's understanding"[170] and "hearing the word of God with the heart."[171] He acknowledged that "all moral virtues are connected *in genere,*"[172] that "faith is the foundation of all the other virtues,"[173] that "a virtuous man is not able to lose all of the virtues except by committing mortal sin,"[174] and that "it is impossible for anyone to commit mortal sin except to the extent he is lacking in faith."[175] The same idea was expressed elsewhere:

> . . . it is impossible for a person to commit a mortal sin except from a lack of faith; since if he sins in that way, he does not possess faith at that time or his faith is unstable. Therefore, Saint James the Apostle appropriately says that "faith without works is dead." For in a certain sense whenever a person does not love God above all things, his faith has been immediately deadened in this way; and since whenever he sins mortally he does not love God at that time, the obvious truth is that when anyone sins mortally he is already lacking in his faith.[176]

In trying to maintain a healthy tension between true belief and obedience to the commands of God, Hus was definitely inconsistent due to his description of faith as both *substancia* and *fundamentum,*[177] but there is also a substantial causal link between Christ as the foundation of the church and the confessed faith of believers.[178] He was also thoroughly convinced in his overall outlook that the nature of true saving faith is the kind of faith which is always connected with other virtues and issues forth in good works.[179] True faith is not merely a "verbal confession" that does not "fulfill the will of God."[180] So while one might justifiably state that Hus showed evidence of expressing and adhering to the *material* principle of the Reformation, his understanding was deeply engrossed in scholastic terminology and did not even remotely resemble a mature form at all; as such, it was no doubt of a different variety than both previous and later expressions of other centuries. For example, Luther disparaged the concept of "faith formed by love" in his *Commentary on Galatians*:

> If they were to distinguish between a "formed faith" and a false or counterfeit faith, their distinction would not offend me at all. But they speak of faith formed by love; and they posit a double faith, namely formed and unformed . . . For if love is the form of faith, then I am immediately obliged to say that love is the most important and the largest part in the Christian religion. And thus I lose Christ, His blood, His wounds, and all His blessings.[181]

Czech theologian and church historian Martin Wernisch explains:

Plana fide—sola fide. A certain exemplary monk in Erfurt whose own extreme struggles led him only to despair and not towards love in freedom would later come to express it similarly. Certainly, in Hus's case this truth was intimated in a much more unassuming manner than his confession of *sola gratia*, which was always a general adherence among proper medieval theologians with an Augustinian background, and in a more modest manner than his confession of *sola scriptura*, which he helped to unearth and bring to light; nevertheless, it is a sign that even the third principle was intertwined with the other two as a categorical necessity, since we are created for [the exercise of] rationality and volition, although we can actually be predestined only to faith. There is hardly any other term which would rightly designate, explain, and entail man's relationship with God in both its totality and all the decisive points. Only faith from the word and in the word will lead to us becoming "one cake" with God.[182] It is not merely an Aristotelian subject which is united with its object by faith, but the human and divine I and Thou, without the disjunction of reason and the will, turning the whole man into a living conscience, listening to his God . . . who can no longer remain merely an axiomatic spark of moral syllogisms. Only the one-hundred-years-younger professor of theology Martin Luther would express it as distinctly and clearly and in many ways much more crystal-clearly, but he would not be wrong at all to recognize the "revised" Hus as his predecessor in the illustration and example of a "seed" that had to fall "to the ground," since in the end the development of Hus' thought quite clearly points towards his reformation discovery as well.[183]

Hus could affirm that "believing in Christ, therefore, is faith which justifies the ungodly" while clarifying that believing is when a person is changed spiritually or "a certain spiritual transition," since believing to some extent directs and moves itself by means of faith and love.[184] While faith is the foundation of the spiritual life, both faith and love are the means of clinging to Christ in intimate communion.[185] Even in his works where he distinguished between faith, hope, and love, Hus always maintained an inseparable unity of their operation since they are all founded "in Christ." Hus did, however, also link faith and works in a manner which at times might appear to make them symmetrical or congruous.[186] In nearly every context where Hus discussed faith, he distinguished between a sincere faith (*fide non ficta*) and a dead and false faith which did not believe "the word of truth" that gives life, which is Christ and his gospel.[187] Hus taught that there is no other way of coming to Christ at all except through faith.[188] Therefore, when we recognize his motivation for explaining the difference between a true living faith and a false dead faith, it is not inaccurate to state that the overall key for grasping Hus's position is realizing that Hus's understanding of the phrase *fides sine operibus* essentially meant *fides sine dilectione operante.*[189]

While Protestants tend to disagree with almost all understandings of the phrase *fides caritate formata,* and Roman Catholics also tend to deny nearly every conception of the phrase *sola fide,* Hus used both seemingly incompatible phrases with their own nuanced positive meanings without any sense of contradiction (at least in his own mind). However, it is not the formula or particular phrase which bears the greatest need for investigation, but the underlying meaning of his expressions in light of his whole teaching, especially the inconsistencies between principle and practice concerning his concepts of predestination, union with Christ, grace, the relationship between faith and obedience, hope, repentance, dwelling in grace, the assurance of salvation, perseverance, etc. In general, everyone who studies Hus will agree that ascribing concrete positions to him is difficult due to his sometimes glaring inconsistencies, but his biblical attitude forces one to realize that Hus was at least fully convinced that his explanations were entirely faithful to Christ and not contradictory to divine revelation, tradition, or reason.

Czech theologian Zdeněk Trtík summarized Hus's overall concept of faith with this explanation: "Faith is the *principium essendi,* while works are the *principium cognoscendi* of salvation."[190] The same author also concluded elsewhere that

> predestinating grace actualized by faith as an incorporation into Christ and his mystical body created a categorically different relationship of such faith to that kind of faith the church understood from the epistle written by James . . . Hus's connection of justifying faith with predestinating grace and along with it the canceling of *ex opere operato* of the sacraments is a theological feat which was truly reformational . . . Hus understood Christian existence as a unity of faith, hope, and love . . . Through a direct connection of formed love with the predestinating grace in Christ, Hus traversed the traditional meaning of the term *fides caritate formata* in the direction toward the biblical concept of justifying faith . . . the saving form of faith along with its works is Christ himself as *charitas.* Thus, Hus's emphasis in the question of justification does not lie upon a "factual aspect" of faith, but rather on the entire agape character of faith existing by the grace of Christ . . . But only formed faith, as Hus understood it differently than the traditional formulation, is biblical faith, because in it Christ is not only an object, but also the source and shaping (i.e., forming) power; therefore, this kind of faith is incorporation into him, inner communion, and identification with him in a relationship of obedient hope and love . . . The biblical character of Hus's meaning of *fides caritate formata* also appears in this: that faith according to Hus involves an existential transformation with a genuine *sanctificatio* . . . There can be no doubt concerning the fact that through his explanation of the traditional unbiblical terms of faith, Hus essentially returned to the biblical conception of justifying faith.[191]

FAITH AND REASON

In addition to his views on Scripture and salvation, another noteworthy point of interest is how Hus viewed reason and knowledge in the light of revelation.[192] He viewed both reason and knowledge as being entirely dependent upon "the first truth"[193] (*prima veritas*): the true and holy God who loves us and reveals himself to us, so that faith always gifts us with understanding.[194] Thus, Hus was in no way the predecessor of modern rationalism, but rather his judges in Constance could be considered as such—the nominalists Jean Gerson (1363–1429) and Pierre d'Ailly (1351–1420). His conception of knowledge and faith did not deviate much from the normal framework of scholasticism as Thomas Aquinas had classically formulated it. Hus taught that "the revealed truth cannot contradict reason, because if reason as well as the knowledge of experience is to remain in the truth, they cannot do otherwise than confirm the content of faith."[195] All of the dozens of references to the doctrine of the Trinity throughout Hus's corpus can be measured by the above-mentioned characteristics describing reason and faith in relation to his concept of salvation, since the actions of the Father, Son, and Holy Spirit are distinct but inseparable.[196]

Even from this very brief overview of some of his beliefs, it is quite simple to ascertain the truth for which Hus lived, struggled, and died: the Truth of the living God—Jesus Christ himself. In fact, all of "the cultural, national, social, moral, and political significance"[197] of Hus's understanding of truth are united together under the power and authority of Jesus Christ—who is the Truth himself (John 14:6). Thus, the following assertion made by our most prominent Hussitologue, Amedeo Molnár (1923–1990), concerning Hus's view of truth is both relevant and appropriate indeed:

> Hus's concept of truth is not primarily marked by intellectual speculation as was generally the case with scholastic logicians, but by moral passion in relation to the person of Jesus in the New Testament, and the truth which was further handed down in the patristic and later Christian theology . . . This is precisely because from the perspective of freedom (i.e., the liberating aspect of truth), divine truth is Christ himself and Christ's work. For Hus, God is the source of the truth. God speaks the truth, and from the very moment it has been spoken, his word continues to speak to us, and this word is identical to Christ. When we as human beings look upon Christ who came and dwelt among us as a human being, he is the person who has made the truth of the uncreated Trinity accessible and understandable. Christ accomplished this by drawing near to us in his humanity, and although the path to the truth is able to be accessed and understood, it is only understood truly by following and imitating Christ. Therefore, this ethical passion is also a noetic principle at the same time. According to Hus,

refusing to follow Christ intimately by faith would mean convicting God and the whole divine Trinity of lying.[198]

The truth that captivated and empowered Hus was the grace of God, and it was this redemptive grace of God revealed to him which compelled Hus to act courageously: to fight against the evil abuses in the church and the discord in society to the point where he was always willing to stand up for those who most desperately needed the grace of God. Standing in the truth which he had come to know and love is exactly what led him to the stake in Constance. Concerning the impact and consequences of living in the revealed truth, Hus gladly quoted from a commentary on the gospel of Matthew attributed to John Chrysostom, the Archbishop of Constantinople: "Even as a priest is bound to preach freely the truth which he has heard from God, so a layman who is not a priest is likewise obligated to defend faithfully the truth which he has heard the priest explaining from the Scriptures; if he does not do so, then he is a traitor to the truth."[199] Whoever has come to know the truth must also lay his own life down in order to bring forth the future victory. Hus was faced with the ultimate decision of faithfully defending the truth or becoming a traitor to the truth when Cardinal Francesco Zabarella (1360–1417) challenged him for opposing witnesses, prelates, doctors, and other notable men who testified against him. Hus's response confirms his commitment to his Lord and his conscience: "As the Lord God and my conscience are my witnesses that I have neither preached nor taught those articles which they have now deposed against me nor have they ever even entered into my heart—even if all of my adversaries were to depose them against me, what else can I do? It will ultimately not hurt me either."[200]

Once we become more aware of Hus's concept of truth and understand its ramifications, then without any reluctance we will become more capable of understanding the *pathos* which marks the graves of "God's Warriors" who also later defended the truth during the Hussite Revolution.[201]

NOTES

1. See: Jan Milič Lochman, "Zum Wahrheitsverständnis von Hus," in *Jan Hus: Zwischen Zeiten, Völkern, Konfessionen*, 121–126; Jiří Kejř, "Husova pravda," *Theologická revue* 77 (2006): 232–243; idem, *Z počátků české reformace*, 12–48; Amedeo Molnár, "Réflexion sur la notion de vérité dans la pensée de Jean Hus," *Listy Filologické* 88 (1965): 121–131; Alexander Patschovsky, "Pravda a poslušnost v Husově chápání církve," in *Jan Hus na přelomu tisíciletí: Mezinárodní rozprava o českém reformátoru 15. století a o jeho recepci na prahu třetího milénia. Papežská lateránská univerzita Řím, 15.–18. prosince 1999* (Ústí nad Labem: Albis

International, 2001), 155–167; Joseph Seifert, "Pravda jako fundament svobody a svědomí. (K etice Jana Husa)," in *Jan Hus na přelomu tisíciletí: Mezinárodní rozprava o českém reformátoru 15. století a o jeho recepci na prahu třetího milénia. Papežská lateránská univerzita Řím, 15.–18. prosince 1999* (Ústí nad Labem: Albis International, 2001), 281–301.

2. See: Thomas Fudge, "'Infoelix Hus': The Rehabilitation of a Medieval Heretic," *Fides et Historia* 30/1 (1998): 57–73; Jiří Kejř, *Husovo odvolání od soudu papežova k soudu Kristovu* (Ústí nad Labem: Albis International, 1999); idem, "Husův proces z hlediska práva kanonického," in *Jan Hus na přelomu tisíciletí: Mezinárodní rozprava o českém reformátoru 15. století a o jeho recepci na prahu třetího milénia. Papežská lateránská univerzita Řím, 15.–18. prosince 1999 (Husitský Tábor: Supplementum 1)*, eds. Miloš Drda, František J. Holeček, and Zdeněk Vybíral (Ústí nad Labem: Albis International, 2001), 303–309; Jiří Kotyk, *Spor o revizi Husova procesu* (Prague: Vyšehrad, 2001).

3. See Hus's references to Christ's personification as the Truth in various letters: *Korespondence*, 13: ". . . *secundum veritatis testimonium* . . ."; 21, 38, 150, 170. For Hus's explanation of the beatific vision, see *Dcerka* (*MIHOO*, 4:181–184).

4. Cf. *Dcerka* (*MIHOO*, 4:166).

5. See his critique of Stanislav of Znojmo and Štěpán Páleč for violating their consciences in his *Letter to Jan Kardinál of Rejštejn* (*Korespondence*, 170–171).

6. *Responsiones ad Articulos Páleč* (*MIHOO*, 24:278): "*Patet ex hoc, quia aliquod est iudicium discrete et abscondite arbitracionis in foro consciencie et aliud iudicium potestative iurisdiccionis in foro ecclesie.*"

7. *Dcerka* (*MIHOO*, 4:166).

8. *Super Quattuor Sententiarum,* 2.39.5.

9. *Česká nedělní postila* (*MIHOO*, 2:457).

10. *Česká nedělní postila* (*MIHOO*, 2:234, 244).

11. This is Jana Nechutová's personal comment in *Jan Hus ve Vatikánu*, 78.

12. For an account of some of Hus's friends, see Michal Svatoš, "Husovi přátelé," in *Jan Hus mezi epochami, národy a konfesemi: Sborník z mezinárodního sympozia, konaného 22.–26. září 1993 v Bayreuthu, SRN*, ed. Jan Blahoslav Lášek (Praha: Česká křesťanská akademie, 1995), 63–67; see also Jaroslav Hrdlička, "Hus a Páleč," in *Jan Hus mezi epochami, národy a konfesemi: Sborník z mezinárodního sympozia, konaného 22.–26. září 1993 v Bayreuthu, SRN*, ed. Jan Blahoslav Lášek (Praha: Česká křesťanská akademie, 1995), 81–83; see also František M. Bartoš, "Hus a jeho učitelé a kolegové na bohoslovecké fakultě Karlovy univerzity," *Jihočeský sborník historický* 13 (1940): 41–47.

13. See Phillip N. Haberkern, *Patron Saint and Prophet: Jan Hus in the Bohemian and German Reformations* (New York: Oxford University Press, 2016).

14. See Stefan Swieżawski, "Jan Hus—A Heretic or a Saint?," *Occasional Papers on Religion in Eastern Europe* 14, no. 2, art. 5 (1994): 36–42; see also Vilém Herold, "Jan Hus—a Heretic, a Saint, or a Reformer?," *Communio Viatorum* 45 (2003): 5–23 [trans. Zdeněk V. David].

15. The most comprehensive evaluations of Hus's theology remain by Kybal and de Vooght. See: Vlastimil Kybal, *M. Jan Hus: Život a Učení*, 3 vols. (Prague: Jan

Laichter, 1923–1931); Paul de Vooght, *L'hérésie de Jean Huss*, 2nd ed. (Louvain: Publications Universitaires de Louvain, 1975). See also Pavlína Rychterová, "The Vernacular Theology of Jan Hus," in *A Companion to Jan Hus*, eds. František Šmahel and Ota Pavlíček (Leiden: Brill, 2015), 170–213.

16. See Martin Dekarli, "The Law of Christ *(Lex Christi)* and the Law of God *(Lex Dei)*—Jan Hus's Concept of Reform," *The Bohemian Reformation and Religious Practice* 10 (2015): 49–69 [trans. Zdeněk V. David].

17. See Amedeo Molnár, *Pohyb teologického myšlení: Přehledné dějiny dogmatu: Skripta pro stud. účely Komenského evangelické bohoslovecké fak.* (Praha: Ústřední církevní nakladatelství, 1982) 193–209; idem, "Husovo místo v evropské reformaci," *Československý časopis historický* 14/1 (1966): 1–14; see also Kamil Krofta, "John Huss," *Cambridge Medieval History, vol. 8: The Close of the Middle Ages,* eds. C. W. Previté-Orton and Z. N. Brooke (Cambridge: Cambridge University Press, 1936), 45–64; see also Pavel Soukup, *Jan Hus*, 159–165.

18. See K. Hagen, "Hus's 'Donatism,'" *Augustinianum* 11/3 (1971): 541–547; see also Spinka, *John Hus's Concept of the Church*, 151–289.

19. Jaroslav Pelikan, *The Riddle of Roman Catholicism* (New York: Abingdon Press, 1959), 49. For patristic and classic Christian teachings on justification and good works, see: Thomas C. Oden, *The Justification Reader* (Grand Rapids: Eerdmans Publishing Co., 2002); idem, *The Good Works Reader* (Grand Rapids: Eerdmans Publishing Co., 2007).

20. Miloslav Kaňák, "K pramenům názorů Husových," in *Hus stále živý: Sborník studií k 550. výročí Husova upálení*, ed. Miloslav Kaňák (Praha: ÚCN, 1965), 17.

21. Our understanding of the term "formal principle" is taken from Congar's explanation concerning Martin Luther's reform: ". . . the formal principle of his doctrinal reform: everything must be judged according to the criterion of Scripture." Yves Congar, *Tradition and Traditions: An Historical and a Theological Essay,* trans. Michael Naseby and Thomas Rainborough (New York: Macmillan, 1967), 140.

22. For a range of resources which help correct improper definitions and misguided notions in conversations around *sola Scriptura*, cf. Keith Mathison, *The Shape of Sola Scriptura* (Moscow: Canon Press, 2001), 237–281; D.H. Williams, "The Search for Sola Scriptura in the Early Church," *Interpretation* 52, no. 4 (1988): 354–366; Lewis W. Spitz, "Luther's Sola Scriptura," *Concordia Theological Monthly* 31, no. 12 (1960): 740–745; Kevin Vanhoozer, *Biblical Authority after Babel: Retrieving the Protestant Solas in the Spirit of Mere Protestant Christianity* (Grand Rapids: Brazos Press, 2016), 109–146; James R. Beck, "Sola Scriptura: Then and Now," in *Psychology & Christianity Integration: Seminal Works That Shaped the Movement,* ed. Daryl H. Stevenson, Brian E. Eck, and Peter C. Hill (Batavia: Christian Association for Psychological Studies, 2007), 75–81; C. D. Allert, "What Are We Trying to Conserve? Evangelicalism and *Sola Scriptura*," *Evangelical Quarterly* 76 (2004): 327–348; Heiko A. Oberman, *The Harvest of Medieval Theology: Gabriel Biel and Late Medieval Mysticism* (Cambridge: Harvard University Press, 1963), 361–393; John C. Peckham, "Sola Scriptura: Reductio ad Absurdum?" *Trinity Journal NS* 35, no. 2 (2014): 195–223. For a substantial academic analysis of *sola Scriptura* including critiques and reappraisals from systematic, biblical, historical,

and practical theological perspectives, see especially *Sola Scriptura: Biblical and Theological Perspectives on Scripture, Authority, and Hermeneutics*, ed., Hans Burger, Arnold Huijgen, and Eric Peels (Leiden: Brill, 2018).

23. Thus, depending on one's presuppositions of what a proper definition of *sola Scriptura* entails, the following statements by Hus concerning Scripture could (perhaps) be claimed by both sides as evidence that he was a proponent of either view, although from our perspective they appear to be conclusively in favor of *sola Scriptura*.

(1) "Ulterius admitto omnes sanctorum doctorum sentencias ipsam legem fideliter declarantes, veneror eciam omnia concilia generalia et specialia, decreta et decretales et omnes leges, canones et constitutiones, de quanto consonant explicite vel implicite legi Dei" (De Fidei Sue Elucidacione in MIHOO, 24:84).

(2) "Ubi tangitur, quod preceptor debet solum consona legi precipere et obedienciarius de tanto debet illis obedire et numquam contra omnipotentis Dei voluntatem" (Responsiones ad Articulos Páleč in MIHOO, 24:273–274).

(3) "... quod continetur omnis veritas in scriptura" (Tractatus de Ecclesia, 177).

(4) "... ex lege, que omnen implicat credibilem veritatem ..." (Tractatus de Ecclesia, 138).

(5) "... primum mendacium quod solam scripturam sanctam in talibus materiis pro iudice habere volumus. In quo dicto asserit, quod nec deum nec apostolos nec sanctos doctores nec universalem sanctam ecclesiam habere vellemus pro iudice ... Hoc tamen debet scire doctor, quod nec sibi nec omnibus sibi adherentibus volumus in fidei consentire materia, nisi de quanto se fundaverunt in scriptura vel racione" (Tractatus de Ecclesia, 132–133).

(6) "Nam scripture sacre nec licet discredere nec licet contradicere" (Tractatus de Ecclesia, 56).

(7) "... et tercio, scripturam sacram consulite, si precipiunt conformiter ad Christi consilium, et secundum hoc credite eis, vel discredite secundum eius oppositum" (Tractatus de Ecclesia, 181).

(8) "Patet quia nemo tenetur quicquam credere, nisi ad quod movet eum deus credere, sed deus non movet hominem ad credendum falsum ..." (Tractatus de Ecclesia, 38).

(9) "Nec debet credi talibus, nisi de quanto sua dicta fundaverint in scriptura" (Tractatus de Ecclesia, 125).

(10) "Ecce, ista Scriptura cum Cristo, qui est sacratissima Scriptura, iudicabit et me et fictorem in die iudicii ..." (Contra Stephanum Palecz in MIHOO, 24:260).

(11) "Quicunque docuerit me secundum vel iuxta legem Dei, sive superior, sive alius, sive fictor, volo humiliter acceptare. Sic enim lex Dei erit dux et iudex superior illo docente, quem ducem et iudicem papa cum cardinalibus et fictor cum suis adherentibus debent sequi" (Contra Stephanum Palecz in MIHOO, 24:269).

(12) "Nec dabitur disparitas, nisi ostensa fuerit ex Scriptura" (Contra Iohannem Stokes in MIHOO, 22:63).

(13) "... quod non debet sibi credi, nisi de quanto se fundaverit in Scriptura" (Contra Octo Doctores in MIHOO, 22:379).

(14) "... *fideles non debent ipsam credere esse fidem katholicam, nisi ipsam fundaverint in Scriptura"* (*Contra Stanislaum de Znoyma* in *MIHOO,* 22:280).

24. For Hus's understanding of the authority of Scripture and authority in general, see Enrico Selley Molnar, "Wyclif, Hus and the Problem of Authority," in *Jan Hus: Zwischen Zeiten, Völkern, Konfessionen: Vorträge des internationalen Symposions in Bayreuth vom 22. bis 26. September 1993* (München: Oldenbourg, 1997), 167–182, though it must be noted that Molnar offered no definition of *sola Scriptura* before his blanket statement that Hus "did not teach the principle of *sola Scriptura* of the later Protestant Reformation" (176). A more reliable portrayal of Hus's position is found in John C. Peckham, "We Must Obey God Rather Than Men: Jan Hus on the Authority of Scripture in Relation to Church and Conscience," *Andrews University Seminary Studies* 54, no. 1 (2016): 71–102. See also Ivana Dolejšová, "Nominalist and Realist Approaches to the Problem of Authority: Páleč and Hus," *The Bohemian Reformation and Religious Practice* 2 (1998): 49–55.

25. Zdeněk Trtík, "Husův odkaz a oba principy reformace," *Hus stále živý: Sborník studií k 550. výročí Husova upálení,* ed. Miloslav Kaňák (Praha: Blahoslav, 1965), 39.

26. See *Super Quattuor Sententiarum,* 1.1.3–11 (*Incepcio*); 1.2.1–7 (*Questio*).

27. For Wyclif's own use of analogy, see: *De Veritate Sacra Scripturae,* 1:7–15; *Tractatus de Logica,* ed. Michael Henry Dziewicki (London: Trübner & Co., 1893–1899), 1:10; 2:19–24.

28. Wyclif, *De Veritate Sacra Scripturae,* 1:107–138.

29. Johannes Wyclif, *De Dominio Divino,* ed. Reginald Lane Poole (London: Trübner & Co., 1890), 1:42–43. Cf. *Česká nedělní postila* (*MIHOO,* 2:112).

30. *Česká nedělní postila* (*MIHOO,* 2:191).

31. *Česká nedělní postila* (*MIHOO,* 2:300).

32. *Česká nedělní postila* (*MIHOO,* 2:367).

33. *Česká nedělní postila* (*MIHOO,* 2:371).

34. Wyclif, *De Veritate Sacra Scripturae,* 1:109; Hus, *Contra Stephanum Palecz* (*MIHOO,* 22:260).

35. *Defensio Libri de Trinitate* (*MIHOO,* 22:53).

36. Wyclif, *De Veritate Sacra Scripturae,* 1:394; Hus, *Tractatus de Ecclesia,* 133–134, 170–173.

37. Richard Muller, *Post Reformation Reformed Dogmatics,* vol. 2 (Grand Rapids: Baker, 1993), 51.

38. Arnold Huijgen, "Alone Together: *Sola Scriptura* and the Other Solas of the Reformation," in *Sola Scriptura: Biblical and Theological Perspectives on Scripture, Authority, and Hermeneutics,* 87 fn. 38: "In research on *sola scriptura,* the term often goes undefined. A loose definition based on 'authority' seems better than both a narrow definition that could be criticized for being either too specific or so general as to have no boundaries at all."

39. Matthew Barrett, *God's Word Alone: The Authority of Scripture. What the Reformers Taught and Why It Still Matters* (Grand Rapids: Zondervan, 2016), 10.

40. Matthew Barrett, "Sola Scriptura in the Strange Land of Evangelicalism: The Peculiar but Necessary Responsibility of Defending Sola Scriptura Against Our Own Kind," *The Southern Baptist Journal of Theology* 19, no. 4 (2015): 19.

41. See *De Fidei Sue Elucidacione* (*MIHOO*, 88).

42. The term *inerrant* here must be understood from within the medieval context of truthfulness and not directly conflated with modern debates concerned with issues of textual criticism. For various perspectives on the meaning of inerrancy, see John Merrick and Stephen M. Garrett, eds., *Five Views on Biblical Inerrancy* (Grand Rapids: Zondervan, 2013).

43. Huijgen, "Alone Together: Sola Scriptura and the Other Solas of the Reformation," 85, 87.

44. John Frame, *The Doctrine of the Word of God* (Phillipsburg: P&R Publishing, 2010), 383.

45. *Documenta*, 293: "*Ego dico, quod haereticus, qui talis esset, primo deberet pulchre, pie, humiliter scripturis sacris et rationibus ex illis elaboratis instrui, sicut fecerunt sancti Augustinus et alii cum haereticus disputantes . . . semper dico, quod debet praecedere instructio talis ex scripturis etc.*"

46. Anthony N. S. Lane, "Sola Scriptura? Making Sense of a Post-Reformation Slogan," in *A Pathway into the Holy Scripture*, eds. Philip E. Satterthwaite and David F. Wright (Grand Rapids: Eerdmans, 1994), 324.

47. *Tractatus de Ecclesia*, 47, 56, 167, 210. Hus provided one poignant example in his *Letter to All the Faithful Czechs*, written on June 26, 1415: "Oh if had you only seen that Council which calls itself the most holy Council and [one] that cannot err, you would surely have seen the greatest abomination! I have even heard it commonly said by the Swabians that their city Constance [Kostnice] would not purge itself of the sins which that Council has committed in their city for thirty years" (*Korespondence*, 318).

48. *Tractatus de Ecclesia*, 36, 82, 166, 176, 194.

49. *Česká nedělní postila* (*MIHOO*, 2:169). His Czech phrase also communicates the idea of the "plain" or "naked" truth.

50. *Sermones de tempore qui Collecta dicuntur* (*MIHOO*, 7:187).

51. *Contra Stanislaum de Znoyma* (*MIHOO*, 22:348): ". . . *quia Scriptura sacra, cum sit veritas infallibilis, non potest dicere, nisi quod vere est vel quod vere non est*"; cf. *Tractatus de Ecclesia*, 133.

52. G.R. Evans, *The Language and Logic of the Bible: The Road to Reformation* (Cambridge: Cambridge University Press, 2009), 31.

53. *Appellacio ad Jesus Christum Supremum Judicem* (*Korespondence*, 133).

54. *Tractatus de Ecclesia*, 76: "*Et notandum quod licet sola trinitas habet huiusmodi potestatem autenticam principalem.*"

55. *Tractatus de Ecclesia*, 165–166, 211.

56. *Documenta*, 319. "*Numquam fui, sed nec sum pertinax, sed semper desideravi et die hodierna desidero informationem efficaciorem ex scripturis.*"

57. This statement is intended as a slightly facetious remark, since Luther was an excellent rational thinker due to his scholastic education and called for the use of reason at the Diet of Worms in 1521, though he also elsewhere referred to reason as a "whore" (LW 51:371–380; WA 51:126–132). This was surely another instance of Luther's frequent usage of hyperbolic rhetoric, rather than an unmitigated disdain of reason. For various issues concerning Luther's view on reason and his influence on

philosophy, see Jennifer Hockenbery Dragseth, ed., *The Devil's Whore: Reason and Philosophy in the Lutheran Tradition* (Minneapolis: Fortress Press, 2011).

58. Ján Liguš, "Husovo pojetí Písma podle jeho kázání," in *Jan Hus mezi epochami, národy a konfesemi: Sborník z mezinárodního sympozia, konaného 22.–26. září 1993 v Bayreuthu* (Praha: Česká křesťanská akademie, 1995), 187. Heiko Oberman likewise clarified that Hus's "insistence on the authority of Holy Scripture is not *sola scriptura* in the sense that it would exclude Tradition understood as the ongoing interpretation of Scripture. The *sola* is restrictive in that the law of God is sovereign and sufficient to determine alone—*without ecclesiastical law*—all cases that have to be tried by the Church." See Oberman, *The Harvest of Medieval Theology*, 377.

59. Zdeněk Trtík, "Husův odkaz a oba principy reformace," 39–40.

60. In his *Letter to Master Křišťan of Prachatice*, Hus clarified his beliefs concerning the pope in terms of principle and practice: "I consider the pope as the vicar of Christ in the Roman Church, but for me this is not of the faith . . . If the pope is one of the predestined and exercises his pastoral office by following Christ in his morals and principles, then he is the leader of as much of the church militant that he rules; and if as the leader he rules according to the law of Christ the entire church militant which exists now, then he is its true leader under the supreme headship of the Lord Jesus Christ. However, if he lives contrary to Christ, then he is a 'thief and a robber, climbing in by some other way' (John 10:1) and a 'ravenous wolf' (Matthew 7:15), a hypocrite, and presently the preeminent Antichrist among all pilgrims . . . For indeed what greater 'abomination of desolation standing in the holy place' (Matthew 24:15) could exist (i.e., in the holy dignity of that place) than if in that holy place where sat the most holy, the most upright and faithful, the most gentle, the most humble, the poorest, the most diligent, the most long-suffering, the most virtuously pure man—now in that holy place (i.e., in actual holiness) sits a man called 'most holy' but in reality is the most wicked, the most hard-hearted, the most vindictive, the most arrogant, the wealthiest in the world, the laziest, the most impatient and intolerant, the most impure? Is it not the 'abomination of desolation' from an abstract point of view?" (*Korespondence*, 167). In another letter to Master Křišťan he also wrote, "Indeed, what more can the Antichrist do to 'exalt himself over everything that is called God' (2 Thessalonians 2:4)—that is, above the deity and humanity of Christ—than to claim that God cannot give his church any successors other than the pope and his cardinals? If they had asserted that God cannot give his church any *worse* successors than the pope and his cardinals, then they would have greater evidence for their statement! As occasions arise, I suppose that by their invented schemes God is revealing to us the Antichrist along with his disciples. But God will surely grant us knowledge and the 'spirit of fortitude' (2 Timothy 1:7) to fight against such seducers."

61. *Tractatus de Ecclesia*, 56: "*Et isto modo tenetur quilibet christianus credere explicite vel implicite omnem veritatem, quam sanctus spiritus posuit in scriptura. Et isto modo non tenetur homo dictis sanctorum preter scripturam nec bullis papalibus credere, nisi quid dixerint ex scriptura vel quod fundaretur implicite in scriptura . . . Nam scripture sacre nec licet discredere nec licet contradicere, sed bullis aliquando licet et discredere et contradicere dum vel indignos comendant vel preficiunt vel avariciam sapiunt vel iniustos magnificant et innocentes deprimunt*

vel mandatis dei vel consiliis implicite contradicunt." Cf. *Responsiones ad Articulos Páleč* (*MIHOO,* 24:280).

62. *Super Quattuor Sententiarum,* 1.2.3 (*Questio*): *"Et sic scriptura sacra est verbum Dei Christus cum hiis, que per ipsum generi humano sunt dicta et revelata, ut sub obtentu eterne beatitudinis ab hominibus teneantur firmiter et credantur. Ex quo sequitur, quod omnis veritas directiva hominis, ut debite serviat Deo suo, est scriptura sacra vel explicite vel inplicite credenda ab hominibus et tenenda, cum omnis talis est lex necessario per fidem hominum adinplenda iuxta Salvatoris illud iuramentum Matth. 5: 'Amen dico vobis, donec transeat celum et terra, iota unum aut unus apex (i. nulla veritas per os meum dicta) preteribit, donec omnia fiant.'"* See Matthew 5:18.

63. Jindřich Mánek, "Husuv spor o autoritu," in *Hus stále živý: Sborník studií k 550. výročí Husova upálení,* ed. Miloslav Kaňák (Praha: Blahoslav, 1965), 31.

64. Matthew Spinka, "John Hus, Advocate of Spiritual Reform," in *Advocates of Reform: From Wyclif to Erasmus,* ed. Matthew Spinka (Philadelphia: The Westminster Press, 1953), 194.

65. Karl Josef von Hefele, *Conciliengeschichte. Nach den Quellen bearbeitet,* vol. 7 (Freiburg im Breisgau: Herder, 1874), 217. Cf. David Schaff, *Jan Hus,* 284. For the context, see Hefele's comments in §763 (211–228).

66. Jan Milič Lochman, "Zum Wahrheitsverständnis von Hus," in *Jan Hus: Zwischen Zeiten, Völkern, Konfessionen: Vorträge des internationalen Symposions in Bayreuth vom 22. bis 26. September 1993* (München: Oldenbourg, 1997), 123.

67. Congar, *Tradition and Traditions,* 175. One should remember, however, an important clarification of this term made by Scott Hahn: "It should be noted that *prima scriptura* does not imply the superiority of Scripture, but rather, its relative primacy for Catholic theology." See Scott Hahn, *Scripture Matters: Essays on Reading the Bible from the Heart of the Church* (Steubenville: Emmaus Road Publishing, 2003), 180 fn. 24.

68. See *De Sufficiencia Legis Cristi* (*MIHOO,* 24:39–79); *Explicatio Epistola Secunda Beati Petri* (*Historia et Monumenta,* 2:289); *Super Quattuor Sententiarum,* 1.1.7–10 *(Incepcio)*; *Postilla adumbrata* (*MIHOO,* 13:324).

69. *Enarratio psalmorum* (*MIHOO,* 17:356).

70. *Česká nedělní postila* (*MIHOO,* 2:267, 275, 460).

71. *Tractatus de Ecclesia,* 106–107.

72. *Tractatus de Ecclesia,* 56; *O víře* (*MIHOO,* 4:338).

73. *Contra Stanislaum de Znoyma* (*MIHOO,* 22:348).

74. *Super Quattuor Sententiarum,* 4.18.3; *Responsiones ad Articulos Páleč* (*MIHOO,* 24:265); *Letter to Master Křišťan of Prachatice* (*Korespondence,* 164–168). Hus even went as far as claiming that many popes not only ratified errors and heresies, but that they were heretics themselves. *Tractatus de Ecclesia,* 143: ". . . *quia certum est, quod multi eorum ratificaverunt errores et hereses, quia fuerunt heretici.*"

75. *Česká nedělní postila* (*MIHOO,* 2:215, 224–225).

76. *Česká nedělní postila* (*MIHOO,* 2:265, 270–271).

77. *Česká nedělní postila* (*MIHOO,* 2:86–88, 108, 137, 237–238, 348, 358–362, 404–405); *Tractatus de Ecclesia,* 161–165; *Korespondence,* 144–145).

78. *Tractatus de Ecclesia,* 134; *Contra Stephanum Palecz* (*MIHOO,* 22:259–261).

79. *Tractatus de Ecclesia,* 174–208, especially 176–178; *Česká nedělní postila* (*MIHOO,* 2:336); *Responsiones ad Articulos Páleč* (*MIHOO,* 24: 273–274, 276–278); *Questio de indulgentiis* (*MIHOO,* 19A:71–72, 75–76).

80. *Tractatus de Ecclesia,* 106–107.

81. *Tractatus de Ecclesia,* 53, 67, 125; *Česká nedělní postila* (*MIHOO,* 2:201; 336).

82. *Česká nedělní postila* (*MIHOO,* 2:274, 280).

83. *Contra Stephanum Palecz* (*MIHOO,* 22:259); cf. *Česká nedělní postila* (*MIHOO,* 2:234).

84. *Tractatus de Ecclesia,* 53.

85. *Tractatus de Ecclesia,* 133.

86. *Documenta,* 267.

87. *Korepondence,* 89–92, 120–121; *Tractatus de Ecclesia,* 152, 177–178, 190; *O víře* (*MIHOO,* 4:341); *O šesti bludiech* (*MIHOO,* 4:280–282).

88. *Tractatus de Ecclesia,* 161.

89. *Výklad na vieru* (*MIHOO,* 1:106).

90. *Super Quattuor Sententiarum,* 3.25.3.

91. *Česká nedělní postila* (*MIHOO,* 2:65, 67, 77–78, 100, 127, 193, 197, 353, 421, 440). In context, Hus referred to biblical passages from Matthew, Mark, Luke, John, Acts, and Revelation.

92. *Česká nedělní postila* (*MIHOO,* 2:95–96).

93. *Česká nedělní postila* (*MIHOO,* 2:119, 205, 381). Hus mentioned each member of the Trinity as bearing witness to "future truths" which the apostles declared and wrote down as Scripture (*MIHOO,* 2:234–235).

94. *Česká nedělní postila* (*MIHOO,* 2:65). Hus also referred to the confirming "testimony" of the Father's own spoken word which John the Baptist and the crowd heard at Jesus's baptism. John's declaration that Jesus is the Lamb of God "bore witness" to the truth (*MIHOO,* 2:73–75). The Holy Spirit also bears witness to the preaching and miracles of Christ by giving believers an "inner" testimony (*MIHOO,* 2:244).

95. R. Francis Martin, "Sacra Doctrina and the Authority of Its Sacra Scriptura: According to St. Thomas Aquinas," *Pro Ecclesia* 10/1 (2001): 84.

96. Zdeněk Trtík, "Husův odkaz a oba principy reformace," 39.

97. The same caution concerning certain improper definitions of *sola Scriptura* mentioned earlier applies for definitions of *sola fide* as well. The apparent inconsistencies in some of Hus's theological formulations should cause hesitation in labeling him as a strict proponent of certain understandings of *sola fide.* For useful articles on *sola fide* from various perspectives, see Son Eun-Sil, "*Sola fide* or *fide caritate formata*: Two Incompatible Principles? From Martin Luther to Thomas Aquinas," *Revue des sciences philosophiques et théologiques* 103, no. 1 (2019): 93–112; Henri Blocher, "Justification of the Ungodly (Sola Fide): Theological Reflections," in *Justification and Variegated Nomism, vol. 2: The Paradoxes of Paul,* eds. D.A. Carson, Peter T. O'Brien, and Mark A. Seifrid (Grand Rapids: Baker Academic, 2004), 465–500; A. E. McGrath, "Justice and Justification: Semantic and Juristic Aspects of the Christian Doctrine of Justification," *Scottish Journal of Theology* 35, no. 5 (1982): 403–418; W. Robert Godfrey, "Faith Formed by Love or Faith Alone? The Instrument of Justification," in R. Scott Clark, ed., *Covenant, Justification, and*

Pastoral Ministry: Essays by the Faculty of Westminster Seminary California (P&R Publishing, 2007), 267–284; Nick Needham, "Justification in the Early Church Fathers," *Justification in Perspective: Historical Developments and Contemporary Challenges*, ed. Bruce L. McCormack (Grand Rapids: Baker Academic, 2006), 25–53; Robert Louis Wilken, "*Fides Caritate Formata*: Faith Formed by Love," *Nova et Vetera* 9, no. 4 (2011): 1089–1100; Josef Smolík, "Truth in History according to Hus' Conception," *Communio Viatorum* 15 (1972): 97–109; Arthur L. Mulka, "'FIDES QUAE PER CARITATEM OPERATUR' (GAL 5,6)," *The Catholic Biblical Quarterly* 28, no. 2 (1966): 174–188.

  98. See *Tractatus de Ecclesia*, 53–56.

  99. Ján Liguš, "Husovo pojetí Písma podle jeho kázání," 185–186: "There is a generally widespread opinion among the scholars focusing on Hus that his conception of faith oscillates between faith in God's saving grace and between good works which are necessary for salvation. Thus, many Hus scholars have come to the conclusion that the relationship between Christian faith which mediates the forgiveness of sins to good works is an unresolved issue within the theology of Hus, and it confirms his deeper moorings in medieval piety rather than in biblical thinking. It is possible to agree that there is a tension between justifying faith and good works in Hus's thought, but it is not a completely unresolvable issue. I will try to illustrate this concerning two practically contradictory statements of Hus. The first testifies in favor of saving faith, that is, justification by faith alone: '*Fides, quae sine operibus salvat.*' The other statement confirms that true faith is unthinkable without good works and that it is always: '*Fides caritate formata.*' This tension between '*fides sine operibus*' and '*fides caritate formata*'—which at first glance appears unclear or ambiguous in Hus as possibly applying to the necessity of faith and also to the necessity of works for salvation—can be satisfyingly resolved despite all of its dubiousness through ontology. From this resolution it will become obvious that according to Hus, the soteriological honor belongs to faith, not to works . . .

  "In other words, to believe means to be in God, to be in salvation, namely, to be in Christ. A Christian first is, and only then does he act. Good works always flow forth from 'being-in-God's-grace.' The relationship between faith and works appears here as follows: faith in Christ enables a Christian to be in God, and a Christian's works are not the outcomes of mere human effort nor of a sheer human quality, but they are understandable only as the results of a man being in Christ through faith. It also follows from this that good works cannot be the ground nor establish man's salvation, but true faith cannot exist without them either. Just as being cannot be separated from thinking, similarly Christian faith is inseparably united with good works as fruit is linked with a good tree . . . In summary, it is possible to say the following about Hus' understanding of faith and works: that it is precisely this ontological recognition which helped Hus both to overcome the medieval soteriological overestimating and over-evaluating of good works, and also (to use the words of Bonhoeffer) to evade and avoid cheap grace. Simultaneously with this, Hus anticipated (according to my opinion) the truth of Holy Scripture's [teaching] 'by faith alone and by grace alone' discovered by the European Reformation, with the difference that he never understood justification as *actus forensis*, as it was in the post-reformation era. It seems that the conception of faith as *'fides caritate formata' helped Hus to walk along the middle path between the abstract theological-scholastic intellectualism, whether of the Aristotelian or Platonic character, and ecclesiological sacramentalism, which very often had lost the personal experience of faith."*

100. *Výklad na vieru* (*MIHOO*, 1:67); see also *Tractatus de Ecclesia*, 53–56.

101. Ivana Dolejšová, "Eschatological Elements in Hus's Understanding of Orthopraxis," *The Bohemian Reformation and Religious Practice* 4 (2002): 132.

102. *Super Quattuor Sententiarum*, 3.23.1–5; *Tractatus de Ecclesia*, 51, 53–54; *Responsiones ad Articulos Páleč* (*MIHOO*, 24:280).

103. Peter Lombard, *Libri Quattuor Sententiarum*, 3.23.3; 3.36.1–2.

104. *Super Quattuor Sententiarum*, 3.36.3.

105. WA 40.1:228–229.

106. *Tractatus de Ecclesia*, 54: "*. . . fides est fundamentum aliarum virtutum . . .*"

107. *Explicatio in Epistola Jacobi* in *Historia et Monumenta*, 205.

108. *De Sanguine Christi*, 11; *De omni sanguine Christi glorificato* (*Historia et Monumenta*, 1:194).

109. *Explicatio in Epistola Jacobi* (*Historia et Monumenta*, 190): "*gratis, sine meritis nostris . . . non ex operibus nostris, quae fecimus . . .*"

110. *Explicatio in Epistola Jacobi* (*Historia et Monumenta*, 205–208).

111. *Menší výklad na vieru* (*MIHOO*, 1:111); see also his exposition of the *Apostles' Creed* (*MIHOO*, 1:106).

112. *Výklad na vieru* (*MIHOO*, 1:63).

113. *Tractatus de Ecclesia*, 42; *Česká nedělní postila* (*MIHOO*, 2:262–263).

114. *Výklad piesniček Šalamúnových* (*MIHOO*, 4:125).

115. *Česká nedělní postila* (*MIHOO*, 2:202).

116. *Tractatus de Ecclesia*, 80.

117. *Tractatus de Ecclesia*, 78: "*contricio . . . et ista in necessitatis articulo sufficeret homini ad salvandum.*"

118. *Explicatio in Epistola Jacobi* (*Historia et Monumenta*, 2:207).

119. *Provázek třípramenný* (*MIHOO*, 4:148).

120. *De Fidei Sue Elucidacione* (*MIHOO*, 24:86); cf. Augustine, *In Joannis Evangelium Tractatus* 29.6.

121. *Provázek třípramenný (MIHOO*, 4:149).

122. *Super Quattuor Sententiarum*, 2.27.5.

123. *Korespondence*, 56; cf. 151.

124. *Korespondence*, 225.

125. *Tractatus de Ecclesia*, 112.

126. *Tractatus de Ecclesia*, 62.

127. *Česká nedělní postila* (*MIHOO*, 2:113).

128. See *Enchiridion*, 18.67–69; *De Gratia et Libero Arbitrio*, 7.16–18; 8.19–20. Some have argued that Augustine taught the doctrine of *sola fide*. See Article 20 of the *Augsburg Confession* (1530) concerning good works. See also Dongsun Cho, "Divine Acceptance of Sinners: Augustine's Doctrine of Justification," *Perichoresis* 12, no. 2 (2014): 163–184.

129. LW 25:152.

100 Chapter 5

130. LW 27:64. See also LW 26:269: ". . . as we also distinguish between a counterfeit faith and a true faith."
131. *Patrologia Latina* 114:481–482.
132. *Explicatio Epistola Secunda Beati Petri* (*Historia et Monumenta*, 2:280).
133. *Tractatus de Ecclesia*, 27.
134. WA 56:272.
135. *Tractatus de Ecclesia*, 27; cf. *Responsiones ad Articulos Páleč* (*MIHO*, 24:258–260).
136. *Documenta*, 296; *O hřieše* (*MIHOO*, 4:336). It should be noted that in context Hus was referring to venial sin.
137. *Tractatus de Ecclesia*, 53–54.
138. *Explicatio in Epistola Jacobi* (*Historia et Monumenta*, 2:205); Cf. *Tractatus de Ecclesia*, 57.
139. *Explicatio in Epistola Jacobi* (*Historia et Monumenta*, 205–208).
140. *Explicatio in Epistola Jacobi* (*Historia et Monumenta*, 2:205).
141. *Tractatus de Ecclesia*, 88; 112: ". . . . cum fide formata et perseverancia."
142. *Letter to the Faithful in Prague* (*Korespondence*, 151).
143. *Česká nedělní postila* (*MIHOO*, 2:152).
144. *Česká nedělní postila* (*MIHOO*, 2:336–337).
145. *Tractatus de Ecclesia*, 45.
146. *Super Quattuor Sententiarum*, 4.19.5; Cf. Augustine, *In Iohannis Evangelium Tractatus* 26.15 (*Patrologia Latina*, 35:1613–1614). It is also interesting to note that in this same homily Augustine mentioned "the righteousness which [God] gives to someone so that he might be righteous" (26.1).
147. *Explicatio in Epistola Jacobi* (*Historia et Monumenta*, 2:205).
148. *Explicatio in Epistola Jacobi* (*Historia et Monumenta*, 2:205).
149. *Super Quattuor Sententiarum*, 3.25.1: ". . . quod fides, spes et caritas et operacio secundum aliquid equalia sunt in presenti, quia quantum credimus, tantum speramus, et quantum credimus et speramus, tantum amamus."
150. *Česká nedělní postila* (*MIHOO*, 2:457).
151. *Česká nedělní postila* (*MIHOO*, 2:272).
152. *Česká nedělní postila* (*MIHOO*, 2:439–441).
153. *Česká nedělní postila* (*MIHOO*, 2:457).
154. *Česká nedělní postila* (*MIHOO*, 2:382).
155. *Letter to an Unnamed Priest* (*Korespondence*, 109); cf. *Česká nedělní postila* (*MIHOO*, 2:453; cf. *Tractatus de Ecclesia*, 58.
156. *Explicatio in Epistola Jacobi* (*Historia et Monumenta*, 2:205).
157. *Responsiones ad Articulos Páleč* (*MIHOO*, 24:260); *Super Quattuor Sententiarum*, 3.31.3; 3.32.6.
158. *Contra Stephanum de Palecz* (*MIHOO*, 22:242).
159. *Tractatus de Ecclesia*, 62.
160. *Contra Stephanum de Palecz* (*MIHOO*, 22:242).
161. *Super Quattuor Sententiarum*, 3.23.4.
162. *Super Quattuor Sententiarum*, 2.27.4: "Sic ergo patet, quod virtus, gracia et caritas, qua homo vel creatura racionalis dicitur cara Deo, sunt idem; et iuxta hoc

debet consequenter dici, quod omnis virtus moralis est qualitas infusa, quamvis non omne opus virtutis est qualitas infusa. Exemplum superius de lumine et colore illumi-nato. Nam lumen infunditur, sed non color illuminatus, et patet veritas questionis."
163. *Katechismus* (*MIHOO*, 4:327).
164. *Explicatio in Epistola Jacobi* (*Historia et Monumenta*, 2:205): *"Penitus nihil fides talis, sed illa quae operatur per charitatem."*
165. *Česká nedělní postila* (*MIHOO*, 2:335).
166. *Explicatio in Epistola Jacobi* (*Historia et Monumenta*, 2:205).
167. *Explicatio Beati Joannis Apostoli Tertia* (*Historia et Monumenta*, 2:362).
168. *Explicatio in Epistola Jacobi* (*Historia et Monumenta*, 2:207).
169. *Explicatio in Epistola Jacobi* (*Historia et Monumenta*, 2:207): *"Et ex operibus fides consummata est, id est, augmentata, confirmata, vel manifestata, vel consum-mata, quia per eam justificatus est."; Cf. "Quoniam ex operibus, scilicet, sequentibus fidem, justificatur homo, id est, magis justus efficitur"* (2:207).
170. *Česká nedělní postila* (*MIHOO*, 2:289).
171. *Explicatio in Epistola Jacobi* (*Historia et Monumenta*, 2:190–191).
172. *Tractatus de Ecclesia*, 66.
173. *Tractatus de Ecclesia*, 54.
174. *Tractatus de Ecclesia*, 183.
175. *Tractatus de Ecclesia*, 54–55.
176. *Česká nedělní postila* (*MIHOO*, 2:105); cf. *Responsiones ad Articulos Páleč* (*MIHOO*, 24:263–264).
177. *Dominica in Octava Pasche* (*MIHOO*, 7:187); *Tractatus de Ecclesia*, 54; *Super Quattuor Sententiarum*, 3.23.3; *Explicatio in Epistola Jacobi* (*Historia et Monumenta*, 2:182).
178. *Tractatus de Ecclesia*, 57–72.
179. A similar view is found in the *Westminster Confession of Faith*: "Faith . . . is ever accompanied with all other saving graces, and is no dead faith, but worketh by love" (11.2).
180. *Česká nedělní postila* (*MIHOO*, 2:338).
181. LW 26:269–270. See also LW 3:169–170; 26:88–90, 146, 160, 208, 279; WA 40.1:229; LW 26:168: ". . . what the sophists have taught about 'faith formed by love' is merely a trick of Satan." See also *Commentarium in Epistolam S. Pauli ad Galatas*, 201–202: ". . . *sola fide, non fide formata caritate, nos justificari. Quare non isti for-mae gratificanti tribuenda est vis justificandi, sed fidei, quae apprehendit et possidet in corde ipsum Christum salvatorem. Haec fides sine et ante caritatem justificat."* Since terms and concepts function differently for nominalists and realists, one needs to be careful to distinguish between critiques of concepts and ideas or the mere terms or phrases which represent those concepts.
182. See Luther, *Erlanger Ausgabe*, 19:365. In English, see Martin Luther, *All Become One Cake: A Sermon on the Lord's Supper*, trans. Matthew C. Harrison (St. Louis: The Lutheran Church—Missouri Synod, 2005).
183. Martin Wernisch, "Ratio voluntatis M. Johannis Hus. Zur Rolle von Vernunft und Willen in der Lehre Hussens," in *Jan Hus: Zwischen Zeiten, Völkern, Konfessionen: Vorträge des internationalen Symposions in Bayreuth vom 22. bis 26.*

September 1993 (München: Oldenbourg, 1997), 153–154. Wernisch cites two important passages as support: *"Hoc tamen ex plana fide scio, quod Salvator noster non gratis passus est miserias et mortis supplicium . . ."* (*Super Quattuor Sententiarum*, 1.40.4; cf. 4.9.6). Wernisch's view is contrary to Oberman. See Heiko A. Oberman, "Hus und Luther. Der Antichrist und die zweite reformatorische Entdeckung," in *Jan Hus: Zwischen Zeiten, Völkern, Konfessionen* (339): "Hus had not yet rightly distinguished between faith and works and made both of them the ground of justification."

184. *Quaestio de Credere* (*MIHOO*, 19A:62).

185. *Výklad piesniček Šalamúnových (MIHOO*, 4:123).

186. *Explicatio in Epistola Jacobi* (*Historia et Monumenta*, 2:208): *"Cum autem adest tempus operandi, tunc nec sola fides, nec opera tantum sine fide, sed utrumque necessarium est ad salutem et justitiam";* ". . . *ita omnes per opera fidei justificati sunt, non justificante sola fide, quia sicut corpus sine spiritu, qui dat vitam corpori . . ."* (2:208). In this context, however, Hus used *justificata* and *justum* with two different meanings. In Rahab's case, *justificata* related to liberation from temporal death (*liberata a morte temporali*), and so *"consecuta est salutem ex fide simul et operibus."* For Abraham, *justum* meant that he "believed God and it was counted to him as righteousness" (James 2:23), so Hus explained the biblical phrase *reputatum est ei ad justitiam* with *"illud quod credidis magna promittenti, et difficilia praecipienti"* (2:206). *Justificatus* for Abraham was related to works after faith, thus the biblical phrase *reputatum est ei ad justitiam* is again explained with *"scilicet ampliorem, qui per fidem, quam per gratiam ei Deus infudit, justum cum reputavit"* (2:207).

187. *Explicatio in Epistola Jacobi* (*Historia et Monumenta*, 2:190): *"Verbo veritatis, id est, per verbum, quod est veritas, Joan 14. Ego sum via, veritas, et vita. Vel verbo veritatis, id est, verbo Evangelii tanquam semine spirituali, Lucae 8."* Hus's exposition of James at times uses exact phrases drawn from Nicholas of Gorran's *In VII epistolas canonicas expositio*. In his remarks on the last section of James 2, Hus cited several other biblical passages to explain his interpretation of faith (e.g., Genesis 15, 22; John 15; Matthew 14, 15; Luke 17; Colossians 2; Romans 4; Malachi 1; Psalm 51; Hebrews 11; Luke 23; 1 John 3; 1 Timothy 1; Ephesians 4, 6, etc.), particularly emphasizing Habakkuk 2:4: *"Justus ex fide vivit"* (2:206–208).

188. *Dominica Quarta Post Octavam Epyphanie* (*MIHOO*, 9:283–284): *"Venite, scilicet per me, post me, ad me. Per me, quia via sum, post me, quia veritas sum, ad me, quia vita sum. Venite per me, et hoc quia via sum. Unde venite ad me per fidem, quia qui extra istam viam est, ad Cristum venire non potest . . . Venite eciam post me, scilicet per bonam operacionem, et venite ad me per finalem in merito consumacionem."* In context, Hus was explaining Matthew 11:28.

189. *Explicatio in Epistola Jacobi* (*Historia et Monumenta*, 2:208).

190. Zdeněk Trtík, "Husův odkaz a oba principy reformace," 41; see also idem, "K Husovu pojetí víry," *Theologická revue* 43 (1972): 158.

191. Zdeněk Trtík, "K Husovu pojetí víry," *Theologická revue* 43 (1972): 157–165. Trtík earlier clarified that "within the framework of the traditional term *fides caritate formata* Hus returned to the biblical meaning of justifying faith and purged the traditionally envisaged faith from an erotic structure" (160).

192. See *Super Quattuor Sententiarum*, 2.24.6.

193. *Výklad na vieru* (*MIHOO,* 1:68, 73).
194. *Česká nedělní postila* (*MIHOO,* 2:153).
195. Molnár, *Na rozhraní věků,* 17.
196. Hus was of course drawing his understanding from Augustine. See *De Trinitate,* 1.2.7; 9.4.4–7.
197. Zdeněk Trtík, "Husův odkaz a oba principy reformace," 38.
198. Amedeo Molnár, *Na rozhraní věků: Cesty reformace* (Praha: Vyšehrad, 1985), 12–13.
199. *Výklad delší na desatero přikázanie* (*MIHOO,* 1:280). The original source is Pseudo-Chrysostomus, *Opus imperfectum in Matthaeum* (*PG* 56.762): *"Nam sicut sacerdos debitor est, ut veritatem quam audivit a Deo libere praedicet: sic laicus debitor est, ut veritatem, quam audivit quidem a sacerdotibus probatam in Scripturis, defendat fiducialiter. Quod si non fecerit, proditor est veritatis."* Hus was citing from *Decretum Gratiani* C.11. q.3 c.86 (*Corpus Iuris Canonici,* 1:667). Hus also used this citation in his letter written to the people of Plzeň; see Novotný, *Korespondence a dokumenty,* 106–107.
200. *Documenta, 278: "Et si dominus deus et conscientia mea mei testes sunt, quod id, quod jam contra me deponunt, nec praedicavi, nec docui, nec in cor meum ascendit, et si omnes adversarii contra me deponerent, quid ego possum, nec hoc mihi finaliter nocet."*
201. "God's Warriors" is a term which appears often in Hussite sources. Perhaps the earliest occurrence is found in the fifteenth-century Hussite war song *Ktož jsú boží bojovníci (You Who Are the Warriors of God).* See *Výbor z české literatury doby husitské,* vol. 1, ed. Bohuslav Havránek, Josef Hrabák, Jiří Daňhelka, et al. (Praha: ČSAV, 1963), 324–325.

6

The Preaching of Jan Hus: His Commitment to Proclaiming Truth

Bethlehem Chapel was destined to become a place of great importance for preaching not only due to the work of Master Jan Hus, but also due to those who preceded and followed the great Bohemian reformer.[1] Many people in Prague who were greatly influenced by the enthusiastic preaching of Jan Milíč of Kroměříž really had nowhere to go to listen to God's word after Milíč's death in 1374.[2] Although there were a plethora of churches in Prague, there was no specific place which particularly focused on preaching the word of God in Czech. During the final years of the reign of Emperor Charles IV and especially after his death, a wave of deep dissatisfaction from ordinary people concerning the corruption of the church was flowing throughout the land. Expectancy for moral and social change had reached its peak, and these disquieted moods were complemented by strong eschatological expectations, since according to the general conception of that time, the situation could not possibly become any worse than it already was. Based on several biblical passages, many believed that the reign of the Antichrist had already commenced, but also maintained the hope and belief that he would soundly be defeated and the millennial reign of Christ would soon be established.

Bethlehem Chapel was built on the initiative of two devout Christian men, the royal courtier Hanuš of Mühlheim and a Prague merchant named Jan Kříž.[3] It was built between the years 1391 and 1394 in the garden behind a house belonging to Kříž. Sermons were to be preached there every Sunday and on every feast day and sometimes several times a day. The benefactors wanted it to serve as a place for preaching in the native Czech language, and it certainly fulfilled its purpose in that regard, although of course Hus sometimes preached in Latin for students and certain members of academia. The chapel itself was an impressive undertaking for its time, since it could accommodate around three thousand standing listeners. However, the existence of Bethlehem Chapel provided clear testimony that there was a great hunger for hearing God's word being preached in the native tongue. Hus had several predecessors in the chapel, and not all of them respected Hus or became his followers. Among those who labored in the chapel before Hus were Jan Protiva of Nová Ves (d. 1430),[4] a later opponent of Hus, Jan Štěkna (d. c. 1407)— who later became a professor in the faculty of theology at the University of Kraków[5]—and also Master Štěpán of Kolín (d. 1406).[6] They were all united by a love of the Czech language and a sense of duty that preaching in Czech was a necessity for the spiritual well-being of the people. No one, however, could have foreseen the specific direction in which the reform efforts would proceed and which particular form they would later take on.

Jan Hus was appointed as preacher in Bethlehem on March 14, 1402, when he received permission and authorization from the archbishop's vicar.[7] According to most estimates, Hus delivered more than three thousand sermons, since according to the foundation charter he would have been required to preach twice on Sundays and holy days, in addition to his preaching on fast days and weekdays. Thus, he would have preached many times a week and sometimes several times a day, perhaps even up to seven times on *nativitas Domini*.[8] From the extant collections of his sermons, we notice that Hus's preaching ministry was founded on diligent preparation and that he consulted the primary theological resources at his disposal. His well-rounded and studious approach allowed him to preach clearly and intelligibly, exerting genuine effort and paying close attention in his attempts to avoid theological speculation, and giving him the freedom to use familiar illustrations drawn from the practical life of his listeners. This practice explains to some extent why Hus was such a popular preacher among the people: he was not simply a scathing critic of the contemporaneous conditions, nor was he some kind of admirable social reformer merely seeking to uplift the difficult social conditions of his surrounding environment. The primary concern which lay heavy upon his heart was how to help his listeners attain salvation.[9] He persistently announced what his listeners should do in order to attain eternal salvation and viewed the courageous yet dangerous task of preaching not only as a perfectly legitimate calling, but also the main calling and responsibility of a preacher, and of course the primary calling of God in his own life. Thus, it is quite obvious that he often touched on the social conditions and circumstances of his time, and that he criticized both the corrupt church and the dominant secular powers. To attain salvation, a person had to be established upon the foundation of Jesus Christ and be united with him by faith, hope, and love, since Christ himself is the essence and foundation of all virtues for those who will be saved.[10] He preached that people should wholeheartedly believe in Jesus Christ as the living Son of God, while also emphasizing that it was necessary for Christians to live a pure and virtuous life according to the commandments of Christ.[11]

One important and decisive aspect of Hus's popularity related to his own personal pursuit of holiness. Gradually, large segments of the Czech-speaking population came to hear Hus preach at Bethlehem Chapel due to his own lifestyle. Hus lived a life of purity and piety and endeavored to practice what he preached—a fact which did not go unnoticed by the people or his friends. Although he certainly had several enemies (e.g., Štěpán Páleč and Michael de Causis) who used some "choice descriptions" against him, in general not even Hus's enemies found fault with the integrity of his life. Many contemporary priests were also critical of the rampant corruption and pervasive immorality, but they were unable to be critical of themselves; they did not live according to what they preached themselves and did not follow that which they demanded of others. This, of course, was one of the many reasons why some of his contemporaries expressed malice or ill-will against Hus. As wicked priests, they became irritated and even irate when people began to notice the holiness and spiritual devotion of Hus's life as a priest. We could say that in many regards, Hus's personal commitment to living a life of purity, devotion, and commitment and imitation of Christ was thus a contributing factor to Hus's overall popularity among the people. Other priests tried to preach in a reforming way, yet their deeds did not always correspond to their words. Since many of Hus's sermons rail against sins of blatant hypocrisy, it was undeniably a serious concern, not only for other priests and commoners, but also for his own spiritual life, as Hus confessed his own sins in his writings numerous times.

Hus reflected upon this unfortunate truth of the lack of morality and virtue in his tract *Knížky o svatokupectví* [*On Simony*] with the following words:

> I myself have carefully listened to the lectures of masters about humility, patience, poverty, courage, and other virtues; they expressed themselves so persuasively and eloquently as if no one else could ever be better than them, as if they themselves actually practiced all of these virtues. However, I did not find any of those virtues in their deeds, yea, they were full of pride, avarice, impatience, and cowardice. And just as the beloved Christ described it, they lay heavy burdens on men's shoulders, imposing their own regulations on them, insisting on [being given] the highest ecclesiastical dignities; and when other men do not bow down before them as if they were bowing before gods, they become infuriated; and when they are seated at the place of honor at the table, [their chests] strangely swell with pride.[12]

The age-old adage that good role models attract like-minded people was proven true in his case. The people before Hus's pulpit began to pursue the truth and to realize and appreciate their own dignity as the unique image-bearers of God,[13] but at the same time they found themselves unable to accept the nearly unbearable environment of moral corruption in which they lived. These Czech homilies in the vernacular must have been really animated and dynamic if they corresponded at all to the preaching notes Hus made in his preparatory materials, where he often included a note that he should expound this part of the text as much as possible. Such notes give an indication of the kind of lucid interpretation and straightforward applications which he intended to preach to the congregation. Unfortunately, not all of Hus's Latin or Czech sermons are extant, but those which we do have at our disposal bear unequivocal testimony that Hus was a masterful preacher. His *Czech Sunday Postil (Česká nedělní postila)*,[14] a revised "homiletical-literary" work which originated from Hus's previous preparations for sermons from 1410 to 1411, was completed at Kozí Hrádek in 1413 while in exile and is distinctly representative of Hus's excellent sermons.[15]

One can only surmise how Hus personally approached the pastoral task of sermon preparation, since not all of his actual resources and examples are entirely known. We assume that he would have found (at least at the outset of his ministry) some inspiration from other preachers whom he had heard while at university and on other occasions. However, based on his own testimony, it is beyond any question whatsoever that after his conversion to Christ, Hus's unyielding commitment to understand Holy Scripture and to follow Jesus Christ himself in imitating his virtues (*imitatio Christi*) was the predominant aim of his life.[16] The particular choice of biblical texts was not random, since Hus used (as was the custom in the Western Church) the established lectionary with its texts intended for the entire church year, especially for Sundays and feast days. The lectionary provided one great advantage in that believers could hear different sermons on the same texts each year. He was certainly familiar with other Czech versions of the biblical texts, and apparently translated a version of the Bible himself.[17] Still, it appears that Hus primarily used the Latin Vulgate, and when he preached in Czech he simply translated the biblical texts into Czech himself.[18] He used all the texts included in the pericopes for his preaching, and did not shy away from the Old Testament texts, which he usually interpreted Christocentrically. The "promised Messiah" is the Redeemer of the world who has been sent by God for his people. The redemptive work of the Father sending his one and only Son for our salvation

> has been accomplished powerfully, graciously, wisely according to his infinite goodness . . . And through whom has it been accomplished? Through his Son— through whom all things have been made and apart from whom not even one thing was made that has been made. And for whom has he accomplished it? For the world—a multitude of impure and corrupted sinners. O defiled world, let it weigh upon your heart that the One who is unable to be corrupt was given for you in order to cleanse you and redeem you from damnation and bring you home to eternal life. And you will immediately know why God sent his Son unto

death: in order to redeem you, world, from death due to sin and from the death of eternal damnation. For the Redeemer of the world himself says, "For God loved the world in this way: He gave his one and only Son, so that everyone who believes in him will not perish but have eternal life."[19]

The lectionary also proved to be a disadvantage in some ways, since not all of the biblical texts were incorporated. When Hus needed to use additional texts as cross references to the predetermined pericope, he did not hesitate to include them within his interpretation of the specific passage. He also benefited from certain preaching manuals used for the interpretation itself, of which there were many of varying quality. Hus's explanation of biblical passages in his sermons is always intertwined with corresponding citations from church fathers, thus demonstrating that he was determined to incorporate all of the available resources at his disposal in order to understand and explain the given verses.

With the advent of modern textual criticism a minor issue which Hus had no way of foreseeing presents itself here. Many of the writings attributed to John Chrysostom, Augustine, Bernard of Clairvaux, or other fathers or teachers of the church were actually pseudonymous compositions which were merely attributed to them by previous church tradition. Although we recognize several of the works cited by Hus as properly belonging to another writer, during his era they were considered the authentic word of church tradition. Hus honestly and humbly strove to honor church tradition and viewed it as a vital aspect of the life of the church; he certainly did not view himself as deviating in any basic way from the tradition of the Western Church, nor did he wish to denigrate Christ's church at all, as he viewed the church as *summa creatura*.[20] Hus did, however, measure all of church tradition against the standard of the Bible, and if some well-known quotations from early church fathers and teachers were found to be at variance, he either did not use them at all or he moderately disputed with them and sought to clarify them in his interpretation. In his so-called independent or innovative interpretations of the lectionary texts, Hus sought to follow exclusively the clear meaning of the Scriptures. He never argued against Scripture, since "Holy Scripture can neither be discredited nor contradicted,"[21] and so even the tradition of the church must be judged according to the Scripture. The extensive preaching ministry of Hus formally followed the homiletical tradition as it gradually developed from antiquity to the High Middle Ages. He preached interpretive and reflective sermons or homilies in the sense of the original meaning of *homilia*: an assembly, a gathering, a meeting, a conversation, or a crowd.[22]

Originally, homilies were rhetorical performances during which the audience in the church either applauded or, in the event of disagreement, made their disapproval very obvious by shouting or throwing everything at hand at the preacher. For example, the famous ancient homilies of Augustine, John Chrysostom, or Gregory the Great remain a valuable source for scholarly research not only due to the interpretive skill and spiritual motivation contained within, but also for the insightful words which these famous classics of Christian homiletics spoke concerning historical events and the respective responses of their congregations. Although the tradition of interacting with listeners at religious gatherings through homilies practically continues to this day, various contemporary models of preaching usually include a wide range of emphases (e.g., exegetical competency, relevant cultural sources used in addition to Scripture and tradition, emotional and engaging appeals to public action, etc.).

Medieval homilies included the reading and "interpretation" of a biblical text and reflective remarks of the preacher. Moreover, topical sermons not necessarily based on a specific biblical reading were commonly associated with a certain feast day or specific events on the church calendar. Homilies were divided into higher and lower, with the "lower" basically comprising interpretations of a given text verse by verse and the preacher's brief expressions of his opinion. In "higher" homilies, the preacher chose one central idea contained in the biblical text, explained it, then offered a portrayal of how various church authorities had approached the same issue. The same homiletical divisions hold true for Hus, but in both cases, his primary intention centered around presenting his interpretation and analysis of the text (i.e., exegesis). Only in the latter case did he make extensive use of ancient and medieval commentaries. In both cases, his applications of the texts he explained were suitable and very relevant for his times.

Czech theologian Rudolf Horský (1914–2001) drew proper attention to both the sharp and piercing tone of Hus's words in the case of the well-known text from the Gospel of Luke (2:42–52) when Jesus was lost and then found by his parents in the temple.[23] Hus's interpretation was quite standard, but his application was already steered in the direction of castigating contemporary problems in the church. Hus first explained why the twelve-year-old Jesus was in the temple: he was instructing those who were gathered there to help them understand the law of the Lord. Then Hus immediately proceeded to give his application of the passage: "But regrettably, the bishops and priests of today, and especially the canons and absentee altar-thanes, just cannot wait for the worship service to be finished as soon as possible so that they can go to the pub or other places to return to their unspeakable practices unworthy of priests, lamentably even to dancing."[24] Jesus was found teaching in the temple, not drinking in a pub, nor dancing, nor playing games. Hus then presented the following practical application for his listeners: "It is well-known that there are many masters, doctors, and other priests who sin by not wisely listening, asking questions, and giving answers, but according to their own desire and false witnesses; they condemn others even as Susanna was condemned without guilt by two old priests; and if any Scripture is against their customs and own interests, they curiously interpret it in a strange way."[25] Hus's point was to demonstrate how the priests did not actually desire to serve God, but instead merely wanted to scamper away from their spiritual duties in order to indulge in worldly pleasures. In a following particular point of application, he urged parents not to hinder their children who want to serve God.

Hus sincerely desired to remain faithful to the truth at all costs while also speaking of contemporary interests and appropriately applying truth to the current circumstances of his listeners. He was fully aware that if he were to reach them with saving knowledge of God, he had "to speak their language," or else no one would listen to him. The result of his commitment to preaching the truth faithfully and plainly is seen in the sheer number of listeners who continually thronged to Bethlehem Chapel.

One of the primary accents which we find in Hus's preaching is his emphasis that sin is overcome and grace is mediated not only through the sacraments but especially by the Word of God. Although proclamation of the gospel was not the exclusive means, according to Hus, preaching certainly was an essential and effectual means of salvation: "Here is the teaching that by asking and hearing about Jesus, people come to the knowledge of faith and thus to salvation, as Saint Paul deduces in the tenth chapter of Romans, saying that 'faith comes by hearing' and hearing cannot exist without speaking or preaching."[26] As an essential means of salvation, preaching affected the whole person: reason, emotions, and will. The purpose and priority of preaching was to proclaim both God's divine work of redemption accomplished for sinners and also man's responsibility to repent of sins, believe in the Redeemer Jesus Christ, and follow him in a new life of loving obedience.[27] In a sense, Hus's preaching basically represented a return to the early Christian era when the Christian message was a profound, joyful, and life-changing message of good news which brought about new life, and participation in the Lord's Supper for believers was a vivid confirmation of this new reality of life, since believers decided to participate due to their belief and experience of the living Word. The fathers of the church were also deeply aware of the importance of preaching; in the fourth and fifth centuries, Augustine stated that the Lord's Supper was still *verba visibile* received by all of the senses.[28] This vital concept gradually disappeared from the Church, and a more mechanical concept prevailed in the Middle Ages, which led to the importance of the living Word of God greatly declining.

A preacher whose unambiguous message and communication style resonated deeply with such a significant percentage of the entire population of a large town like Prague was not a matter of common occurrence at the time. There were many preachers who no doubt noticed the dissension and corruption in the church, but they raised their concerns and preached about problems mostly in Latin and only for a certain section of the population. This explains why some of Hus's "predecessors" who preached clear messages in the language of the people also became popular preachers. However, none of them seemed to strike a good balance between theory and practice or between the academic language of Latin and the common language of the people. For the sake of comparison, Konrad Waldhauser did not speak Czech, and his sermons in Latin and in German were directed more towards the Prague German patricians. Jan Milíč of Kroměříž was a compassionate and understandable preacher, but his overall ministry presents him as more of a visionary, though he was of course able to reach and transform certain classes of society with the message of reconciliation and renewed lives. Matěj of Janov was a typical intellectual reformer whose works were not completely understandable or accessible to everyone. In contrast, Hus evidently preached with a distinctive "aura of unmistakable clarity" so that all of his listeners could comprehend his message. Hus walked among the people, lived in the midst of them, and understood what was relevant to them, what needed to be explained at particular moments, and in which particular manner or expression he should preach the truth.

His public declarations from the pulpit were heard by thousands of people, yet Hus was also well aware that his listeners were not identical; not everyone was treated equally in that feudalistic society, especially women. Although Hus did issue warnings against women in relation to their fickle nature even in spirituality, he still respected women and approached them within the social boundaries of his time.[29] In his Easter homily on the text of the conclusion of the gospel of Mark (Mark 16:1–7), he emphasized that it was the women to whom the resurrection of Christ was first declared. He even affirmed the right of women to rebuke unworthy priests for their immoral behavior.

> Well, priests: when you offend others by failing to follow Christ, if a woman rebukes you, receive it gladly. I myself want to receive it gladly whenever any old woman teaches me something valuable, and especially when it concerns teaching me how to live virtuously. But others consider it utter foolishness that good women should rebuke them or teach them anything good at all, just like the disciples of Christ considered that which the holy women told them about Christ from his commandment was nonsense, as Saint Luke says in the twenty-fourth chapter.[30]

This was a unique perspective quite unheard of at that time. While in exile, Hus composed a delightful little treatise on Christian spirituality specifically written for a community of women living in a house near Bethlehem Chapel. *The Little Daughter: On Knowing the True Path to Salvation* is a devotional text based on Psalm 45:10 which explains in ten short chapters some of the main themes of medieval spirituality: self-knowledge, the image of God, the conscience, temptations, *contemptus mundi,* the three enemies of mankind, repentance, the soul, the future judgment, the kingdom of heaven, and loving God.[31]

Of course, Hus did severely criticize certain excesses in both men and women. For example, he did not hesitate to warn of the unpredictable temptations which dancing could arouse, as dancing at that time was still considered something either sinful or inappropriate by many, even as it was in the early church. Still, Hus's underlying concern was the welfare of the people, as confirmed by a letter written to a noblewoman in which Hus critiqued dancing.

> Oh, who there among those dancing, watching them, or idly standing around is without sin? Let us see who is with God or without God! Yea, lamentably, many mortal and even unspeakable sins are committed there through lascivious and impure thoughts, flirting and teasing, indecent appearance, inconspicuous glances, a lot of vain and obscene words, touching of body parts, groping, hugging and cuddling, and other unholy deeds. There is too much amusing laughter, quarrels and deafening clamor, pompous pride, envy, feelings of wrath, and other resentful grievances. They forsake valuable time for doing better activities in order to commit such evil deeds by utterly wasting their time there, and the souls of many are eternally damned. They encounter diabolical and cunning temptations there, and the maidens and the young men greatly defile their own heart.
>
> For when they leave home and attend a dance, not having personal knowledge of certain sins, they return home with an evil imagination, lazy, and restless disposition for their work, having already depleted their physical strength and energy and torn their dress and shoes. Some of the youth and maidens lose their "pure white shirt" [i.e., virginity, widowhood, or marriage] which is worth more than all the wealth in the whole world and which as Saint Jerome says, even God himself cannot restore even though he is all-powerful. Likewise, a widow and a wife and even a virgin, being filled with evil desires, returns home from the dance having defiled her own estate.[32]

Hus's Czech expositions were intended for ordinary people and were therefore designed to reflect the daily realities of life with which his listeners were most familiar. Even while reacting to the stark realities of his medieval era in preaching against many sins, his authoritative statements do not possess any hidden agenda, as his motivation for denouncing sin was simply to proclaim the truth and strive for the salvation of his flock.

Much like prophets in the Old Testament, Hus did not feel the least inhibition in pronouncing sharp words of criticism when he considered them necessary, and he apparently showed little reservation in attempting to temper his speech. When Hus sometimes resorted to coarser and rougher expressions (not only in relation to women), we may safely assume that his motivation for using such unconventional language from the pulpit served as a viable means of encouraging closer relationships with his listeners—but not so much perhaps with his enemies! In short, Hus was seeking first the reign of God's majesty and his kingdom (Matthew 6:33) and preaching the truth so that people would live according to God's commandments. Unfortunately, it seems as if he found nothing else except the exact opposite in the sins of his culture at large. As well, Christian teachings in his time had gradually merged with folklore, fables, and legends, and in Hus's mind had deteriorated to the point where the church began elevating custom and tradition over biblical truth, something which Hus opposed in principle since it was foreign to his commitment to Christ and Scripture. He earnestly desired for people to follow the Ten Commandments, and he especially made mention of God's command to "remember the Sabbath day, to keep it holy" (Exodus 20:8) so that people would be aware of the deep meaning and significance which the Lord's Day has for Christians. He criticized those who celebrated important Sundays or kermesses with unrestrained merriment.

> For the sake of custom, they are no longer willing to call sin what it is—sin— even showing it in words and deeds, for even the priests dance on Sunday, and claim that it is not a sin to dance, yea, even as Saint Augustine says, that it would be better for a woman to do some other work such as hand-spinning rather than to dance on holy days, and especially on Sunday, which God himself has commanded to be kept holy.[33] Woe to the people with their "holy days!" Keeping them holy by sinning! Is this the way to keep Sunday holy: by playing, committing gluttony, dancing, flirting and teasing, quarreling and fighting, drinking all day long, and buying and selling? Oh! To keep Sunday or another day holy, however, means to abstain from sinning, to refrain from physical labor and urgent worldly endeavors, and to contemplate God, to serve him, and take pleasure in applying all of your efforts toward pursuing your salvation. And this is what Lord God demands from everyone, which he especially emphasized in the third commandment in this way: "Remember the Sabbath to keep it holy." (Exodus 20:8)

Even with all of Hus's fiery lambasting against sin, none of his at times severe words should give the idea that Hus was somehow a killjoy; he was certainly not against participating in wedding festivities or against people rejoicing. He simply did not want solemn events which served as reminders of the important moments in the history of salvation to degenerate into worldly merriment where the original meaning and purpose of the holy feast days would be forgotten. Thus, a thoughtful liturgical appreciation and genuine biblical seriousness accompanied the whole of Hus's preaching ministry.[34]

Hus's preaching is sometimes criticized for using a large number of allegories which gave the biblical texts meanings different from the author's original intention. Engaging in allegorical interpretation was a widespread practice in the Middle Ages, but the use of allegory was not as decisive for Hus as it appears. Of course, he did use allegories in his texts at times, but never in the specific cases which are central to the history of salvation. Hus was simply wise enough to use allegories as a helpful aid in narrating biblical stories and historical realities that were far removed from his modern listeners. It cannot be maintained that the allegories he used as an auxiliary method jeopardized the Christocentric content of his explanations in any way. From the number of allegorical interpretations used by Hus, Hus's exposition of the parable of the Good Samaritan (Luke 10:30–37) serves as a good example. Hus wrote: "'But a certain Samaritan' means Christ; he is called a Samaritan because he is the guardian of all his faithful, since Samaritan is interpreted as a guardian . . . 'and poured oil' means mercy, 'and wine' means repentance, suffering, or comfort. 'And having put him on his own beast' means having suffered for him in his own body . . . "[35] Horský commented:

> So we see then that the Samaritan is Christ, the wounded one signifies humanity, the oil signifies mercy, the wounds signify sin, the wine signifies repentance, the putting of the man on his own animal signifies his vicarious suffering, bringing him to the inn signifies bringing him into the congregation of holy people, that he greatly cared for him signifies that he lived more than thirty-two years in affliction for the sake of mankind, the other day signifies the time of grace, the taking out of two coins signifies the Old and New Testaments, and giving them to the inn-keeper signifies giving them to a priest who should know and understand both of the Testaments, etc.[36]

These allegorical explanations serve rather to illustrate the spiritual meaning and content of the biblical text. His interpretation was not based on producing fanciful allegorizations, but rather his intentional emphasis centered on explaining the meaning of the passage and the intended application in response to the word of God for his own audience.[37]

Hus's sermons prove that he was keenly aware of the various and distinct dimensions of social and cultural elements at work within his own environment. Due to the moral degradation of his time, this meant first and foremost that he came face to face with the sins of the people. Therefore, he preached boldly and openly against every imaginable sin or vice, especially against the greed of secular lords and the simony of the priests. He insisted that each human should live a holy life in accordance with the law of Christ, called for a consistent pursuit of the imitation of the life of Christ, and promoted divine justice as the standard by which the affairs of the world should be regulated.

According to him, divine justice or righteousness is set forth and laid out in Scripture, and each person's calling before God is to put the word of God into practice in his or her own daily life. The greatest commandments—to love God with all of one's heart, soul, mind, and strength and to love one's neighbor as oneself—were not mere platitudes of pious morality, but the very essence of true Christian spirituality.[38] And based on the testimony of his friend Jakoubek, we can here again affirm that Hus practiced what he preached. In a sermon preached in Bethlehem Chapel only a few years after Hus's death, his faithful friend reminisced over the fact that Hus was not only a zealous preacher of the gospel, but that he loved and showed compassion to all men, including his enemies and those who had persecuted him.[39]

There is scant evidence that Hus ever called for a violent revolution or for people to take matters of justice into their own hands away from legitimate structures of authority. Although his preaching did arouse and lead to emotional and sometimes improper responses by the people, claims that he was a violent revolutionary are entirely inappropriate. Revolutionary in a certain sense—yes! but violent—no! Hus's only "revolutionary" actions were disobeying papal bulls which were not founded in Holy Scripture, appealing to Jesus Christ himself as the supreme Judge against the pope and canon law, and preaching the gospel of Christ in spite of papal injunctions and excommunication. In a *Notarial Instrument of Appeal* written to Pisan Pope John XXIII protesting and appealing against the ban on preaching in chapels and the burning of Wyclif's books, Hus and several of his supporters wrote: "We do not intend to submit or obey," since they had "a reasonable and just cause" to disobey: the ecclesiastical judgments were "frivolous and void of all truth and destitute of any justice by reason of its premises"—premises which they interpreted as opposed to Scripture and reason.[40] Of course, it can be argued that Hus encouraged disobedience to superiors, as evidenced in the second half of *Tractatus de Ecclesia*,[41] but that fact is nothing more than a basic acknowledgement that for Hus the law of Christ was superior to human mandates and that many of the mandates which ecclesiastical superiors demanded at that time were patently opposed to the law of Christ. A constant refrain running throughout all of the struggles in his life and ministry was the well-known declaration of Peter and the other apostles: "We must obey God rather than men" (Acts 5:29).

Obedience for Hus primarily meant trusting the promises of God and fulfilling the commandments of Christ. He believed that every vice, every sin, all moral corruption, all dissension, and all of the wickedness experienced by humanity were the consequence of human sin. He pleaded with people of every age and social background to return to a saving relationship with their Creator and Redeemer as the main path of expunging every measure of injustice. Hus's *Sermo de Pace* clearly expressed his belief that a man must first be reconciled to God and experience peace with God before he can live in peace with his fellow man in society. Hus wrote:

> There are three diverse aspects of peace: peace with God, peace with one's own self, and peace with one's neighbor. All of these aspects of peace stand firmly in observing the commandments. The first kind of peace, namely a person's peace with God, is such a powerful virtue that every other kind of peace is unimaginable without it, but whoever has this peace, possesses both of the other two following kinds [of peace] as a consequence. Indeed, nothing frustrates peace with God except sin, because only sin separates God and man according to that [prophecy] of Isaiah: "Your sins have separated you from your God" (Isaiah 59:2).[42]

It is therefore surprising that radical socialists and Communists in the twentieth century considered Jan Hus as one of their "predecessors."[43] Moreover, it is important to realize that the violence one encounters in the later Hussite movement was a direct result of overbearing and incessant provocation— namely, that on March 17, 1420, Pope Martin V (1369–1431) issued a bull (*Omnium plasmatoris domini*) which ordered a crusade against Hussite Bohemia.[44] Violence inevitably stirred up reactionary violence, and the social ramifications of a crusade in many regards demanded that personal defense become a virtual necessity. In the case of Hus, we must pose the legitimate question as to whether or not he was even aware of the fact that the harsh historical circumstances of his era were indeed so intolerable that violence would unavoidably follow.

By evaluating the specific Czech terms of Hus's expositions of the *Apostles' Creed*, the Lord's Prayer, and the Decalogue and relating them to similar stylistic expressions in his other shorter Czech writings (e.g., *Dcerka*) and especially his *Czech Sunday Postil*,[45] we can at least find a useful window into which we can peer to understand what Hus's actual preaching might have sounded like to his original listeners. While attending the university, he had diligently studied and utilized the common tools and techniques of medieval rhetoric,[46] as in his academic discourses we see the fruits of his labors demonstrated in persuasive rhetorical questions, interjections, logical syllogisms, and appeals to etymology, authority, and emotion. Not only was Hus a highly educated priest, but he was also a full-blooded Bohemian, speaking Czech perfectly and even explicitly playing with the language at times through idiomatic expressions, puns, and other forms of figurative language which testifies to his linguistic prowess. While there is no definitive consensus concerning its authorship,[47] Hus is still recognized and accepted by many as the author of *Orthographia Bohemica*, a very remarkable work which made a unique contribution to Czech orthography.[48] While many of the same figurative elements are evident in his *Czech Sunday Postil,* one may also notice a careful attention to the grammatical structures and meaning of the biblical text. Any perceived embellishments of the certain meanings of words were employed only in service of his overall didactic and exhortatory purposes. Although Hus admitted in the preface that he was writing his text in a different manner not exactly commensurate to the way in which he usually preached, his *Czech Sunday Postil* no doubt provides a harmonious example of his speaking capabilities, even while accounting for the various distinctions which surely existed between Hus's spoken and written language.[49] Generally speaking, Hus's language never appears to be turgid, vague, abstract, or pretentious. The Czech expressions in *Postila* are descriptive yet clear, creative yet understandable, imaginative yet reasonable, and firm yet compassionate. Thus, if we assume a consistent relation between his written and spoken language, we can accordingly affirm that his harsh denouncements against sin and his pressing the necessity of repentance were matched by compassionate calls to receive mercy and grace; his general pronouncements for the entire congregation also evinced a conversational and personal tone; and his emotionally stirring illustrations were always closely connected to reasonable explanations of the truth. Although he often used recognizable illustrations from daily life which were easily understandable (and thus more credible as a matter of experience for his listeners), Hus's message was never "watered down" even when he sought to make it accessible to the widest audience possible: the "common people" of whom he often spoke.[50] Hus's preaching ministry represents a classic example of what is sometimes called "tough love"—a loving invitation to understand and embrace the truth accompanied with an uncompromising challenge which demands personal response in terms of active obedience to it.

Therefore, Hus's linguistic proficiency and presentation of biblical truths in understandable language for the masses was not the sole significant factor in how Hus gained the confidence and support of his listeners; it was principally due to his personal desire to lead people to repentance and salvation, since they longed to hear a "living word" that would touch upon and explain their own circumstances, desires, and questions.[51] In contrast, his Latin sermons were intended for scholarly circles, but at the same time in comparison to other contemporary academic sermons they do appear to be rather lengthy. Any kind of theological analysis would lead one to regard his academic sermons not merely as intellectual discussions on morality or disputed topics, but spiritual exhortations to pursue truth and a call to live in light of the truth, even though their structure and style are of course different from his popular Czech sermons, which were intended for the broadest strata of society.

Vernacular hymns also played an important role in Hus's pastoral ministry at Bethlehem.[52] Despite a ban on singing songs in Czech in Prague churches issued by Archbishop Zbyněk Zajíc of Házmburk in 1408, Hus regularly practiced the singing of Czech songs during worship services and even included songs which were not approved. *"Hospodine pomiluj ny"* ("Lord, Have Mercy on Us") or *"Svatý Václave"* ("Saint Wenceslaus") and a few other songs were exceptions to the prohibition, but they were mostly sung only during special occasions. Among the most common hymns whose Czech lyrics have been attributed to Hus are *"Navštiv nás Kriste žádúcí"* ("Visit Us, O Desirable Christ"), *"Jezu Kriste, štědrý kněže"* ("O, Jesus Christ, Bountiful Priest"), *Králi slavný, Kriste dobrý* ("O Glorious King, Good Christ"), *"Vstalť jest bóh z mrtvých"* ("God Has Risen from the Dead").[53] He also revised and translated the older Latin hymn *Jesus Christus nostra salus* into Czech.[54] According to Hus, spiritual songs served to prepare the listeners to hear and understand God's word properly. Later the use of Czech songs was further adapted and developed, and the singing of hymns became an integral part of the Bohemian Reformation both as a theological concept and practice. Songs were written not only by Hussite (Utraquist) theologians in the fifteenth century,[55] but also in the sixteenth century by major representatives of the Unity of Brethren such as Jan Augusta (1500–1572),[56] Jan Blahoslav (1523–1571),[57] Jan Roh (1490–1547),[58] and Jan Amos Komenský (1592–1670).[59] In fact, the first Czech hymnal of the Unity of the Brethren, printed in Prague in 1501, was the first hymnal printed in Europe.[60] Therefore, although congregational singing in the vernacular had already been used by Konrad Waldhauser, Hus's fostering of the practice definitely had a significant influence on this important aspect of lay participation in worship, at least in terms of uniting the community of common people and providing an opportunity for the active expression of their desires rather than passive "participation" in a language they could not understand.[61] Thus, in both preaching and singing in the vernacular, Bethlehem Chapel "is a liturgical landmark on the landscape of religious thought."[62]

The entire course of Hus's life, with both its successes and failures, certainly bears testimony to his irresistible and passionate desire to preach the truth of the living God. To say that preaching was paramount for Hus would be an understatement, since Hus lived and breathed the preaching of the truth. Even while in exile, his mind was still engaged with fulfilling his calling of being a preacher. In a letter written to the people of Prague sometime shortly before December 25, 1412, Hus concluded with these memorable words:

> You who are zealous for the Word of God to which you are being conformed,
> would be glad in your love to see me as a neighbor for your own good. I too
> would like to see you and preach the Word of God to you. The other priests also

must seek those things with the greatest amount of diligence. Woe to the priests who consider the Word of God as nothing! Woe to those who are duty-bound to preach and yet do not preach! Woe to those who hinder preaching and hearing! But praise be to those who hear the word and keep it, for it is Christ himself who grants them his "indulgences," saying, "Blessed rather are those who hear the Word of God and keep it" (Luke 11:28).

May this blessedness and this hearing be granted to you by the good pleasure of God the Father, the Son, and the Holy Spirit, one eternal God, blessed forever. Amen.[63]

The latter part of Hus's life in relation to his influential preaching was marked by unavoidable controversy. He mentioned in his *Postila* that the Archbishop of Prague Zbyněk along with the canons purchased from Pope Alexander V a bull which had forbidden preaching in chapels. Never bowing down to the powers that be when they contradicted the truth, Hus stood his ground and protested. His protests are summarized most succinctly and his own attitude toward preaching was most clearly expressed in a few personal comments he made in his explanation of Luke 14:

The Lord God granted me the passionate desire to stand up and protest and disobey the injunctions of that bull [which were] against his gospel. And with his help *I preached* even in spite of the anathema and unjust suspension of the worship services, *I am still preaching* now, and if God grants me his holy grace, *I will continue to preach* so that I might lead anyone who is poor, weary, blind, or faltering to the banqueting table of the family of Christ.

NOTES

1. On the chapel itself, see Alois Kubíček, *Betlémská kaple,* 2nd ed. (Praha: Státní nakladatelství krásné literatury, hudby a umění, 1960); see also Václav Novotný, František Michálek Bartoš, Ferdinand Hrejsa, and Karel Guth, *Betlémská kaple: O jejích dějinách a zachovaných zbytcích* (Praha: Společnost Husova Musea, 1922).

2. For an edition of his sermons, see Vilém Herold and Milan Mráz, eds., *Iohannis Milicii de Cremsir Tres sermones synodales* (Prague: Academia, 1974). For his role as a preacher, see Peter C. A. Morée, "The Role of the Preacher According to Milicius de Chremsir," *The Bohemian Reformation and Religious Practice* 3 (2000): 35–48.

3. See Otakar Odložilík, "The Bethlehem Chapel in Prague: Remarks on Its Foundation Charter," *Studien zur Älteren Geschichte Osteuropas [Wiener Archiv für Geschichte des Slawentums und Osteuropas 2,1]* (Graz and Cologne, 1956): 125–141.

4. See Kamil Krofta, "Kněz Jan Protiva z Nové Vsi a Chelčického mistr Protiva Zdrojový dokument," *Časopis Musea Království českého* 74 (1900): 190–220.

5. See František M. Bartoš, "Husův učitel Dr. Jan Štěkna a kaple Betlémská," *Věstník České akademie věd a umění* 58 (1949): 5–13.

6. See Otakar Odložilík, *M. Štěpán z Kolína* (Praha: Nákladem Společnosti Husova musea, 1924).

7. For an excellent overview of Hus's preaching ministry, see Pavel Soukup, "Jan Hus as a Preacher," in *A Companion to Jan Hus*, eds. František Šmahel and Ota Pavlíček (Leiden: Brill, 2015), 96–129; see also Anežka Vidmanová, "Hus als Prediger," *Communio viatorum* 19 (1976): 65–81.

8. Václav Flajšhans, ed., *Mistra Jana Husi Sebrané spisy*, vol. 6 (Prague: J.R. Vilímek, 1904), iv (Epilogue); ibid., vol. 4, ix (Prologue); see also Spinka, *John Hus*, 51.

9. Even when in exile, Hus wrote a spiritual treatise entitled *O poznání cěsty pravé k spasení (On Knowing the True Path to Salvation). See Dcerka (MIHOO*, 4:163–186). Though it is commonly referred to as *Dcerka, the oldest manuscript has the longer title. See Drobné spisy české (MIHOO*, 4:13–14).

10. *Česká nedělní postila (MIHOO*, 2:454–457).

11. *Česká nedělní postila (MIHOO*, 2:453).

12. *Knížky o svatokupectví (MIHOO*, 4:251).

13. *Česká nedělní postila (MIHOO*, 2:374, 407).

14. See Anežka Vidmanová-Schmidtová, "Kdy, kde a jak psal Hus českou Postilu," *Listy filologické* 112 (1989): 144–158.

15. The critical edition is Amedeo Molnár, ed., *Magistri Iohannis Hus Postilla adumbrata: Liber cura Commissionis ad Hussii Opera omnia edenda ab academico Collegio historiae creatae vulgatus* (Prague: Academia: 1975); republished as Bohumil Ryba and Gabriel Silagi, eds., *Magistri Iohannis Hus Postilla adumbrata (Magistri Iohannis Hus Opera omnia; tomus XIII; Corpus Christianorum. Continuatio mediaevalis 261)* (Turnhout: Brepols Publishers, 2015).

16. See *Tractatus de Ecclesia*, passim. Cf. *Defensio Libri de Trinitate (MIHOO*, 22:41–42).

17. For support of Hus's authorship, see: F.M. Bartoš, "Hus a jeho účast na staročeské bibli," *Strahovská knihovna* 3 (1968): 86–112; Antonín Zeman, "K biblickému textu Husovy postily," *Listy filologické* 101 (1978): 13–16.

18. See the introductions to each sermon found in *Česká nedělní postila (Magistri Iohannis Hus Opera Omnia,* vol. 2).

19. *Česká nedělní postila*, 2:73, 261–262.

20. *Tractatus de Ecclesia*, 4. Hus was citing Augustine. See Augustine, *Enchiridion de fide, spe et charitate*, 15.56.

21. *Tractatus de Ecclesia*, 56.

22. Ernest Klein, *A Comprehensive Etymological Dictionary of the English Language: Dealing with the Origin of Words and Their Sense Development Thus Illustrating the History of Civilization and Culture*, 2 vols. (Amsterdam: Elsevier Publishing Company, 1966), 1:739.

23. Rudolf Horský, "Kazatelské a pastýřské dílo M. Jana Husi," in *Hus stále živý, sborník studií k 550 výročí Husova upálení*, ed. M. Kaňák (Prague: Blahoslav, 1965), 45–68.

24. *Česká nedělní postila (MIHOO, 2:86).*

25. Ibid.

26. *Česká nedělní postila (MIHOO, 2:137; cf. 2:363).*

27. For an insightful evaluation of Hus's preaching priorities, see Reid S. Weber, "A Preacher's Priorities: Jan Hus and Late Medieval Homiletics" (PhD dissertation, University of Florida, 2014).

28. Augustine, *Contra Faustum Manichaeum,* 19.16; *De Doctrina Christiana,* 1.2.2; 2.3.4; *In Iohannis Evangelium Tractatus* 80.3 (*Patrologia Latina,* 35:1840).

29. Hus mentioned this in his letters to Martin of Volyně (*Korespondence,* 204–205; 276–279) and Havlík (*Korespondence,* 214–216).

30. *Česká nedělní postila (MIHOO, 2:188).*

31. *Dcerka: O poznání česty pravé k spasení (MIHOO,* 4:163–186). (English translation forthcoming.)

32. Hus also critiqued dancing in a *Letter to a Noblewoman (Korespondence,* 16). For the citation of Jerome concerning virginity, see Jerome, *Letter to Eustochium* 22.5 (*Corpus Scriptorum Ecclesiasticorum Latinorum*), 54:149–150. See also "O Tanci," in *Mistra Jana Husi Sebrané spisy,* 5:4–6.

33. Augustine, *Sermones de Scripturis* in *PL,* 38:77 (*Sermo 9: De Decem Chordis*).

34. See David R. Holeton, "Liturgická a svátostná teologie mistra Jana Husa: Byl Jan Hus reformátorem liturgie?" *Theologická revue* 67/1 (1996): 9–12; idem, "O felix Bohemia—O felix Constantia," *Liturgická úcta Mistra Jana Husa in Jan Hus mezi epochami, národy a konfesemi: Sborník z mezinárodního sympozia, konaného 22.–26. září 1993 v Bayreuthu, SRN* (Praha: Česká křesťanská akademie, 1995), 154–170. His biblical seriousness is evidenced by the fact that he preached against dancing mainly because he believed that "dancing is a grave and mortal sin . . . condemned by many declarations of Holy Scripture" (*Korespondence,* 17).

35. *Česká nedělní postila (MIHOO, 2:376).*

36. Horský, "Kazatelské a pastýřské dílo M. Jana Husi," 58.

37. For an overview of ancient allegorical interpretations of this parable, see Riemer Roukema, "The Good Samaritan in Ancient Christianity," *Vigiliae Christianae* 58 (2004): 56–74.

38. See "Confirmata corda vestra," in Iohannes Hus, *Positiones, recommendationes, sermones,* ed. Anežka Schmidtová (Prague: Státní pedagogické nakladatelství, 1958), 119–130; see also *Dcerka (MIHOO,* 4:184–186).

39. Jacobelli de Misa, "Sermo habitus in Bethlehem a quodam pio in memoriam novorum martyrum M. Johannis Hus et M. Hieronymi," in *Fontes Rerum Bohemicarum,* 8:238.

40. *Korespondence,* 62–63: "*. . . predicte bulle surrepticie et vehementer de falsificacione suspecte processibusque et sentenciis predicti domini Sbinconis archiepiscopi inde fulminatis et secutis, tamquam frivolis et nullis et omni veritate et iusticia destitutis, ex causis premissis et aliis infra scriptis parere et obedire non intendimus, quousque ex certa sedis apostolice sciencia de singulis premissis ac eius determinacione, deo et iusticia mediante, plene et expresse non fuerimus docti et informati.*"

41. See *Tractatus de Ecclesia,* 148–237.

42. *Sermo de Pace* (*MIHOO*, 24:5): "*Ista autem pax tripliciter variatur: est enim pax hominis ad Deum, hominis ad seipsum et hominis ad proximum, et tota illa pax consistit in observancia mandatorum. Et prima pax, scilicet hominis Deum, est tante virtutis, quod sine illa non valet pax alia, sed ipsa habita utraque posterior consequitur. Nichil enim dissolvit pacem cum Deo, nisi peccatum, quia solum ipsum dividit inter Deum et hominem iuxta illud Ysaie 59: 'Iniquitates vestre diverserunt inter vos et Deum.'*"

43. The following works represent varying Marxist perspectives on Hus: Josef Macek, *Husitské revoluční hnutí* (Praha: Rovnost, 1952); idem, *Jan Hus: Studie s ukázkami Husova díla* (Praha: Svobodné slovo, 1963); idem, *Jean Hus et les traditions hussites (XVe–XIXe siècles)* (Paris: Plon, 1973); Robert Kalivoda, *Husitská ideologie* (Praha: ČSAV, 1961); Zdeněk Nejedlý, *Hus a naše doba,* 2nd ed. (Prague: Svoboda, 1946); Milan Machovec, *Husovo učení a význam v dějinách českého národa* (Praha: ČSAV, 1953). See also Martin Weis, "M. Jan Hus v ideologii Komunistické strany Československa ve světle díla Zdeňka Nejedlého a archivních dokumentů," *Studia Theologica* 17 (2015): 113–123.

43. Oddone Colonna was elected pope at the Council of Constance on November 11, 1417. On February 22, 1418, he issued two bulls (*In eminentis* and *Inter cunctas*) in which he approved all of the basic verdicts, edicts, and decrees of Pope John XXII and the Council of Constance aimed against the followers of Wyclif, Hus, and Jerome. See Petr Čornej, *Jan Žižka: Život a doba husitského válečníka* (Praha: Paseka, 2019), 127, 234. (An English translation is forthcoming.)

44. There are several editions. See: *Postylla svaté paměti M. Jana Husi, mučedlníka božího, na evangelia, kteráž se čtou přes celý rok. K nížti přidané jsou mnohé jiné knihy téhož M. Jana Husi. Kteréž jsou ještě nikdy nebyly imprimované a již nyní teprv na světlo vydané* (Nuremberg: Johann Montanus and Ulrich Neuber, 1563); Karel Jaromír Erben, ed., *Mistra Jana Husi Sebrané spisy české, vol. 2* (Praha: Bedřich Tempský, 1866); Jan Hus, *Postilla*, trans. Václav Flajšhans (Praha: Josef R. Vilímek, 1899–1900); Jan Hus, *Postilla: Vyložení svatých čtení nedělních*, ed. Josef B. Jeschke (Praha, Komenského evangelická fakulta bohoslovecká, 1952); Jan Hus, *Česká nedělní postila. Vyložení svatých čtení nedělních*, ed., Jiří Daňhelka (Praha: Academia, 1992) (*Magistri Iohannis Hus Opera omnia*, vol. 2).

45. For matters of rhetoric at the University of Prague in the Middle Ages, see Josef Tříška, *Rétorický styl a pražská univerzitní literatura ve středověku: Stilus rhetoricus et litterae Universitatis Pragensis medio aevo florentes* (Praha: Univerzita Karlova, 1975).

46. See "Instead of Conclusion: Jan Hus as Writer and Author," in *A Companion to Jan Hus*, 398–401. In support of his authorship, see František Šmahel, *Jan Hus*, 146–147.

47. See Johann Schröpfer, ed., *Hussens Traktat "Orthographia Bohemica." Die Herkunft des diakritischen Systems in der Schreibung slavisher Sprachen und die älteste zusammenhängende Beschreibung slavischer Laute* (Wiesbaden: Harrassowitz, 1968). For a modern Czech and English translation, see *Orthographia Bohemica*, ed. Kateřina Voleková (Praha: Akropolis, 2019). See also F. M. Bartoš, "K Husovu spisku o českém pravopise," *Jihočeský sborník historický* 18 (1949): 33–38;

see also Anežka Vidmanová, "Ke spisku Orthographia bohemica," *Listy filologické* 105 (1982): 75–89.

48. *Česká nedělní postila* (*MIHOO*, 2:60). See also Kateřina Voleková, *Česká lexikografie 15. století* (Praha: Academia, 2015), 93–94.

49. See footnote 3 in Appendix 1.

50. See Enrico C. S. Molnar, "The Liturgical Reforms of John Hus," *Speculum* 41/2 (1966): 298. Molnar noted, "The introduction of the vernacular language into the services of the Church in Bohemia was one of the important achievements of the Hussite Reformation."

51. See David Holeton and Hana Vlhová-Wörner, "The Second Life of Jan Hus: Liturgy, Commemoration, and Music," in *A Companion to Jan Hus*, 289–324. Despite some reservations, Nejedlý's work *Dějiny husitského zpěvu* still provides valuable insights on the issue of singing within the Hussite movement. See Zdeněk Nejedlý, *Dějiny husitského zpěvu*, vols. 1–6 (Prague: ČSAV, 1954–1956).

52. See *Drobné spisy české* (*MIHOO*, 4:27–30, 348–359).

53. *Jesus Kristus, naše spása* (*MIHOO*, 4:355–356).

54. See Jiří Daňhelka, ed., *Husitské písně* (Praha: Československý spisovatel, 1952), 29–184.

55. See the biographical sketches in *The Music of the Moravian Church in America*, ed. Nola Reed Knouse (Rochester: University of Rochester Press, 2008), 268ff; see also Aneta Mladějovská, "Několik písní Jana Augusty v novém kontextu," *Bohemica litteraria* 18/1 (2015): 13–39.

56. See Thomas Paul Sovík, "Music Theorists of the Bohemian Reformation: Jan Blahoslav and Jan Josquin," *Kosmas* 6 (1987): 104–145; idem, "Music Theorists of the Bohemian Reformation: Translation and Critique of the Treatises of Jan Blahoslav and Jan Josquin" (PhD dissertation, Ohio State University, 1985); see also M. T. Brown, *John Blahoslav—Sixteenth-Century Moravian Reformer: Transforming the Czech Nation by the Word of God* (Bonn: Verlag für Kultur und Wissenschaft, 2013).

57. For brief remarks on his personality, see Amedeo Molnár, *Boleslavští bratří* (Praha: Komenského evangelická fakulta bohoslovecká, 1952), 24, 94–95, 140–141, 151–152, 158–160, 209, 270–271.

58. See Olga Settari, "Jan Amos Komenský a hudba," *Studia Comeniana et historica* 45 (1991): 47–62; *Jan Amos Komenský, Kancionál*, ed. Olga Settari (Praha: Kalich, 1992).

59. See Jan Kouba, "Der älteste Gesangbuchdruck von 1501 aus Böhmen," *Jahrbuch für Liturgik und Hymnologie* 13 (1968): 78–112.

60. Against certain priests denouncing singing in the vernacular in Bethlehem Chapel, Hus mentioned that the common people would continue to joyfully sing songs of praise to their merciful Savior in spite of any complaints from the priests, teachers, or lawyers. See *Česká nedělní postila* (*MIHOO*, 2:183–184).

61. Enrico C. S. Molnar, "The Liturgical Reforms of John Hus," 303.

62. *Letter to the Praguers* (*Korespondence*, 160).

Conclusion: The Contemporary Struggle for Truth

Our own contemporary struggle for truth forces us to admit that modern society is facing a significant challenge in terms of discerning truth from lies, right from wrong, good from evil, and love from hate. It for this very reason that we must possess the same courage that Hus exhibited as a prerequisite even for us to ask ourselves what particular significance Jan Hus still embodies for us and our modern society. Although this challenging yet pertinent question is certainly not easy to answer, any kind of fidelity to Hus's message and teachings certainly means no less than following and living in a knowledge of the truth (i.e., in the "truth known and understood"),[1] which is exactly the same truth as the truth which Hus confessed. Today, "truth which conquers all"[2] merely faces a different set of circumstances. Hus testified to the truth at the beginning of the fifteenth century when conflict and confusion abounded; we are bearing witness to the same truth now in a century whose different contours appear in many ways to be just as turbulent and divisive. Within the context of his own struggle, Hus's personal convictions concerning the truth never wavered even in the face of loss of friends or freedom. From our humble perspective, we are persuaded that what our contemporary society needs perhaps more than anything else is to reconsider its own view of truth and come to share the same underlying attitude and prevailing conviction of Hus concerning the truth: *Super omnia vincit veritas*.

We cannot predict whether or not our own present-day situation and circumstances will somehow become any easier for us than in Hus's day, since the present era is perhaps just as complicated and unsettled as the medieval period. The internal situation—namely, the struggle for the proper identity of the church (especially the Czechoslovak Hussite Church) and for the profile of the ecumenical community—is connected with the external situation: the watching world is still waiting . . . not only for our word of truth but also for our witness to the truth. Unfortunately, the testimony of the church to the truth has not always been "in action and in truth," and many times it still does not represent the faithful witness and example of Jan Hus. We must confess with deep regret that the significance of the truth which has allegedly captivated and inspired many people has still not made its full impact in terms of our own personal witness within society.

All of the Protestant churches in the Czech Republic profess to maintain and support the enduring legacy of Master Jan Hus, most notably the Evangelical Church of Czech Brethren (*Církev českobratrské evangelická*), which was established in 1919 through the merger of the Czech Lutheran and Reformed Churches.[3] Hus has also been revered by the Orthodox Church of the Czech Lands and Slovakia (*Pravoslavná církev v českých zemích a na Slovensku*).[4] The Catholic Church in the former Czechoslovakia, however, maintained a rather reserved attitude towards Hus until the overall situation began to change and develop after the Second Vatican Council (1962–1965), although free and open dialogue concerning religious traditions in the Czech lands was hardly possible at all until 1989. The important symposiums in Bayreuth, Germany (1993),[5] and at the Pontifical Lateran University in Rome (1999)[6] marked a significant step forward in the ongoing discussion of Hus's life and intellectual heritage. For many people, the public statement made by Pope John Paul II (1920–2005) on December 17, 1999, to a general audience of participants at the international symposium that Jan Hus "belongs among the reformers of the church"[7] was at least an irenic public gesture in terms of seeking to improve ecumenical relations.[8]

The Czechoslovak Church has also honored and celebrated the life and legacy of Jan Hus from its very beginning. Hus's truth is the same truth which guided and led several Catholic Czech priests who were earnestly seeking reform: Josef Dobrovský (1753–1829),[9] Bernard Bolzano (1781–1848),[10] František Náhlovský (1807–1853),[11] and Vincenc Zahradník (1790–1836).[12] The same truth along with an accompanying desire for a greater degree of the flourishing of humanity captivated and motivated Karel Farský (1880–1927),[13] Matěj Pavlík (1879–1942),[14] František Kovář (1888–1969),[15] Gustav Procházka (1872–1942),[16] and other priests faced with making a difficult decision (similar to Hus's) of following their own conscience when they separated from the Catholic Church in January 1920.[17] We also promoted Hus's truth and honored his legacy by changing the name of the Czechoslovak Church in 1971 to the Czechoslovak Hussite Church.[18] Hopefully, that momentous occasion will not only stand for us as a mere declaration, but also a sincere commitment to truth which will become a testament and commitment to the life, work, and witness of the Czechoslovak Hussite Church in our nation.

In conclusion, we would like to reiterate that the most important aspect of Hus's worldview and thought was the inseparable union of his conception of truth and his commitment to the truth. Nowhere does the intricate connection between orthodoxy and orthopraxy find a clearer and more profound expression than in Hus's sermons and in his *Appeal to Jesus Christ the Supreme Judge*. Every sincere Christian who aims to follow his own conscience especially in matters of ultimate concern will find in Jan Hus a kindred spirit.

Despite having various confessions of faith, all Christians can agree that church tradition is certainly important, but here again each person is forced to ask himself a most daunting question which requires an honest answer from the deepest depths of his own conscience: how would it even be possible for any church tradition to exist at all if there is no living Jesus Christ? Christians from a multitude of backgrounds disagree on the precise meaning and role of tradition (e.g., its binding nature and relationship to freedom of conscience), but if they are able and willing to agree on the fact that church tradition should be rooted in Jesus Christ, then controversies over tradition will have to be concerned with understanding the extent to which tradition in its forms and expressions is or is not actually following Jesus Christ himself. In particular, certain necessary disputes and painful moments arise when we come to the persuasion that the traditions of the Church are at variance and disagree with the will of Christ and the words of Holy Scripture. Intense dialogue over controversial aspects of tradition belongs to the essence and experiences of church history as a theological discipline, although it definitely requires the virtues of humility and mutual respect and must be accompanied with authentic efforts to seek, understand, and grow closer to the truth that is *with* us and *above* us. Maintaining and expressing such a commitment will surely honor the legacy of Hus's own attitude to truth: "If I cannot liberate the truth to pervade in all things, at least I refuse to be an enemy of the truth . . . It is better to die virtuously than to live wickedly."[19]

"I hope by the grace of God that I will never retreat from the known truth."[20] What does this relentless conviction and distinctive approach to truth reveal for contemporary man—whether or not they consider themselves as a follow of Jesus Christ—if not a profound *challenge* united with a *promise* of great reward? Until "restless and unquiet hearts"[21] have embraced the challenge to "seek the truth," then the promise that those who diligently seek the truth will find it will only be met with doubt, resignation, or despair.[22] Each individual, no matter his or her status in life, is encouraged to ask honest and difficult questions in order to "hear the truth" and "learn the truth." And according to Hus, all questions—whether theological, historical, ecclesiastical, sociological, or philosophical—must ultimately become *personal* questions in order for a person to be able to "love the truth" and "adhere to the truth."

Like Hus, since our adherence to the truth will always be in accordance with human reason, emotion, and volition, we must strive to live according to the convictions of our own conscience, while never forgetting, as Hus explained: "A person should always search the Scriptures in order to inform his conscience."[23] In his defense at Constance, Hus cited a passage from Paul's first letter to the church in Corinth: "But if we were more discerning with regard to ourselves, we would not come under such judgment."[24] With that compelling reminder, each of us must be willing to accept the *challenge* to seek and pursue the truth as well as to embrace the *promise* that "the truth will set you free."[25] Yet, if freedom depends upon truth as its very foundation, we must listen carefully to this appropriate reminder from Hus concerning the difference between falsehood and truth: "It is obvious that no one is bound to believe anything except that which he is moved by God to believe, but God does not lead any person to believe untruth."[26] Thus, the thought-provoking call of Jan Hus to all Christians everywhere to "speak the truth" and faithfully to "defend the truth" until death is a reflection of Hus's resilient confidence and enduring hope that the truth will prevail for all of eternity: "I wholeheartedly trust in [our] beloved God that he will not allow slanderous people, adversaries of the truth, to overcome and defeat the truth."[27]

Fortunately, Hus's inspiring words were not destined to be forgotten, since "after his death, the truth which Hus preached and defended was later asserted as the unique expression of the people's desire for a greater standard of humanity and as a justification of their corporate social responsibility."[28] May Hus's faithful life and example help us to rise to the occasion and testify to our being among those courageous people who desire to be faithful witnesses to the truth both in our theological orientation, in our social responsibilities to others, and in our own individual lives *coram Deo*. The life of the Bohemian reformer Jan Hus in some regard serves as a paragon of freedom of speech, freedom of conscience, religious liberty, and equality,[29] but first and foremost his personality and the whole trajectory of his life present him as a *faithful witness to truth* in both life and death. This simple acknowledgement explains one of the main reasons why the liberating power of the truth which Hus preached and the clarion call of Hus's prophetic voice still resonate deeply in the hearts of men and women both in his homeland[30] and in other places across the world:

> Therefore, faithful Christian, seek the truth, hear the truth, learn the truth, love the truth, speak the truth, adhere to the truth, and defend the truth until death; for the truth will set you free from sin, the devil, spiritual death, and ultimately from eternal death, which is eternal separation away from the grace of God and away from the fullness of blessed happiness, and whoever believes in God and in Jesus Christ, who is true God and true man, will enter into that joy.[31]

NOTES

1. Hus used this phrase in a letter written to Jan of Chlum: "*Spero de dei gracia, quod a cognita veritate numquam sim recessurus*" [I hope by the grace of God that I will never retreat from the known truth]. He also used it in a letter to the members of the University of Prague: "*Ceterum, amantissimi in Christo Ihesu, state in cognita veritate, que super omnia vincit et invalescit usque in eternum*" [Moreover, dearly

beloved in Christ Jesus, stand firm in the truth you have come to know, for it conquers all things and increases in strength forever]. See *Korespondence*, 240, 323.

2. *Korespondence*: *Letter to Jan Kardinál of Rejštejn* (170); see also *Letter to the Praguers* (145) and *Letter to the Members of the University of Prague* (323).

3. For the Protestant reception of Jan Hus in other lands, see Tom Schwanda, "The Protestant Reception of Jan Hus in Great Britain and the American Colonies," *Journal of Moravian History* 16, no. 2 (2016): 65–89.

4. See Jiří Jakub Jukl, "Hus v myšlení a tradici pravoslavné církve," *Studia Theologica* 17/4 (2016): 259–271.

5. See *Jan Hus mezi epochami, národy a konfesemi: Sborník z mezinárodního sympozia konaného 22.–26. září v Bayreuthu*, ed. Jan Lášek (Praha: Česká křesťanská akademie, 1995).

6. For the proceedings of the symposium, see *Jan Hus na přelomu tisíciletí: Mezinárodní rozprava o českém reformátoru 15. století a o jeho recepci na prahu třetího milénia. Papežská lateránská univerzita Řím, 15.–18. prosince 1999 (Husitský Tábor: Supplementum 1)*, ed. Miloš Drda, František J. Holeček, and Zdeněk Vybíral (Ústí nad Labem: Albis International, 2001).

7. *Jan Hus ve Vatikánu: Mezinárodní rozprava o českém reformátoru 15. století a o jeho koncepci na prahu třetího tisíciletí*, eds. Jaroslav Pánek and Miroslav Polívka (Prague: Historický ústav AVČR, 2000). The pope's address is on pages 111–113. Surprisingly, the German, English, French, Portuguese, and Spanish translations on the Vatican's official website have not translated the Italian word *riformator* as reformer, but rather as "one who aspired to reform the church." However, the Czech translation in *Jan Hus ve Vatikánu* and the Czech and German translations in *Jan Hus na přelomu tisíciletí* use their respective words for reformer (i.e., Czech *reformátor* on page 685 and German *Kirchenreformator* on page 687), as well as the Italian version on the Vatican's website. Pope John Paul II also delivered a speech at Prague Castle on April 21, 1990, in which he declared, "It will be the task of experts—in first place Czech theologians—to define more precisely the place which Jan Hus occupies among the reformers of the Church . . ." See *L'Osservatore Romano (English Edition)* 17:1127 (April 23, 1990): 4–5. For individual participants' reflections on the symposium in reference to Hus being called a reformer, see *Jan Hus ve Vatikánu*, 45, 61, 65, 82, 87, 95, 134, 140, 151. See also Marco Politi, "E il papa polacco riabilita Jan Hus," *La Repubblica* (December 18, 1999). For the responses to the symposium by Czech media, see: Libor Budinský, "Vatikán uzná Husa reformátorem církve," *Lidové noviny* (December 15, 1999); Josef Kašpar, "Katolická církev směřuje k uznání úsilí Jana Husa," *Mladá fronta Dnes* (December 16, 1999); Jiří Sládek and Johanna Grohová, "Papež: Hluboce lituji kruté smrti Jana Husa," *Mladá fronta Dnes* (December 18, 1999); Martin C. Putna, "Husovská omluva z Říma: Přece, ale pozdě," *Mladá fronta Dnes* (December 22, 1999); Czech News Agency, "Vlk čeká politování církve nad upálením Jana Husa," *Právo* (December 16, 1999); Jaroslav Zbožínek, "Papež vyjádřil lítost nad upálením Jana Husa," *Právo* (December 18, 1999).

8. See Ivana Noble, "The Ecumenical Reevaluation of the Heritage of Jan Hus in the Czech Churches," *Lutheran Forum* 49/4 (2015): 45–48.

9. Josef Dobrovský was the patriarch of Slavonic studies who is considered the greatest personality of the Czech National Revival. He was a philologist whose

research in Slavic languages is still recognized throughout Europe. He was influential in helping to found the National Museum in 1818. Some of his most important works include *Geschichte der Böhmischen Sprache und ältern Literatur (History of the Bohemian Language and Older Literature) and Institutiones linguae slavicae dialecti veteris.*

10. Bernard Bolzano was a Bohemian theologian, mathematician, and philosopher who wrote in German and made significant contributions in the realm of mathematical theory. He was appointed to the chair of philosophy of religion in 1805. Some of his important works have been translated to English, including *Theory of Science* and *The Mathematical Writings of Bernard Bolzano.* See Paul Rusnock and Jan Šebestík, *Bernard Bolzano: His Life and Work* (Oxford: Oxford University Press, 2019). Bolzano's entire corpus is being published under the auspices of Frommann-Holzboog. See Bernard Bolzano, *Gesamtausgabe*, eds. Eduard Winter, Jan Berg, Friedrich Kambartel, Jaromír Loužil, Edgar Morscher, and Bob van Rootselaar (Stuttgart-Bad Cannstat: Fromann-Holzboog Verlag, 1969–). For Bolzano's influence on theological thought within Bohemia, see Kamila Ververková, *Bernard Bolzano: A New Evaluation of His Thought and His Circle*, trans. Angelo Shaun Franklin (Lanham: Lexington, 2022).

11. František Náhlovský was an ordained priest who worked to promote national education. He served as director of the Lusatian Seminary and outlined his program for church reform during a meeting of many priests in 1848 near Charles Bridge. It is recorded in *Versammlung der Geistlichen, gehalten zu Prag am 18. und 22. Mai 1848.*

12. Vincenc Zahradník was a Catholic priest who was appointed professor of pastoral theology at Litoměřice in 1820. As one of the first people to write philosophy in the Czech language, he helped to develop certain Czech philosophical terms. Some of his works include *Bájky i básně (Fables and Poems)* as well as five volumes of *Filosofické spisy (Philosophical Writings).*

13. Karel Farský was a priest, theologian, and the founder and first patriarch of the Czechoslovak Hussite Church. He served from 1924 until 1927. He wrote several important works, including *Český problém církevní (The Czech Problem of the Church), Náboženství v národě československém (Religion in Czechoslovakia), Papežství a národ český (The Papacy and the Czech Nation).*

14. Matěj Pavlík was originally ordained as a Roman Catholic priest in 1902, was consecrated as bishop for the Czechoslovak Church in 1921, then later converted in 1924 and became a bishop of the Orthodox Church. He is well known for sheltering the paratroopers who assassinated Reinhard Heydrich. He was executed on September 4, 1942.

15. František Kovář was a priest, theologian, and translator, and the third patriarch of the Czechoslovak Hussite Church (1946–1961). He also served as dean of Hus's Czechoslovak Evangelical Faculty of Theology (1949–1950). He was a prolific writer, whose major works include *Království Boží na Zemi: K ideovým základům církve československé (The Kingdom of God on Earth: The Ideological Foundations of the Czechoslovak Church), V zápase o pravou zbožnost: Exegetické úvahy novozákonní (In the Struggle for True Devotion: Exegetical Reflections on the New Testament),* and *Základy novozákonní theologie: Studijní pomůcka z oboru novozákonní vědy (Fundamentals of New Testament Theology: A Guide from the Field of New Testament Studies).*

16. Gustav Procházka was co-founder along with Karel Farský and František Kovář of the Czechoslovak Hussite Church and later served as the second patriarch from 1928 to 1942. From 1935 to 1939 he taught as a professor of {the} Hus Czechoslovak Protestant Theological Faculty. One of his important works is *Křesťanský humanism a československá církev (Christian Humanism and the Czechoslovak Church)*. See Ferdinand Prášek, *Vznik československé církve a patriarcha G. A. Procházka* (Prague: Ústřední rada Čsl. Církve, 1932).

17. The Czechoslovak Hussite Church was founded on January 8, 1920.

18. Until 1971 the Czechoslovak Hussite Church was known as the Czechoslovak Church. For the definitive work on its history, see Rudolf Urban, *Die tschechoslowakische hussitische Kirche* (Marburg/Lahn: J.G. Herder-Institut, 1973).

19. *Korespondence*, 170: *"Et si ego non possum libertare veritatem per omnia, saltim nolo esse inimicus veritatis . . . Melius est bene mori, quam male vivere."* Cf. 1 Maccabees 3:59 and Ecclesiasticus 40:29.

20. *Korespondence*, 240.

21. See Augustine, *Confessiones*, 1.1.1: "For You have made us for Yourself, and our hearts are restless until they rest in You."

22. See Deuteronomy 4:29; Proverbs 8:17.

23. *Dcerka* (*MIHOO*, 4:166).

24. 1 Corinthians 11:31 NIV.

25. John 8:31–32.

26. *Tractatus de Ecclesia*, 38: *"Patet quia nemo tenetur quicquam credere, nisi ad quod movet eum deus credere, sed deus non movet hominem ad credendum falsum . . ."*; cf. *Super Quattuor Sententiarum*, 3.24.5.

27. *Korespondence*, 196.

28. Molnár, *Na rozhraní věků*, 21.

29. Each of these categories (e.g., freedom of speech and freedom of conscience) which represent modern concerns are found in the centuries-old *Four Articles of Prague*. See Kamila Veverková, *The Four Articles of Prague within the Public Sphere of Hussite Bohemia: On the 600th Anniversary of Their Declaration (1420–2020)*, trans. Angelo Shaun Franklin (Lanham: Lexington Books, 2021), vii–xi, 7–16.

30. See Ladislav Holy, *The Little Czech and the Great Czech Nation: National Identity and the Post-Communist Transformation of Society* (Cambridge: Cambridge University Press, 1996), 40. Holy noted that the words of Hus gave rise to the national motto *pravda vítězí* ("the truth prevails").

31. *Výklad na vieru* (*MIHOO*, 1:69).

Appendix: Homily on the Feast Day of the Holy Trinity (John 3:1–15)

By Jan Hus
Translated from Latin and with explanatory
notes by Angelo Shaun Franklin

Now there was a man of the Pharisees, named Nicodemus, a ruler of the Jews (a teacher of the Jews).[1] This man came to Jesus (humbly wanting to learn the faith) at night (for fear of the Jews) and said to Him, "Rabbi, we know that You have come from God as a teacher; for no one (human being) can do these signs that You do unless God is with him" (through power and grace). Jesus responded and said to him, "Truly, truly, I say to you, unless someone is born again he cannot see the kingdom of God" (eternal joy). Nicodemus said to Him, "How can a person be born when he is old? He cannot enter his mother's womb a second time and be born, can he?" Jesus answered, "Truly, truly, I say to you, unless someone is born again (spiritually), he cannot enter the kingdom of God. That which has been born of the flesh is flesh, and that which has been born of the Spirit is spirit. Do not be amazed that I said to you, 'You must be born again.' The wind blows where it wishes, and you hear the sound of it (hears the voice of the Holy Spirit in Scripture), but you do not know where it is coming from and where it is going; so is everyone who has been born of the Spirit" (the Holy Spirit). Nicodemus responded and said to Him, "How can these things be?" Jesus answered and said to him, "You are the teacher of Israel (among the Jews), and yet you do not understand these things? Truly, truly, I say to you, we (my apostles and I) speak of what we know and testify of what we have seen, and you people do not accept our testimony (since the Jews do not accept it). If I told you earthly things and you do not believe, how will you believe if I tell you heavenly things? (such as his being eternally begotten of the Father). No one has ascended into heaven (by his own power), except he who descended from heaven (who became incarnate and is in heaven now): the Son of Man.

And just as Moses lifted up the serpent (bronze) in the wilderness, so must the Son of Man be lifted up, so that everyone who believes in him will not die but have eternal life.

Today the church celebrates the feast day of the Holy Trinity. And since Nicodemus was hereby cleansed from *unbelief* and led to *belief* in the Holy Trinity by this holy gospel, therefore this pericope of the gospel is read today during mass. And some read this pericope of the gospel—"When the Comforter comes" (John 15:26)[2]—which is read on the Sunday after the divine ascension, and may it be read many times, in virtue of the fact that it herein contains a reference to the Father, the Son, and the Holy Spirit—who are the three persons of the Holy Trinity to whom we should now especially give praise today. And because leaders, many intelligent people, often perhaps even teachers, and especially common people err in their beliefs concerning the Holy Trinity, I will therefore declare the truth about the Holy Trinity briefly and in clear and simple terms for the common people.

You common people[3] should know and understand that the Holy Trinity in whom we believe is neither a woman, nor a virgin, nor a Sunday, as many foolish and mad men imagine; but the Trinity is three eternal persons—the Father, the Son, and the Holy Spirit—one God who is the supreme good above which no greater good can be conceived.[4] And so if a common person asks you, "What is the Holy Trinity in whom you believe?" answer and say, "God the Father and the Son and the Holy Spirit." If someone asks, "Who is the Father?" answer, "The eternal God who has an eternal Son." If someone asks you, "Who is the Son?" answer and say, "God begotten of God the Father." If someone asks you, "Who is the Holy Spirit? Say, "God who proceeds from God the Father and from the Son of God." And confess and believe that these three persons are not three gods, but the one and only true God; and again, that these three persons are co-equal in power, in wisdom, and in goodness, as each of the persons is God—*infinitely powerful, infinitely wise*, and *infinitely good*. However, the Father is especially called powerful for the common people, so that they would not assume[5] that he is not as powerful as the Son due to his age. And the Son is called wise so that they would not assume that he is not as wise as the Father.[6] And the Spirit is called good[7] or benevolent, so that they would not assume that he is not as good as the Father and the Son.[8]

Since the soul of man bears the image of the Holy Trinity from whom he is created (thus according to his likeness),[9] even as the Holy Trinity is God (who is Spirit), so the soul of man is spirit. Since the Father is distinct from the Son and the Holy Spirit, and the Son is distinct from the Holy Spirit, therefore the Father is neither the Son nor the Holy Spirit (i.e., the person), and the Son is also not the Holy Spirit (i.e., the person), yet these three persons are one

God. It is the same in the soul of man. The *understanding* is distinct from the *memory* and from the *will*, and memory is distinct from the will; therefore, the understanding is neither the memory nor the will, yet these three powers[10] of the soul are one mind in man.[11] Consequently, believing in the Holy Trinity[12] (from whom he is created and to whom his soul possesses a certain likeness) and having *power* from God the Father, he should diligently protect himself against sin and vigorously progress in virtue. Second, having *wisdom* from the Son of God, he should diligently return that wisdom into praise for God. Third, having a *good will* from the Holy Spirit, he should always stand firm in goodness, and thus finally persevere in good intentions. For when a man endures[13] in this way, it is impossible for him to perish, since he preserves the image and likeness of the Holy Trinity. And when as an impotent, unwise, and indolent[14] man he falls into mortal sin, he then loses the likeness of the Holy Trinity, dishonors the Father, the Son, and the Holy Spirit, and thus each member of the Holy Trinity.[15]

And know that through mortal sin one loses the *likeness* of the Holy Trinity, but not the *image*, which is blemished by sin. For example, it is like when a picture is created which represents the image of some man becomes so disfigured that while the image[16] still remains, it does not possess the likeness of that man; there is something comparable to this in sinning inasmuch as a person who possesses wisdom, understanding, memory, and a will blemishes them through mortal sin, so that he does not maintain such a likeness to the Holy Trinity as he would have possessed if he had not committed mortal sin. And when a man disfigures and defiles himself, then it is impossible for him to attain unto that likeness again except by the power, the wisdom, and the will of the Holy Spirit and in due course by the created triad which is *faith, hope,* and *love*. Likewise a man cannot possess this triad anew except from God: *faith* for every divine truth which physical eyes do not see and which the Scripture leads the soul to believe; *hope* for obtaining grace and glorification; *love* from a whole heart for loving God wholeheartedly.[17] Behold, when a common person believes these truths about the Holy Trinity and believes whatever else should be believed[18]—even though he does not know how to define[19] or eloquently explain these truths—since he believes everything necessary—it is sufficient for salvation, if he fulfills[20] the commandments.

Even Nicodemus was thus instructed in the faith, of whom the gospel says, "There was a man of the Pharisees named Nicodemus, a ruler of the Jews" (i.e., a teacher of other Jews).[21] "This man came to Jesus" (i.e., humbly wanting to learn even more about the faith from Jesus,[22] since he had already believed some things). He came "by night" (v. 2). This means that he was still ignorant and fearful, since he did not truly know Jesus yet, and since he was afraid to come to him because of the Jews, for they had already ostracized[23]

vieſta/abÿ kazdÿ ktoz vierzi wnieho neza

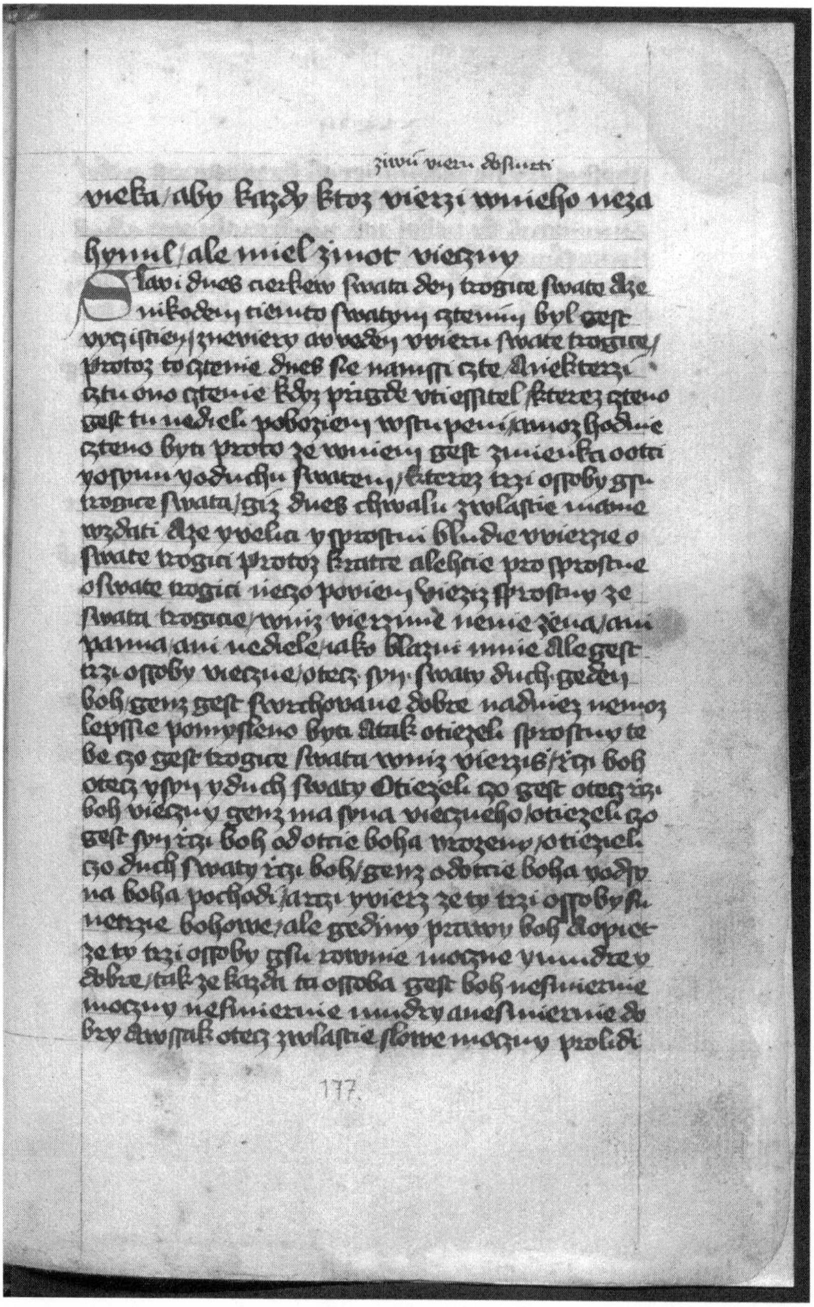

hÿnul/ale miel ziuot vieznÿ

177.

Figure A.1. First page of Hus's Homily on John 3:1–15 from His Czech Sunday Postil.

Source: Česká nedělní postila (Vyloženie svatých čtení nedělních), National Library of the Czech Republic in Prague, MS XVII.A.11, fol. 0177R.

Jesus, and because whoever confessed that Jesus is the Christ would be banished from the Jewish community. And even though Nicodemus was one of the most advanced leaders of the religious community, he did not want to provoke the Jews against him; and that is why he came to Jesus "by night" (v. 2)—so that he could go to learn Jesus's teachings without exasperating them. And he humbly confessed the *humanity* of Christ, saying, "Rabbi, we know that you are a teacher sent from God" (v. 2); and even though he still did not understand his *deity*, he was counted worthy because Jesus taught him even about believing his deity. And he establishes evidence that Jesus is a teacher sent from God and thus a good man by saying, "No one can do these signs which you do unless God is with him" (v. 2). These words show that Jesus is truly a man and is a Teacher exalted above other divine messengers, and thus a Prophet exalted above others. Therefore, the beloved Teacher Jesus, teaching him about the new birth of a man who is spiritually born of God so that he may become a son of God, answers him and says this: "Truly, truly, I say to you, unless one is born again, he cannot see the kingdom of God" (v. 3). It is as if he said, "You already know something about the physical birth of a man and the beginning of belief[24] concerning my humanity from the signs or due to the miracles; but even more than this, you must still be born again spiritually and especially must be an elect son of God. And because this birth cannot happen except by God himself, Nicodemus, you have proof that I am God when I spiritually make you become a child of God."

And Saint John says here in the first chapter and verse twelve that Christ possessed that authority: "To them he gave the right to become children of God, even to those who believe in his name" (John 1:12).[25] And everyone, even a pagan[26] who has been enlightened through reason, is able to understand that whoever gives the right[27] to a man to become a son of God must necessarily be God in order to give that right. For a man can become a son of God, only if God has created him, sustains and shelters him, nourishes him, and above all elects him to an eternal inheritance.[28] Therefore, no one except God alone is able to give a man this right to become an elect[29] child of God. For God alone from eternity elects those whom he pleases unto salvation, whereas a mere man who is not God does not possess the power within himself to become an elect child of God except by the grace of God alone and not according to his own merits, even as Saint Paul says in Titus: "He saved us, not because of works done by us in righteousness, but according to his own mercy" (Titus 3:5). So how then could a mere man give the right to another man to become an elect child of God? For if a man who is not God could actually effectuate this, then he would be able to give sovereign grace to another man even as God himself does.

And perhaps you will respond that Saint Paul writes to the Corinthians in his first epistle in chapter four, saying: "For in Christ Jesus, by the word of

God,[30] I have begotten you" (1 Cor 4:15). And in Galatians in chapter four he says, "My little children, for whom I am again in the anguish of childbirth" (Gal 4:19). Behold, Saint Paul is speaking here about spiritual birth in the grace of God.[31] Know here that it is not as a consequence of a person making someone else a child of God by the word of God, nor is it by holy baptism which directly gives someone the right to become a child of God, nor is it on account of someone choosing him to become a child of God. *For God himself first gave this right to man to become a child of God and first chose him to become an elect child of God.* For example, if an axe by which a carpenter builds a house were able to speak, it would never brag or boast that it had somehow made the house itself.[32] It would rather say in truth that it was the power of the carpenter working through the axe by which the house was built. And so Saint Paul, being as an instrument or divine tool, says in 1 Corinthians 15:10: "But by the grace of God I am what I am, and his grace in me was not in vain. On the contrary, I labored more abundantly than all of them, though it was not I, but the grace of God that is with me." And elsewhere he says, "Not that we are sufficient to claim anything as coming from ourselves, but our sufficiency is from God" (2 Cor 3:5). And again he says, "For when one of you says, 'I am indeed of Paul,' and another, 'I am of Apollos,' are you not acting like mere humans? What then is Apollos? What is Paul? Servants through whom you believed, as the Lord gave {opportunity} to each one. I planted, Apollos watered, but God was causing the growth. So neither the one who plants nor the one who waters is anything, but God who gives the increase or growth" (1 Cor 3:4–7). Paul means that he planted or established[33] the Corinthians in the faith by the word of God, and Apollo the bishop baptized them, and God was the one who gave his grace and thus made them children of God. So Saint Paul discredits his own deeds and even Apollo's deeds compared to the work of God when he says, "Neither the one who plants" (here this means Saint Paul) "nor the one who waters" (understand this as being baptized by Apollo), but God is the one who accomplishes everything.[34] And so we should likewise also profess that if we preach or if we baptize or if we hear someone's confession—and since in this way we lead people to the grace of God—we should attribute it all to the power of God but definitely not to ourselves, nor should we say that we are able to give the right to someone to become a son of God or choose who would become a son of God.

The gospel further says, "Nicodemus said to him (still speaking in an uncouth and carnal[35] manner, not understanding Christ's words concerning spiritual birth), 'How can a man be born when he is old? Can he enter a second time into his mother's womb and be born?'" (v. 4). It is as if he said, "I am an old man, and inquiring of you about my salvation; according to your words, how am I supposed to be born again in order to be saved? Should I enter into my mother's womb and be born again?" Here Saint Augustine says, "The Spirit speaks . . . and he thinks carnally.[36] This man was aware of no other birth of the one from Adam and Eve, but he still did not know about the one from God and the holy church. So you should understand the birth of the Spirit just as Nicodemus understood physical birth. For just as a man cannot be physically born again, neither can baptism be repeated."[37] That is how Augustine explained it. To be sure, neither should these words of Nicodemus be rejected simply because he said, "How can a man be born when he is old? Can he enter a second time into his mother's womb and be born?" (v. 4). For these words are complementary and instrumental in helping us to recognize physical birth and to discern the difference between it and spiritual birth. And just as this uncouth question was beneficial for learning, so other coarse people can also benefit since the ultimate Teacher Jesus immediately sets forth spiritual birth and distinguishes it from physical birth, telling Nicodemus, "Truly, truly, I say to you, unless one is born of water and the Holy Spirit, he cannot enter into the kingdom of God" (v. 5). It is as if he said, "I do not mean a physical birth from the womb and from the seed of man, but I intend for you to understand a *spiritual* birth by which whoever is born of the water which flowed from my side and by the grace of the Holy Spirit." Understand from this that everyone who will be saved (i.e., cleansed from sin) must be baptized by the water and blood which flowed from the side of Christ and by the Holy Spirit.

And understand here that baptism is threefold: the baptism of *water*, of *blood*, and of *spirit*.[38] The *baptism of water* is baptism by which someone is baptized in water {i.e., the material element}, which is baptism as referred to in general terms. The *baptism of blood* is baptism whereby whoever is not baptized in water is cleansed from his sins by shedding his blood for Christ. The *baptism of the Spirit* is baptism whereby whoever truly believes in God and in Jesus Christ desires to be baptized and is cleansed from his sins by the Holy Spirit. And everyone who will be saved must be baptized by this baptism of the Spirit and of the water which flowed from the side of Christ. Yet, a man can be saved without water baptism as it is commonly administered, just as many were saved both in the Old Testament and in the New Testament by the baptism of blood as they were martyred for the sake of Christ, and just as holy infants and many others who believed the apostles or other saints, yet who immediately departed freely to their death without receiving the baptism of water. Therefore, when the Savior says, "Unless one is born of water and of the Holy Spirit" he means the baptism of water which flowed from his side and [the baptism of] the Holy Spirit who by the power of his great might[39] cleanses the soul from sin.

Furthermore, understand how our gracious Teacher teaches the difference between *physical* and *spiritual* birth, saying, "That which is born of the flesh is flesh, and that which is born of the Spirit is spirit" (v. 6). These words show that each person is two parts—spirit and body. From this you should understand that when every person first comes to life, he then immediately undergoes two kinds of birth: first, from the physical side—the body—which existed before it possessed a soul; second, from the spiritual side—the soul—which God then soon afterwards imparted to the body.[40] So while he still is inside the womb, each man is born from both a physical and a spiritual perspective (i.e., body and soul), even though he has not yet been born outside of the woman's womb; and so an angel told Joseph concerning the birth of Jesus in this life: "Joseph, son of David, do not be afraid to take Mary as your wife, for that which is conceived in her is from the Spirit" (Matthew 1:20); thus, know that the child conceived in her was born by the power of the Holy Spirit.

Thus the new birth of a person is spiritual, whereby he becomes a special and supernatural child of God by the power of God. And now our beloved Teacher speaks about this, and wanting to lead the fleshly-minded Nicodemus into deeper knowledge of this birth says, "Do not marvel that I have said to you, 'You must be born again.' The wind blows where it wishes, and you hear its sound, but you do not know where it comes from or where it goes. So it is with everyone who is born of the Spirit" (v. 7–8). Here, according to the exposition of Saint John Chrysostom,[41] Christ is giving a physical example, knowing that although Nicodemus feels the wind, he nevertheless does not know where it begins or ends, for it blows wherever it wants. It is the same for a person who is born spiritually through baptism, because he feels the water in baptism[42] cleansing the body, but the Holy Spirit who accomplishes the cleansing and the grace of God for attaining final blessedness is hidden. And according to this exposition, understand it in the following sense: "the wind" (i.e., the Spirit) "blows" (i.e., breathes) "where it wishes" (i.e., wherever he has the inclination), and "the sound or rustling"[43] (i.e., voice) "you hear" (i.e., with physical ears), and "you do not know" (i.e., with certainty) "where it comes from" (i.e., because you do not know where he comes from or how he is working)[44] "or where it is going" (i.e., where he will complete his work). "So it is with" (understood this to mean that even I myself do not know) "everyone who is born of the Spirit" (v. 8), because he does not know whether he is elect from eternity and if he will be finally saved in the end. For although one who is born again as a son of God has signs and the inspiration of the Holy Spirit, yet without revelation he does not know how the Holy Spirit began his work in him or how he will complete his work.[45] But according to the exposition of Saint Augustine[46] it is understood in this sense: "The Spirit" (i.e., the Holy Spirit) "breathes" (i.e., by his grace) "where" (in whichever man), "he wants" (i.e., freely), and "you hear his voice" (in the Scriptures). For Christ told his disciples, "For it is not you who speak, but the Spirit of your Father who is in heaven" (Matt 10:20). "But you do not know where it comes from" (i.e., its rhyme or reason) "or where it goes" (i.e., final knowledge of those who are baptized). "So it is" (v. 8) means that I myself do not know "who is born of the Spirit" (v. 8). And Nicodemus, being burdened and struggling with difficulty to understand these words of Jesus, said, "How can these things be?" (v. 9). And the merciful Teacher humbly rebukes him, saying, "Are you the teacher of Israel and yet you do not understand these things?" (v. 10). It is as if he said to him, "You should be ashamed of your lack of understanding, since it is suitable and appropriate for a teacher of the Old Testament to understand these things. Why, Nicodemus, don't you understand that which God says through Ezekiel in the thirty-sixth chapter: "I will sprinkle clean water on you, and you will be clean from all of your filthiness" (Ez 36:25). And Nicodemus, Zechariah says in the thirteenth chapter: "A fountain will be opened for the house[47] of Israel and the inhabitants of Jerusalem, to cleanse them from sin" (Zech 13:1).

Oh, Nicodemus, the teacher of the Jews! Do you not understand this—that cleansing from all of your sins you must come through an open fountain—through the wounded side of Christ opened wide from which water was poured out and flowed forth as an inexhaustible[48] fountain for the cleansing of sins? Nicodemus, do you not understand that Ezekiel in the forty-seventh chapter saw "water flowing forth from the right side?" (Ez 47:2). And what is this "right side" from which the water flowed? The one and only Son of God! For then Ezekiel consequently says that "wherever the river goes, every little creature that swarms will live" (Ez 47:9). And he says once again, "Everything will live where the river goes" (Ez 47:9). And what else did Ezekiel see through the Holy Spirit except the cleansing power of the water which flowed forth from Christ on the cross by virtue of which everyone who is born of the Holy Spirit and of this water is spiritually enlivened.

Second, Nicodemus deserved to be rebuked, because at first he praised Christ and said, "We know that you are a teacher who has come from God" (v. 2), yet he still doubts what Christ is saying to him. Therefore, Christ says to him, "Truly, truly, I say to you, that *we* (i.e., I along with my apostles) speak of what we know, and bear witness to what we have seen, but *you* do not receive our testimony" (i.e., you Jews, and especially you scribes and Pharisees).

Third, Nicodemus was rebuked because Christ spoke simple truths[49] to him, and yet he did not understand them. Thus, Christ says, "Since I have spoken to you of earthly things (i.e., to you, Nicodemus, and to your disciples) and you do not believe earthly things (i.e., easily understood truths) such as how people created {from the dust} of the earth[50] are born again spiritually, if I tell you heavenly things (e.g., such as my being eternally begotten of God the Father and about the Holy Trinity) how can you believe?" And so Nicodemus is rebuked for this, because having already believed *simpler* truths, he hesitated to believe *greater* truths of the faith. And because Jesus saw that Nicodemus along with his disciples were afterwards supposed to receive mysterious matters of faith, he therefore instructs him further concerning his *ascension* into heaven, which was going to happen after his *incarnation* and after his dwelling among and *communing with*[51] people, saying, "No one has ascended into heaven except the one who descended from heaven—the Son of Man who is in heaven" (v. 13). It is as though he were saying, "No one ascends into heaven (into heavenly joy) by his own power, except the Son of Man whom you call the Messiah; he is the one who descended from heaven, that is, he has become incarnate and his divine nature is always in heaven." And so the Savior teaches Nicodemus that he, being God, has become incarnate and communes here and that he, being the Son of Man, will ascend into heaven by his own power;[52] and so no other man can enter into heaven by his own power, but everyone who will be in heaven will be drawn in as members of Christ their head by his power.

Now understand this: when Christ says that the Son of Man "descended from heaven," many heretics took this as their starting point,[53] because they claimed that the Son of God had assumed a body in heaven and in that way physically descended from heaven and passed through the womb of the Virgin Mary.[54] And in a similar way painters also illustrate this heresy when they paint an angel who is greeting the Virgin Mary with a little baby above her, as if he somehow wanted to enter into her womb physically from heaven. And this is perhaps the way in which these paintings have been created[55] by these heretical people. But people should not believe that the Son of God abandoned[56] heaven when he became incarnate; for he has always been omnipresent even as he is now omnipresent according to his divine nature;[57] and thus he existed in his divine nature and in grace in the womb of the Virgin Mary, when she consented and said, "May it happen to me according to your word" (Luke 1:38), immediately the Son of God became incarnate in her, and he became truly human.

And because the crucifixion of Christ is the refuge for supporting faith and necessary for salvation and set forth in the Old Testament in types, therefore Christ finally teaches Nicodemus as a teacher of the Old Testament who should have understood what the figures in the Old Testament signify and mean. Consequently, he says, "And as Moses lifted up the serpent in the wilderness, so must the Son of Man be lifted up" (v. 14). Now know this here in order to understand: that when the Jewish people murmured against God in the desert, then God sent fiery serpents upon them; and know this: that they were extremely vicious, mordacious,[58] and poisonous, because those who were bitten died. That is why many people came unto Moses and said, 'We have sinned against God and against you! Pray that the serpents would be taken away from us.' So Moses prayed for the people. And God said to Moses, 'Make a bronze serpent and lift it up as a sign: whoever is bitten will live if he looks at it.' So Moses made a bronze serpent and set it up for a sign, and when anyone wounded (i.e., stung by the serpents) simply looked at it, he would live" (Num 21:7–9). It is written in this way in the book of Numbers, which is the fourth book of Moses in the Old Testament (read the twenty-first chapter).

Jesus introduced and brought this type (i.e., illustration) home to Moses, because even as Moses lifted up the serpent on a pole so that those who were bitten by the serpents could see it and so that they would be healed and would not die—the Son of Man also had to be lifted up on the cross in order to deliver our souls from the stinging wound from the diabolical serpent of sin,[59] so that we would not perish eternally. Therefore, Christ says, "So that whoever believes in him will not perish" forever "but will have eternal life" (i.e., endless satisfaction in eternal joy). So even as they were bitten by the serpents, yet by believing that God had given them a serpent for healing them from physical death they were delivered from death and from pain by looking upon it—we too will be delivered from everlasting death by believing that the Son of Man, Jesus, was given to us by God and lifted up on the cross so that we would seek faith and hope and love in him. And just as the bronze serpent was a sign, merely appearing as if it were poisonous, although it was not actually poisonous, as it was bronze—so the Son of God was sent in the likeness of sinful flesh,[60] since he was sinless and since God can neither suffer nor die,[61] just as the bronze serpent could neither experience pain nor could it die.

And so it is in this manner which the beloved Savior taught Nicodemus very clearly and truly and teaches us along with him about baptism, about his incarnation, about his passion, and about his ascension into heaven. And every Christian should adhere to these four articles. First, because it is impossible for a person to be saved *without baptism*. Second, because Christ, the Son of God, became incarnate, and therefore he is *true God and true man*. Third, because he was *crucified for sinners*. And fourth, because he *ascended into heaven*, and so he will bring his elect who believe in him unto himself in eternal life. May he be pleased to lead us out of this miserable life soon—with the help of our beloved and faithful Teacher who so gently, graciously, and gloriously taught Nicodemus and us the true faith—he is blessed forever! Amen.

NOTES

The source for this translation is the critical edition of the text found in *Česká nedělní postila. Vyložénie svatých čtení nedělních* (*Magistri Iohannis Hus Opera*

Omnia), *vol. 2.*, ed. Jiří Daňhelka (Praha: Academia, 1992), 274–282, 536–538, 635–637, 694–696. For a comparison of similar ideas expressed in a sermon preached on the same Johannine pericope on the Feast Day of the Holy Trinity on June 7, 1411, see: *Mag. Io. Hus Sermones in Capella Bethlehem, 1410–1411*, 6 vols., ed. Václav Flajšhans (Praha: Nákladem Královské české společnosti nauk, 1941), 4:177–183. See also *Sermones de tempore qui Collecta dicuntur* (*MIHOO*, 7:279–283).

1. In the introduction of each homily where Hus cited or translated biblical pericopes, he "elucidated the text of the biblical passage with inscribed notes as a commentary for a correct understanding of the meaning of individual words and phrases." See "Preface," in *Česká nedělní postila*, 11. His explanatory notes are included here in parentheses.

2. See Guillaume Durand, *Rationale Divinorum Officiorum*, ed. Jean Beleth (Naples: Joseph Dura, 1859), 625: "*Evangelium est: Erat homo ex Pharisaeis Nicodemus, in quo habetur de baptismo, qui invocatione sanctae Trinitatis sanctificat baptizatos. In aliis vero Ecclesiis dicitur Epistola: Gaudete perfecti, quae est ad Corinth. c. ult. Et in aliis dicitur: Vidi ostium, quae est Apocal. c.4. Et Evangelium: Cum venerit Paraclitus*" (114.5). See also Josef Vašica, *Staročeské evangeliáře* (Praha: České akademie věd a umění, 1931), 115–121.

3. Or *simple folk, ordinary people*. Hus frequently expressed his deep and compassionate desire to explain biblical truths to the "common people" and critiqued those priests who prevented the commoners or laymen from understanding Scripture. See: *Výklad na vieru* (*MIHOO*, 1:63); *Česká nedělní postila* (*MIHOO*, 2:112, 127, 184, 201, 223, 338).

4. Hus used this same phrase or similar expressions on the supreme goodness of each member of the Trinity in several of his Czech writings. See: *Česká nedělní postila* (*MIHOO*, 2:261–262, 292, 372, 405–408, 453); *Výklad na vieru* (*MIHOO*, 1:73); *Výklad na páteř* (*MIHOO*, 1:357); *Dcerka: O poznání cěsty pravé k spasení* (*MIHOO*, 4:185); *Katechismus* (*MIHOO*, 4:327); *Jádro učení křesťanského* (*MIHOO*, 4:330); *Knížky o svatokupectví* (*MIHOO*, 4:196). Cf. *De Cognicione Dei* in *Magistri Iohannis Hus: Constantiensia*, eds. Helena Krmíčková et al. (*Magistri Iohannis Hus Opera omnia*), 24 (*Corpus Christianorum. Continuatio Mediaevalis*), 274 (Turnhout: Brepols, 2016), 146: ". . . *Deus est bonum, quo melius cogitari non potest.*"; *Sermones in Capella Bethlehem*, 4:178: ". . . *trinitas in divinis est tres persone, sc. Pater, Filius et Spiritus S., unus Deus et una essencia, que est summum bonum, quo melius excogitari non potest.*"; *Letter to the Praguers* (*Korespondence*, 184: "*bonitas summa*"); *Super Quattuor Sententiarum*, 1.1.5; 1.2.4; Hus's specific Czech and Latin formulations of this phrase appear to be a combination of several thinkers: Augustine, Anselm, Boethius, and others. See Augustine, *De Natura Boni Contra Manichaeos*, 1: "*Summum bonum, quo superius non est, Deus est.*"; 22; *Confessiones*, 7.4.6: "*Neque enim ulla anima unquam potuit poteritve cogitare aliquid quod sit te melius, qui summum et optimum es.*"; *De libero arbitrio*, 2.6.14.54. See also Anselm of Canterbury, *Proslogion*, 2–3; 9: "*O immensa bonitas, quae sic omne intellectum excedis.*"; 14: "*Quaerebas deum, et invenisti eum esse quiddam summum omnium, quo nihil melius cogitari potest.*"; 22–23. See also Boethius, *Philosophiae Consolatio*, 3.10: "*Deum rerum omnium principem bonum esse communis humanorum conceptio probat*

animorum. Nam cum nihil Deo melius excogitari quaet, id quo melius est bonum esse quis dubitet." See also Tomáš Štítný, "O sedmy wstupnych," in *Sborník vyšehradský, vol. 1: Úvod a text*, ed. František Ryšánek (Praha: NČSAV, 1960), 198–199: "*Diligere Deum super omnia debemus propter tria: quia bonis est in se, nec tantummodo bonus, sed etiam ipsa bonitas est, quo nihil melius cogitari vel esse potest et quo omne, quod aliquo modo bonum est, bonum est.*" Štítný's composition *O sedmy wstupnych* is a Czech translation of David of Augsburg's scholastic work *De septem processibus religiosorum.* (The Latin citation is from 3.31.)

5. Or *suppose and believe.*

6. Hus was referring to any potential misunderstandings of the Trinity which might ensue because the words "father" and "son" are used to describe the relationship between the Father and the Son. He thought that the common people would somehow naturally assume that the Father was older (thus not as powerful as the Son) and that the Son was younger (thus not as wise as the Father). He explained his rationale in more detail in the first of two sermons he preached on June 7, 1411, and in his treatise *On Simony*. See *Sermones in Capella Bethlehem*, 4:179; *Knížky o svatokupectví* (*MIHOO*, 4:193).

7. Or *gracious and merciful. Cf. Sermones in Capella Bethlehem*, 4:179: "*Patri singulariter ascribitur potencia . . . Et Filio . . . sapiencia . . . Et Spiritui s. bonitas appropriatur . . .*"

8. *Cf.* Augustine, *De Trinitate*, 6.1.1–2; 6.3.5; 6.7.9; 7.1.1.1. Hus also explained this triadic pattern of virtues in relation to the Trinity in his devotional treatise on spirituality. See *Dcerka* (*MIHOO*, 4:164).

9. Or *as a similitude.*

10. *Cf.* Jan Hus, *Super Quattuor Sententiarum*, 1.2.3; 1.3.3–5; 1.11.5; 2:1.1–5 (*Incepcio*); 2.16.1–4; *De Cognicione Dei* (*MIHOO*, 24:144).

11. *Cf.* Augustine, *De Trinitate*, 10.11.17–18; 10.12.19; 14.4.6.

12. Hus adopted the Augustinian threefold distinction of different kinds of belief: (1) *credere Deum (věřiti boha)*, (2) *credere Deo (věřiti bohu)*, and (3) *credere in Deum (věřiti v boha)*. The Czech preposition *v* (English *in*) is key for him, especially in his Czech writings. Thus, in order to communicate Hus's intended meaning in English, it is important to make the distinction between "believing *in* God" (i.e., where the preposition *in* is used to construe the personal aspect of entrusting oneself to God: *credere in Deum*) and "believing a particular doctrine" (e.g., believing the deity of Christ or believing the church) without the particular preposition *in*. Hus explained the important distinction of using this preposition in: *Tractatus de Ecclesia*, 4; *Výklad na vieru* (*MIHOO*, 1:66–69, 72–73, 87); *Tractatus de Tribus Dubiis (Historia et Monumenta*, 208–210). Hus also mentioned this threefold distinction of belief quite often in both his Latin and Czech writings. See: *Česká sváteční kázání* (*MIHOO*, 3:67); *De Fidei Sue Elucidacione* (*MIHOO*, 24:86–91); *De Mandatis Dei et de Oracione Dominica* (*MIHOO*, 24:120); *Super Quattuor Sententiarum*, 3.23.1–3; *Quaestio de Credere* (*MIHOO*, 24:57–66); *Explicatio in Epistola Jacobi* (*Historia et Monumenta,* 2:206); *Výklad na vieru* (*MIHOO*, 1:66–67); *Katechismus* (*MIHOO*, 4:327); *Provázek třípramenný* (*MIHOO*, 4:149); *O šesti bludiech* (*MIHOO*, 4:274). For the original source, see Augustine, *In Joannis Evangelium Tractatus* in *Patrologia*

Latina, 35:1630–1631 (Tractatus 29.6); see also Peter Lombard, *Libri Quattuor Sententiarum*, 3.23.4.1; see also Thomas Aquinas, *Summa Theologiae*, 2–2.2.2.

13. Or *stands upright*.

14. Or *unstable and indifferent*. This word (*nesetrvavý*) was one of Hus's many unique Czech neologisms. It refers to the lack of a single-minded persistence or discipline in constantly pursuing a goal. See Emanuel Michálek, "Adjektivní neologismy v Husově jazyce," in *Listy filologické* 90/3 (1967): 247–250. *Cf. Sermones in Capella Bethlehem*, 4:181: "... *inpotens, insipiens, inperseverans* ..."

15. *Cf. Knížky o svatokupectví* (*MIHOO*, 4:196); *De Cognicione Dei* (*MIHOO*, 24:144–145). See also Jan Hus, *Betlemské Poselství*, 2 vols., trans. and ed. Anna Císařová-Kolářová (Praha: Jan Laichter, 1947), 1:80–81.

16. The Czech word *obraz* is a homonym with several meanings, including picture, painting, or image.

17. *Cf. Výklad na vieru* (*MIHOO*, 1:67–68).

18. *Cf. Tractatus de Ecclesia*, 53: "*Similiter credendo quicquid vult Christus de se credi, et non credendo de Christo quod vult non de se credi, in hoc credit omnem articulum sive affirmativum sive negativum de Christo credibilem.*"

19. Literally *to contemplate* or *to meditate upon*.

20. Or *keeps and observes*. Hus did, however, make nuanced theological distinctions between fulfilling the law, keeping or following the commandments, and doing God's will. See: *Česká nedělní postila* (*MIHOO*, 2:324); *Výklad piesniček Šalamúnových* (*MIHOO*, 4:122); *Korespondence,* 20, 28, 144, 151: "... *det vobis deus intellectum et perseveranciam, et vestrum desiderium dignetur omnibus bonis per merita Jesu Christi adimplere* ..."; 181: "*venit rex mundi summusque pontifex, ut legem dei operibus suis adimpleret.*"; 208, 270; *Quaestio de Supremo Rectore* (*MIHOO*, 19A:172): "*Ex isto notabili sequitur, quod impossibile est creaturam esse et nullam Dei legem penitus observare.*"

21. Portions of this sermon by Hus were adapted from John Wyclif's sermon on the same pericope. See Jan Sedlák, ed., "Pramen české Postilly Husovy," in *Studie a texty k náboženským dějinám českým: Studie a texty k životopisu Husovu* (Olomouc: Matice Cyrillo-Methodějská, 1914), 1:257–283; see also *Česká nedělní postila* (*MIHOO*, 2:635–637). Wyclif's sermon is found in Johann Loserth (ed.), *Iohannis Wyclif Sermones, vol. 1: Super Evangelia Dominicalia* (London: Trübner & Co., 1887), 215–223 (*Sermo 32*).

22. Or *wanting to be instructed even deeper in his belief*.

23. Or *had driven him away*. This is the same Czech word Hus used elsewhere for excommunication. See: *Česká nedělní postila* (*MIHOO*, 2:222, 243, 245, 247–251, 266); *O šesti bludiech* (*MIHOO*, 4:282–287).

24. Or *initiation into the faith*. Hus was making a play on words since the Czech word (*počátek*) means both "birth" and "beginning."

25. *Cf.* Hus's similar explanation of this verse in *Leccionarium Bipartitum Pars Hiemalis* (*MIHOO*, 9:138–139).

26. It is interesting to note that Wyclif's text from which Hus was borrowing here uses the Latin word *philosophis* (philosopher) while Hus used the Czech word *pohan*

(pagan or heathen). In his *Česká nedělní postila*, Hus referred to Aristotle as both a pagan (*MIHOO*, 2:245, 401) and a philosopher (*MIHOO*, 2:397).

27. The Czech noun *moc* is used throughout this sermon twenty-six times. It has various meanings depending on the context; Hus did not use the word interchangeably in all contexts, but expressed distinct theological nuances between power, authority, and right in Czech which are similar to the concepts he also developed in his usage of the Latin word *potestas* in *Treatise on the Church*. See *Tractatus de Ecclesia*, 44, 65, 70, 73–89, 90–95, 112, 121–126, 153, 169–170, 234. For Hus's usage of the Latin terms *auctoritas* and *potestas* related to this Johannine pericope, see *Postilla Adumbrata* (*MIHOO*, 13:251–256).

28. Or . . . *a man cannot become a son of God, unless God* . . .

29. Hus did partially distinguish between election and predestination in *Super Quattuor Sententiarum* (1.35.1–1.48.7), but he often translated the Latin word *praedestinatus* as the Czech word *vyvolený* (chosen or elect). See Pavlína Rychterová, "The Vernacular Theology of Jan Hus," in *A Companion to Jan Hus*, ed. František Šmahel and Ota Pavlíček (Leiden: Brill, 2015), 198 fn84.

30. In this biblical citation, Hus used the phrase "the word of God," although the word "gospel" was used in both the Latin Vulgate (*evangelium*) and in the oldest versions of the gospel readings (*čtenie*) of the Czech Bible. For example, see Vladimír Kyas, *Staročeská bible drážďanská a olomoucká s částmi Bible litoměřicko-třeboňské: Biblia Palaeobohema Codicis Dresdensis ac Olomucensis cum Partibus Codicis Litomericensis-Trebonensis: Kritické vydání nejstaršího českého překladu bible ze 14. století, vol. 2, Epištoly, Skutky apoštolů, Apokalypsa = Epistolae Actus apostolorum Apocalypsis)* (Praha: Academia, 1985), 74–75; see also *Česká nedělní postila* (*MIHOO*, 2:72–74).

31. *Cf.* Hus's similar comments in *Výklad delší na desatero přikázanie* (*MIHOO*, 1:193).

32. Isaiah 10:15: "Shall the ax vaunt itself over the one who wields it, or the saw magnify itself against the one who handles it? As if a rod should raise the one who lifts it up, or as if a staff should lift the one who is not wood!" Hus used a similar illustration of an axe in relation to the power of God in *Super Quattuor Sententiarum* (2.27.5) and in *Výklad na vieru* (*MIHOO*, 1:91); Cf. *Tractatus de Ecclesia*, 170.

33. Literally *embedded*.

34. Hus offered the same exegesis of this passage in *Tractatus de Ecclesia* (58) and *Contra Octo Doctores* (*MIHOO*, 22:424–426).

35. Or *fleshly*.

36. Or *sensually*.

37. Augustine, *In Joannis Evangelium Tractatus* in *Patrologia Latina*, 35:1477–1478 (*Tractatus* 11.5–6).

38. *Cf.* John Wyclif, *Trialogus: Cum Supplemento Trialogi*, ed. Gotthard V. Lechler (Oxford: Clarendon Press, 1869), 285–288.

39. Ephesians 1:19; 3:7; 6:10.

40. Hus also commented on ensoulment in his *Super Quattuor Sententiarum*, 2.18.6; *Cf.* Augustine, *De Natura et Origine Animae*, 1.16–20; *De Civitate Dei*,

5.11; *Cf.* Thomas Aquinas, *Summa Theologiae*, 1.75.1–4; 1.78.1; 1.118.2–3; *Summa Contra Gentiles*, 2.89.1–23.

41. John Chrysostom, *Commentarius in Sanctum Joannem Apostolum et Evangelistam* in *Patrologia Graeca*, 59:154–155 (Homilia 26.1–2).

42. Or *baptism of water*.

43. Or *the sound of the wind blowing*.

44. Or *the manner in which he is operating*.

45. *Cf.* Hus's similar comments in: *De Ecclesia*, 36, 38, 51, 107–108, 110, 129, 143; *Česká nedělní postila* (*MIHOO*, 2:457–458); *Korespondence*, 37–38, 121; *Articuli a Michaele de Causis Romam missi anno 1412* (*Documenta*, 171).

46. Augustine, *In Joannis Evangelium Tractatus* in *Patrologia Latina*, 35:1486–1487 (*Tractatus* 12.5).

47. Literally *generation or posterity*.

48. Or *generous and bountiful*.

49. Literally *easy things*.

50. Genesis 2:7: "Then the LORD God formed the man out of the dust from the ground and breathed the breath of life into his nostrils, and the man became a living being."

51. The Czech word used here (*obcovat*) is the exact opposite of excommunicate (*vyobcovat*). It means to associate or consort with someone and involves social interaction and communication with people, but usually maintains the connotation of a more intimate relationship of sharing as in fellowship or communion.

52. See Thomas Aquinas, *Summa Theologiae*, 3.57.3.

53. Hus used an interesting and complex play on words here where the Czech word (*pochop*) has several meanings. It signifies a starting point or foundation, but also means conceptus (i.e., the embryo in the uterus during the early stages of pregnancy); the Czech verb (*pochopit*) means to grasp something and understand it as a concept. Hus is saying that the heretics falsely took this idea of the Son of man descending (from the phrase "descended from heaven") as the foundation of their understanding of Christ's conception, but they grasped it improperly. See also *Výklad delší na desatero přikázanie* (*MIHOO*, 1:209, 317); *Provázek třípramenný* (*MIHOO*, 4:150).

54. Hus also mentioned the heresy of the Patarines in his *Menší výklad na vieru* (*MIHOO*, 1:109). In this brief exposition which served as a summary of his larger exposition, Hus commented on both the *Apostles' Creed* (*MIHOO*, 1:105–106) and the *Niceno-Constantinopolitan Creed* (*MIHOO*, 1:107–112), viewing the second creed as a sort of "commentary" on the first one (*MIHOO*, 1:107; *Super Quattuor Sententiarum*, 3.25.3). For an example of medieval heresies concerning the incarnation, see the Cathar text *Interrogatio Iohannis* in Walter L. Wakefield and Austin P. Evans, *Heresies of the High Middle Ages: Selected Sources Translated and Annotated* (New York: Columbia University Press, 1991), 458–465, esp. 462.

55. Literally *invented*. Hus was making another play on words by noting that the idea was "imagined" before the "image" of the idea was created in a painting. Hus was saying that this heretical idea was first "imagined" and then represented in the "images" which supported the invention of the original idea.

56. Literally *moved away from*.

57. *Cf. Menší výklad na vieru* (*MIHOO*, 1:109).

58. Literally *stinging*.

59. Or *from the diabolical stinging serpent of sin.*

60. Romans 8:3: "For what the Law could not do, weak as it was through the flesh, God *did:* sending His own Son in the likeness of sinful flesh and *as an offering* for sin, He condemned sin in the flesh . . ."

61. *Cf. Jádro učení křesťanského* (*MIHOO*, 4:330).

Bibliography

Allert, C. D. "What Are We Trying to Conserve? Evangelicalism and *Sola Scriptura.*" *Evangelical Quarterly* 76 (2004): 327–348.

Antonín, Robert. "The Bishop Andrew of Prague and Church in Bohemia after the Fourth Lateran Council." *Zeitschrift für Ostmitteleuropa-Forschung* 69, no. 4 (2020): 453–469.

———. "S kým se přel biskup Ondřej?: K meandrům v právní krajině Čech na počátku 13. století na základě 'známého' příběhu." *Právní kultura středověku (Colloquia mediaevalia Pragensia 17),* eds. Martin Nodl and Piotr Węcowski, 45–63. Praha: Filosofia, 2016.

Aquinas, Thomas. *Summa Theologica*, trans. Fathers of the English Dominican Province. Westminster: Christian Classics, 1981.

———. *Summa Contra Gentiles*, trans. Anton Pegis, James F. Anderson, Vernon J. Bourke, and Charles J. O'Neil. Notre Dame: University of Notre Dame Press, 1975.

Barrett, Matthew. *God's Word Alone: The Authority of Scripture. What the Reformers Taught and Why It Still Matters.* Grand Rapids: Zondervan, 2016.

———. "Sola Scriptura in the Strange Land of Evangelicalism: The Peculiar but Necessary Responsibility of Defending Sola Scriptura Against Our Own Kind." *The Southern Baptist Journal of Theology* 19, no. 4 (2015): 9–38.

Bartoš, František Michálek. *Světci a kacíři.* Praha: Husova československá evangelická fakulta bohoslovecká, 1949.

———. "V předvečer Kutnohorského dekretu." *Časopis Národního Musea* 102 (1928): 92–123.

———. *Petr Chelčický: duchovní otec Jednoty Bratrské.* Prague: Kalich, 1958.

———. *Literární činnost M. J. Husi.* Praha: České akademie věd a umění, 1948.

———. *Husitská revoluce,* 2 vols. Prague: SAV, 1965–1966.

———. *The Hussite Revolution, 1424–1437.* Translated by John Martin Klassen. New York: Columbia University Press, 1986.

———. "Hus a jeho učitelé a kolegové na bohoslovecké fakultě Karlovy univerzity." *Jihočeský sborník historický* 13 (1940): 41–47.

———. *Čechy v době Husově (1378–1415).* Praha: Jan Laichter, 1947.

152   *Bibliography*

————. "K Husovu spisku o českém pravopise." *Jihočeský sborník historický* 18 (1949): 33–38.

————. "Husův učitel Dr. Jan Štěkna a kaple Betlémská." *Věstník České akademie věd a umění* 58 (1949): 5–13.

————. "Hus a jeho účast na staročeské bibli." *Strahovská knihovna* 3 (1968): 86–112.

Beck, James R. "Sola Scriptura: Then and Now." *Psychology & Christianity Integration: Seminal Works That Shaped the Movement*, ed. Daryl H. Stevenson, Brian E. Eck, and Peter C. Hill, 75–81. Batavia: Christian Association for Psychological Studies, 2007.

Bellito, Christopher M. "The Reform Context of the Great Western Schism." In *A Companion to Great Western Schism (1378–1417)*, eds. Joëlle Rollo-Koster and Thomas M. Izbicki, 303–331. Leiden: Brill, 2009.

De Benedictis, Cristina. "*La Vita del Cardinale Pietro Stefaneschi* di Sebastiano Vannini." *Annali della scuola normale superiore di Pisa: Classe di lettere e filosofia* (series 3, vol. 6, fascicle 3), 955–1016. Pisa: Scuola Normale Superiore di Pisa, 1976.

Benrath, Gustav Adolf. "Wyclif und Hus." *Zeitschrift für Theologie und Kirche* 62, no. 2 (1965): 196–216.

Betts, Reginald Robert. *Essays in Czech History*. London: Athlone Press, 1969.

————. "The Regulae Veteris et Novi Testamenti of Matěj z Janova." *The Journal of Theological Studies* 32, no. 128 (1931): 344–351.

Bláhová, Marie, ed. *Kroniky doby Karla IV.* Praha: Svoboda, 1987.

Blocher, Henri. "Justification of the Ungodly (Sola Fide): Theological Reflections." *Justification and Variegated Nomism, vol. 2: The Paradoxes of Paul*, ed. D. A. Carson, Peter T. O'Brien, and Mark A. Seifrid, 465–500, Grand Rapids: Baker Academic, 2004.

Boethius. *Trost der Philosophie / Consolatio philosophiae: Lateinisch–Deutsch*, ed. Ernst Gegenschatz and Olof Gigon. Berlin/Boston: De Gruyter, 2014.

Bonnechose, Emile de. *Lettres de Jean Hus, écrites durant son exil et dans sa prison*. Paris: L.R. Delay, 1846.

Brown, Marshall T. *John Blahoslav–Sixteenth-Century Moravian Reformer: Transforming the Czech Nation by the Word of God.* Bonn: Verlag für Kultur und Wissenschaft, 2013.

Brundage, James A. "The Medieval Advocate's Profession." *Law and History Review* 6, no. 2 (1988): 439–464.

————. "The Advocates Dilemma: What Can You Tell the Client? A Problem in Legal Ethics." *Medieval Church Law and the Origins of the Western Legal Tradition: A Tribute to Kenneth Pennington*, ed. Wolfgang P. Müller and Mary E. Sommar, 201–210, Washington, D.C.: The Catholic University of America Press, 2006.

Budinský, Libor. "Vatikán uzná Husa reformátorem církve." *Lidové noviny* (December 15, 1999).

Bünz, Enno. "Die Leipziger Universitätsgründung: eine Folge des Kuttenberger Dekrets." *Acta Universitatis Carolinae: Historia Universitatis Carolinae Pragensis: Příspěvky k dějinám Univerzity Karlovy* 49, no. 2 (2009): 55–64.

Burger, Hans, Arnold Huijgen, and Eric Peels, eds. *Sola Scriptura: Biblical and Theological Perspectives on Scripture, Authority, and Hermeneutics.* Leiden: Brill, 2018.

Cattley, Stephen Reed, ed. *The Acts and Monuments of John Foxe, vol. 3.* London: Seeley, Burnside & Seeley, 1844.

Čelakovský, Jaromír. *Codex juris municipalis Regni Bohemiae–Sbírka pramenů práva městského království Českého, vol. 1: Privilegia měst pražských.* Privilegia civitatum Pragensium. Praha: Eduard Grégr, 1886.

Cho, Dongsun. "Divine Acceptance of Sinners: Augustine's Doctrine of Justification." *Perichoresis* 12, no. 2 (2014): 163–184.

Chroust, Anton-Hermann. "Legal Profession during the Middle Ages: The Emergence of the English Lawyer Prior to 1400." *Notre Dame Law Review* 31, no. 4 (1956): 537–601.

Consistorium diaboli. National Library of the Czech Republic, MS VI.A.5, fol. 1r–5v.

Čornej, Petr. *Jan Žižka: Život a doba husitského válečníka.* Praha: Paseka, 2019.

Čornejová, Ivana. "Das Kuttenberger Dekret und die Interpretation der Universitätsautonomie im Wandel der Geschichte." *Acta Universitatis Carolinae: Historia Universitatis Carolinae Pragensis: Příspěvky k dějinám Univerzity Karlovy* 49, no. 2 (2009): 257–262.

Corpus Scriptorum Ecclesiasticorum Latinorum, 85 vols. Vienna: Hölder-Pichler-Tempsky, 1866–.

Coufal, Dušan. "Vědecké bádání o Janu Husovi." *Praha Husova a husitská 1415–2015: Publikace k výstavě: Clam-Gallasův palác, 25. září 2015–24. ledna 2016* (Praha: Scriptorium, 2015), 241–247.

Creighton, Mandell. *A History of the Papacy During the Period of the Reformation, vol. 1.* London: Longmans, Green, and Co., 1882.

Czech News Agency. "Vlk čeká politování církve nad upálením Jana Husa." *Právo* (December 16, 1999).

Daňhelka, Jiří et al., eds. *Staročeská kronika tak řečeného Dalimila: Vydání textu a veškerého textového materiálu.* Praha: Academia, 1988.

———. *Husitské písně.* Praha: Československý spisovatel, 1952.

———. "České glosy v textu Pseudo-Augustinova traktátu Speculum peccatoris v mikulovském rukopise Mk 102." *Listy filologické* 114, no. 2/3 (1991): 176–179.

———, ed. *Česká nedělní postila. Vyložení svatých čtení nedělních.* Praha: Academia, 1992. *Magistri Iohannis Hus Opera Omnia,* vol. 2.

Darlage, Adam W. "Bohemian Church." *Encyclopedia of Martin Luther and the Reformation,* vol. 2, ed. Mark A. Lamport, 79–81. Lanham: Rowman & Littlefield, 2017.

David, Zdeněk. "Masaryk's View of Jan Hus and the Bohemian Reformation." *Kosmas: Czechoslovak and Central European Journal* (2016): 149–171.

Deane, Jennifer Kolpacoff. *A History of Medieval Heresy and Inquisition.* Lanham: Rowman & Littlefield Publishers, 2011.

Dekarli, Martin. "The Law of Christ *(Lex Christi)* and the Law of God *(Lex Dei)*— Jan Hus's Concept of Reform." Translated by Zdeněk V. David. *The Bohemian Reformation and Religious Practice* 10 (2015): 49–69.

Denzinger, Heinrich, and Petrus Hünermann. *Enchiridion symbolorum definitionum et declarartionum de rebus fidei et morum (Lateinisch–Deutsch).* Freiburg im Breisgau: Herder, 1991.

Dobiáš, F. M., and Amedeo Molnár. *Husova výzbroj do Kostnice.* Praha: Kalich, 1965.

Dolejšová, Ivana. "Eschatological Elements in Hus's Understanding of Orthopraxis." *The Bohemian Reformation and Religious Practice* 4 (2002): 132.

———. "Nominalist and Realist Approaches to the Problem of Authority: Páleč and Hus." *The Bohemian Reformation and Religious Practice* 2 (1998): 49–55.

Dragseth, Jennifer Hockenbery, ed. *The Devil's Whore: Reason and Philosophy in the Lutheran Tradition.* Minneapolis: Fortress Press, 2011.

Drda, Miloš, František J. Holeček, and Zdeněk Vybíral. *Jan Hus na přelomu tisíciletí: Mezinárodní rozprava o českém reformátoru 15. století a o jeho recepci na prahu třetího milénia Papežská lateránská univerzita Řím 15.–18. prosince 1999.* Tábor: Husitské museum, 2001.

Duns Scotus, John. *Philosophical Writings: A Selection.* Translated by Allan B. Wolter. Indianapolis: Hackett Publishing, 1987.

Durand, Guillaume. *Rationale Divinorum Officiorum,* ed. Jean Beleth. Naples: Joseph Dura, 1859.

———. *Speculi clarissimi viri Gulielmi Durandi pars tertia et quarta, vna cum Io. Andreae, ac Baldi, Doctorum in vtroque Iure longè praestantißimorum theoremaribus, quàm diligentißimè excusa,* vol. 2. Basel: Frobenius et Episcopius, 1563.

Emler, Josef, ed. *Reliquiae tabularum terrae regni Bohemiae anno MDXLI igne consuptarum—Pozůstatky desk zemských království českého r. 1541 pohořelých,* vol. 2 (Praha: Otto, 1872).

Eun-Sil, Son. "*Sola fide* or *fide caritate formata*: Two Incompatible Principles? From Martin Luther to Thomas Aquinas." *Revue des sciences philosophiques et théologiques* 103, no. 1 (2019): 93–112.

Evans, Austin P. *Heresies of the High Middle Ages: Selected Sources Translated and Annotated.* New York: Columbia University Press, 1991.

Evans, G. R. *The Language and Logic of the Bible: The Road to Reformation.* Cambridge: Cambridge University Press, 2009.

Flajšhans, Václav. "Husovo odvolání ke Kristu." *Český časopis historický* 39 (1933): 237.

———. *Mistr Jan Řečený Hus z Husince.* Prague: Josef R. Vilímek, 1904.

Frame, John. *The Doctrine of the Word of God.* Phillipsburg: P&R Publishing, 2010.

Friedberg, Emil, and Emil Ludwig Richter, eds. *Corpus iuris canonici, 2 vols.* Graz: Akademische Druck, 1995.

Fritz, Wolfgang D., ed. *Die Goldene Bulle Kaiser Karls IV. vom Jahre 1356: Text* in *Monumenta Germaniae Historica. Fontes Iuris Germanici in Usum Scholarum Separatim Editi, vol. 11: Bulla Aurea Karoli IV. Imperatoris Anno MCCCLVI Promulgata.* Weimar: H. Böhlau, 1972.

Fudge, Thomas A. *The Trial of Jan Hus: Medieval Heresy and Criminal Procedure.* Oxford: Oxford University Press, 2013.

———. *Jan Hus: Religious Reform and Social Revolution in Bohemia.* London: I. B. Tauris, 2010.

———. *The Crusade against Heretics in Bohemia, 1418–1437: Sources and Documents for the Hussite Crusades*. NewYork: Routledge, 2016.

———. "The State of Hussite Historiography." *Mediaevistik* 7 (1994): 93–117.

———. "Jan Hus in English Language Historiography, 1863–2013." *Journal of Moravian History* 16, no. 2 (2016): 90–138.

———. "'Infoelix Hus': The Rehabilitation of a Medieval Heretic." *Fides et Historia* 30, no. 1 (1998): 57–73.

———. "The Role of Michael de Causis in the Prosecution of Jan Hus." *The Bohemian Reformation and Religious Practice*, vol. 10, ed. Zdeněk V. David and David R. Holeton, 123–143. Prague: Filosofia, 2015.

Godfrey, W. Robert. "Faith Formed by Love or Faith Alone? The Instrument of Justification." In *Covenant, Justification, and Pastoral Ministry: Essays by the Faculty of Westminster Seminary California*, ed. R. Scott Clark, 267–284. P&R Publishing, 2007.

Goll, Jaroslav, et al., eds. *Fontes rerum bohemicarum. 8 vols*. Prague, Nákladem nadání Františka Palackého, 1873–1932.

Grosseteste, Robert. *The Letters of Robert Grosseteste, Bishop of Lincoln*. Translated by F.A.C. Mantello and Joseph Goering. Toronto: University of Toronto Press, 2010.

Haberkern, Phillip N. *Patron Saint and Prophet: Jan Hus in the Bohemian and German Reformations*. New York: Oxford University Press, 2016.

Hagen, K. "Hus's 'Donatism.'" *Augustinianum* 11, no. 3 (1971): 541–547.

Havránek, Bohuslav, Josef Hrabák, Jiří Daňhelka, et al., eds. *Výbor z české literatury doby husitské, vol. 1*. Praha: ČSAV, 1963.

Hefele, Karl Josef von. *Conciliengeschichte. Nach den Quellen bearbeitet, vol. 2*. Freiburg im Breisgau: Herder, 1856.

———. *Conciliengeschichte. Nach den Quellen bearbeitet*, vol. 7. Freiburg im Breisgau: Herder, 1874.

Helan, Pavel. *Duce a kacíř: Literární mládí Benita Mussoliniho a jeho kniha Jan Hus, muž pravdy*. Brno: L. Marek, 2006.

———. "Mussolini Looks at Jan Hus and the Bohemian Reformation." Translated by Zdeněk V. David. *The Bohemian Reformation and Religious Practice* 4 (2002): 309–316.

Herold, Vilém. "Vojtěch Raňkův of Ježov (Adalbertus Rankonis de Ericinio) and the Bohemian Reformation." *The Bohemian Reformation and Religious Practice* 7 (2009): 72–79.

———. "How Wyclifite Was the Bohemian Reformation." *The Bohemian Reformation and Religious Practice* 2 (1998): 25–37.

———, with Milan Mráz, eds., *Iohannis Milicii de Cremsir Tres sermones synodales*. Prague: Academia, 1974.

———. "Jan Hus—A Heretic, a Saint, or a Reformer?" Translated by Zdeněk V. David. *Communio Viatorum* 45 (2003): 5–23.

Heymann, Frederick G. *John Žižka and the Hussite Revolution*. Princeton: Princeton University Press, 1955.

156 Bibliography

Hilsch, Peter. "Der Kampf um die Libertas ecclesiae im Bistum Prag." *Bohemia Sacra: Das Christentum in Böhmen 973–1973*, ed. Ferdinand Seibt, 295–306. Düsseldorf: Schwann, 1974.

———. *Johannes Hus (um 1370–1415): Prediger Gottes und Ketzer.* Regensburg: Verlag Friedrich Pustet, 1999.

———. *History und warhafftige geschicht wie das heilig Evangelion mit Johannes Hussen im Concilio zu Costnitz durch den Bapst und seinen anhang offentlich verdampt ist im Jare nach Christi unsers Herren geburt 1414: Mit angehenckter Protestation des Schreibers, der bey allen stücken vnd puncten gewesen ist.* Ed. Johann Agricola. Hagenau: Johannes Secerius, 1529.

Hlaváček, Ivan, ed. "Petr z Mladoňovic, Zpráva o Mistru Janu Husovi v Kostnici." *Ze zpráv a kronik doby husitské.* Praha: Svoboda, 1981.

Höfler, Konstantin von. *Magister Johannes Hus und der Abzug der deutschen Professoren und Studenten aus Prag, 1409.* Prague: Tempský, 1864.

Holeton, David R. "Liturgická a svátostná teologie mistra Jana Husa: Byl Jan Hus reformátorem liturgie?" *Theologická revue* 67, no. 1 (1996): 9–12.

———. "The Sacramental Theology of Tomáš Štítný of Štítné." *The Bohemian Reformation and Religious Practice* 4 (2002): 57–79.

———. "Wyclif's Bohemian Fate: A Reflection on the Contextualization of Wyclif in Bohemia." *Communion Viatorum* 32 (1989): 209–222.

———, with Hana Vlhová-Wörner. "A Remarkable Witness to the Feast of Saint Jan Hus." *The Bohemian Reformation and Religious Practice* 7 (2009): 156–184.

Holý, Ladislav. *The Little Czech and the Great Czech Nation: National Identity and the Post-Communist Transformation of Society.* Cambridge: Cambridge University Press, 1996.

Horský, Rudolf. "Kazatelské a pastýřské dílo M. Jana Husi." *Hus stále živý, sborník studií k 550 výročí Husova upálení*, ed. M. Kaňák, 45–68. Prague: Blahoslav, 1965.

Hudson, Anne. "From Oxford to Prague: The Writings of John Wyclif and His English Followers in Bohemia." *The Slavonic and East European Review* 75, no. 4 (1997): 642–657.

Hus in Konstanz: Der Bericht des Peter von Mladoniowitz. Translated by Josef Bujnoch. Graz: Verlag Styria, 1963.

Hus, Jan. *Postylla svaté paměti M. Jana Husi, mučedlníka božího, na evangelia, kteráž se čtou přes celý rok. K nížti přidané jsou mnohé jiné knihy téhož M. Jana Husi. Kteréž jsou ještě nikdy nebyly imprimované a již nyní teprv na světlo vydané.* Nuremberg: Johann Montanus and Ulrich Neuber, 1563.

———. *Betlemské Poselství*, 2 vols. Translated and edited by Anna Císařová-Kolářová. Praha: Jan Laichter, 1947.

———. *Výklady.* Ed. Jiří Daňhelka. Praha: Academia, 1975

———. *Česká nedělní postila: Vyložení svatých čtení nedělních.* Ed. Jiří Daňhelka. Praha: Academia, 1992.

———. *Česká sváteční kázání.* Ed. Jiří Daňhelka. Praha: Academia, 1995.

———. *Quodlibet: Disputationis de Quodlibet Pragae in Facultate Artium Mense Ianuario anni 1411 habitae Enchiridion.* Ed. Bohumil Ryba. Turnhout: Brepols, 2006.

————. *Questiones.* Ed. Jiří Kejř. Turnhout: Brepols, 2004.

————. *Enarratio Psalmorum (Ps. 109–118).* Ed. Jana Nechutová. Turnhout: Brepols, 2013.

————. *Constanciensia.* Ed. Helena Krmíčková, Jana Nechutová, Dušan Coufal, Jana Fuksová, Lucie Mazalová, Petra Mutlová, Libor Švanda, Soňa Žákovská, and Amedeo Molnár. Turnhout: Brepols, 2016.

————. *Drobné spisy české.* Ed. Jiří Daňhelka. Praha: Academia, 1985.

————. *Passio Domini nostri Iesu Cristi.* Ed. Anežka Vidmanová-Schmidtová. Praha: Academia, 1973.

————. *Sermones de tempore qui Collecta dicuntur.* Ed. Anežka Schmidtová. Pragae: Academia scientarum bohemicae, 1959.

————. *Postilla adumbrata.* Ed. Bohumil Ryba. Praha: Academia, 1975.

————. *Magistri Iohannis Hus Polemica.* Ed. Jaroslav Eršil. Turnhout: Brepols, 2010.

————. *Leccionarium bipartitum Pars hiemalis.* Ed. Anežka Vidmanová-Schmidtová. Praha: Academia, 1988.

————. *Dicta de tempore: Magistro Iohanni Hus attributa,* 2 vols. Ed. Jana Zachová. Turnhout: Brepols, 2011.

————. *Dcerka: O poznání cesty pravé k spasení,* ed. František Žilka. Praha: Kalich, 1995.

————. *Iohannis Hus et Hieronymi Pragensis, confessorum Christi Historia et monumenta,* ed. Matthias Flacius Illyricus, 2 vols. Nuremberg, 1558; new edition Nuremberg/Frankfurt, 1715.

————. *Mag. Io. Hus Sermones in Capella Bethlehem, 1410–1411,* 6 vols. Ed. Václav Flajšhans. Praha: Nákladem Královské české společnosti nauk, 1941.

————. *Mag. Joannis Hus Opera Omnia: Nach neuentdeckten Handschriften,* 3 vols. Osnabrück: Biblio-Verlag, 1966.

————. *Dicta de Tempore Magistro Iohanni Hus Attributa II. Corpus Christianorum Continuatio Mediaevalis 239A.* Ed. Jana Zachová. Turnhout: Brepols, 2011.

————. *Listy z Prahy (do r. 1412): Listy z vyhnanství (1412–1414): Listy z Kostnice (1414–1415).* Translated by Václav Flajšhans. Praha: Otto, 1915.

————. *Postilla: Vyložení svatých čtení nedělních.* Ed. Josef B. Jeschke. Praha: Komenského evangelická fakulta bohoslovecká, 1952.

————. *Positiones, recommendationes, sermones.* Ed. Anežka Schmidtová. Prague: Státní pedagogické nakladatelství, 1958.

————. *Česká nedělní postila. Vyložení svatých čtení nedělních.* Ed. Jiří Daňhelka. Praha: Academia, 1992. *Magistri Iohannis Hus Opera omnia,* vol. 2.

————. *Tractatus de Ecclesia.* Ed. Samuel Harrison Thomson. Praha: Komenského evangelická fakulta bohoslovecká, 1958.

————. *The Church by John Huss.* Translated by David S. Schaff. New York: Charles Scribner's Sons, 1915.

————. *O církvi.* Translated by František M. Dobiáš and Amedeo Molnár. Praha: Nakladatelství Československé akademie věd, 1965.

————. *Mistra Jana Husi Sebrané spisy české, 3 vols.* Ed. Karel Jaromír Erben. Praha: Bedřich Tempský, 1865–1868.

————. *Magistri Iohannis Hus Postilla adumbrata. Magistri Iohannis Hus Opera omnia; tomus XIII; Corpus Christianorum. Continuatio mediaevalis 261.* Eds. Bohumil Ryba and Gabriel Silagi. Turnhout: Brepols Publishers, 2015.

————. *Mistra Jana Husi Sebrané spisy,* 6 vols. Ed. Václav Flajšhans and Milan Svoboda. Prague: J. R. Vilímek, 1904–1908.

————. *Sto listů M. Jana Husi.* Translated and edited by Bohumil Ryba. Praha: Jan Laichter, 1949.

————. *Postilla.* Translated by Václav Flajšhans. Praha: Josef R. Vilímek, 1899–1900.

————. *Obrany v praze (r. 1408–1412). Obran Husových,* vol. 1. Translated by Václav Flajšhans. Praha: J. Otto, 1916.

————. *Sermo de Pace/Řeč o míru.* Translated by F.M. Dobiáš and Amedeo Molnár. Praha: Česká křesťanská akademie, 1995.

————. *O Kościele.* Translated by Krzysztof Moskal. Lublin: Towarzystwo Naukowe Katolickiego Uniwersytetu Lubelskiego, 2003.

Janz, Denis R., ed. *Martin Luther's The Church Held Captive at Babylon: Latin-English Edition with a New Translation and Introduction.* Oxford: Oxford University Press, 2019.

John of Paris. *On Royal and Papal Power.* Translated by John A. Watt. Toronto: Pontifical Institute of Mediaeval Studies, 1971.

Jukl, Jiří Jakub. "Hus v myšlení a tradici pravoslavné církve." *Studia Theologica* 17, no. 4 (2016): 259–271.

Kadlec, Jaroslav. *Leben und Schriften des Prager Magisters Adalbert Ranconis de Ericinio.* Münster: Aschendorff, 1971.

————, ed. *Bohemia Sancta: Životopisy českých světců a přátel Božích,* Zvon: České katolické nakladatelství, 1989.

Kalivoda, Robert. *Husitská ideologie.* Praha: ČSAV, 1961.

Kaminsky, Howard. *A History of the Hussite Revolution.* Eugene: Wipf and Stock, 1967.

Kaňák, Miloslav. *Milíč z Kroměříže.* Praha: Ústřední církevní nakladatelství, 1975.

————. "M. Hus a Viklef." *Husův sborník: Soubor prací k 500. výročí M. Jana Husa,* ed. Rudolf Říčan and Michal Flegl, 253–264. Prague: Komenského evangelická fakulta bohoslovecká, 1966.

————, ed. *Hus stále živý: Sborník studií k 550. výročí Husova upálení.* Praha: ÚCN, 1965.

————. *Jan Viklef: Život a dílo anglického Husova předchůdce.* Praha: Blahoslav, 1973.

Kašpar, Josef. "Katolická církev směřuje k uznání úsilí Jana Husa." *Mladá fronta Dnes* (December 16, 1999).

Kavka, František. "Dvorská komora Karla IV. a její nejvyšší mistr Zbyněk Zajíc z Házmburka." In *Pocta Josefu Petráňovi: Sborník prací z českých dějin k 60. narozeninám prof. dr. Josefa Petráně.* Compiled by Zdeněk Beneš, Eduard Maur, and Jaroslav Pánek, 23–36. Praha: Historický ústav Československé akademie věd, 1991.

Kejř, Jiří. *Husovo odvolání od soudu papežova k soudu Kristovu.* Ústí nad Labem: Albis International, 1999.

————. "Johannes Hus als Rechtsdenker." Jan Hus—*Zwischen Zeiten, Völkern, Konfessionen: Vorträge des internationalen Symposions in Bayreuth vom 22. bis 26. September 1993.* Ferdinand Seibt et al., eds. 213–226. Munich: R. Oldenbourg, 1997.

————. "Husovo odvolání ke Kristu." *Dialog Evropa XXI* 5, no. 2 (1994): 15–18.

————. *Z počátků české reformace.* Brno: L. Marek, 2006.

————. "M. Jan Hus o právnictví." *Právněhistorické studie* 1 (1955): 83–100.

————. "Právnické otázky Husova quodlibetu." *Právněhistorické studie* 5 (1959): 33–47.

————. *Stát, církev a společnost v disputacích na pražské universitě v době Husově a husitské.* Praha: ČSAV, 1964.

————. *Žil jsem ve středověku.* Praha: Academia, 2012.

————. "Husova pravda." *Theologická revue* 77 (2006): 232–243.

————. *Husitský právník M. Jan z Jesenice.* Praha: Československé akademie věd, 1965.

————. *Dvě studie o husitském právnictví.* Prague: ČSAV, 1954.

————. *Husův proces.* Praha: Vyšehrad, 2000.

————. "Husův proces z hlediska práva kanonického." *Theologická revue* 71 (2000): 33–39.

————. "Husův proces z hlediska práva kanonického." *Jan Hus na přelomu tisíciletí: Mezinárodní rozprava o českém reformátoru 15. století a o jeho recepci na prahu třetího milénia Papežská lateránská univerzita Řím 15.–18. prosince 1999.* Eds. Miloš Drda, František J. Holeček, and Zdeněk Vybíral, 303–311. Tábor: Husitské museum, 2001.

————. *Die Causa Johannes Hus und das Prozessrecht der Kirche.* Translated by Walter Annuss. Regensburg: Pustet, 2005.

Kelly, J. N. D. *Golden Mouth: The Story of John Chrysostom—Ascetic, Preacher, Bishop.* Ithaca: Cornell University Press, 1995.

à Kempis, Thomas. *The Imitation of Christ.* Translated by Ronald Knox and Michael Oakley. San Francisco: Ignatius Press, 2005.

Klein, Ernest. *A Comprehensive Etymological Dictionary of the English Language: Dealing with the Origin of Words and Their Sense Development Thus Illustrating the History of Civilization and Culture,* 2 vols. Amsterdam: Elsevier Publishing Company, 1966.

Knouse, Nola Reed, ed. *The Music of the Moravian Church in America.* Rochester: University of Rochester Press, 2008.

Kohnle, Armin, and Thomas Krzenek, eds. *Johannes Hus Deutsch.* Leipzig: Evangelische Verlagsanstalt, 2017.

Kotowski, Norbert. "Magister Johannes Hus im Gespräch mit Prag, Kiew, Rom und Wittenberg. Bericht über das internationale Hus-Symposion." *Una Sancta* 2 (1994): 145–152.

————, with Jan Blahoslav Lášek, eds. *Johann Amos Comenius und das moderne Europa.* Fürth: Flacius-Verlag, 1992.

Kotyk, Jiří. *Spor o revizi Husova procesu.* Prague, Vyšehrad, 2001.

Kouba, Jan. "Der älteste Gesangbuchdruck von 1501 aus Böhmen." *Jahrbuch für Liturgik und Hymnologie* 13 (1968): 78–112.

Krofta, Kamil. "Kurie a církevní správa zemí českých v době předhusitské." *Český časopis historický* 10 (1904): 15–36, 125–152, 249–175, 373–391.

———. *Francie a české hnutí náboženské.* Prague: Melantrich, 1935.

———. "John Huss." *Cambridge Medieval History, vol. 8: The Close of the Middle Ages,* ed. C. W. Previté-Orton and Z. N. Brooke, 45–64. Cambridge: Cambridge University Press, 1936.

———. "Kněz Jan Protiva z Nové Vsi a Chelčického mistr Protivazdrojový dokument." *Časopis Musea Království českého* 74 (1900): 190–220.

Krzenck, Thomas. *Johannes Hus. Theologe, Kirchenreformer, Märtyrer.* Gleichen/Zürich: Muster-Schmidt, 2011.

Kubíček, Alois. *Betlémská kaple.* Praha: Státní nakladatelství krásné literatury, hudby a umění, 1960.

Kučera, Zdeněk, Tomáš Butta, and Olga Nytrová, eds. *Hus a Masaryk: Hledání národní tradice a identity: Sborník projevů pronesených na slavnostním setkání u příležitosti 163. výročí narození Tomáše Garrigua Masaryka v budově Poslanecké sněmovny Parlamentu České republiky a dalších příspěvků.* Praha: Církev československá husitská, 2013.

von Kügelgen, Constantin, ed. *Die Gefangenschaftsbriefe des Johann Hus.* Leipzig: Richard Wöpke, 1902.

Kyas, Vladimír. *Staročeská bible drážďanská a olomoucká s částmi Bible litoměřicko-třeboňské: Biblia Palaeobohema Codicis Dresdensis ac Olomucensis cum Partibus Codicis Litomericensis-Trebonensis: Kritické vydání nejstaršího českého překladu bible ze 14. století, vol. 2, Epištoly, Skutky apoštolů, Apokalypsa = Epistolae Actus apostolorum Apocalypsis).* Praha: Academia, 1985.

Kybal, Vlastimil. *M. Jan Hus: Život a Učení,* 3 vols. Prague: Jan Laichter, 1923–1931.

———. *M. Matěj z Janova: Jeho život, spisy a učení,* 2nd ed. Brno: L. Marek, 2000.

Lane, Anthony, N. S. "Sola Scriptura? Making Sense of a Post-Reformation Slogan." *A Pathway into the Holy Scripture,* ed. Philip E. Satterthwaite and David F. Wright, 297–327. Grand Rapids: Eerdmans, 1994.

Langpaul, Ladislav, ed. *Stížný list: České a moravské šlechty proti upálení Mistra Jana Husa 1415–2015.* Okrouhlice: Spolek Za záchranu rodného domu malíře Jana Zrzavého v Okrouhlici, 2015.

Lášek, Jan Blahoslav. *Počátky křesťanství u východních Slovanů.* Praha: Síť, 1997.

———. "Význam náboženství starých Slovanů a proces christianizace Evropy." *Bohové dávných Slovanů,* ed. Martin Pitro and Petr Vokáč, 177–183. Praha: ISV, 2002.

———. "Comenius als Prediger." In *Comenius als Theologe: Beiträge zur Internationalen wissenschaftlichen Konferenz "Comenius' Erbe und die Erziehung des Menschen für das 21. Jahrhundert" (Sektion VII): Anläßlich des 400. Geburtstages von Jan Amos,* ed. Vladimír Dvořák and Jan Blahoslav Lášek, 166–173. Praha: Nadace Comenius, 1998.

———. "Teologické předpoklady pro mír a pokoj v Komenského Všeobecné poradě." *"Rýžoviště zlata a doly drahokamů."* Sborník pro Václava Huňáčka, 493–504. Červený Kostelec: Pavel Mervart, 2006.

———. *Kristův Svědek Mistr Jan Hus.* Praha: Blahoslav, 1991.

———. "Aktuální Husův apel na svědomí." *Jan Hus: 600 let od smrti,* ed. Marek Loužek, 19–22. Václav Klaus Institute, 2015.

———. "Mistr Jan Hus." In *Mistr Jan Hus v proměnách času a jeho poselství víry dnešku,* compiled by Tomáš Butta and Zdeněk Kučera, 9–19. Praha: Církev československá husitská, 2012.

———, ed. *Jan Hus mezi epochami, národy a konfesemi: Sborník z mezinárodního sympozia konaného 22.–26. září v Bayreuthu, SRN.* Praha: Česká křesťanská akademie, 1995.

———. "Preface." In *Jan Hus mezi epochami, národy a konfesemi: Sborník z mezinárodního sympozia konaného 22.–26. září v Bayreuthu,* ed. Jan Lášek, 12–15. Praha: Česká křesťanská akademie, 1995.

———. "Některé specifické úkoly husovského bádání." In *Jan Hus mezi epochami, národy a konfesemi: Sborník z mezinárodního sympozia konaného 22.–26. září v Bayreuthu,* ed. Jan Lášek, 305–310. Praha: Česká křesťanská akademie, 1995.

———. "Konzultace o teologii M. Jana Husa." *Mediaevalia Historica Bohemica* 4 (1997): 408–409.

———. *Husitství ve východních Čechách.* Praha: 1996.

———. "K ekumenické diskusi o životě a díle M. Jana Husa." *Český zápas* 76, no. 14 (1996): 3.

———. "Ke 'sporu' o Husovo pojetí večeře Páně. Zpráva o literatuře." *Theologická revue* 67, no. 3 (1996): 40–41.

———. "Liturgická a svátostná teologie mistra Jana Husa: Byl Jan Hus reformátorem liturgie?" *Theologická revue,* 67, no. 1 (1996): 9–11.

———. "Jak je to s husitstvím?" *Český zápas* 77, no. 14 (1997): 1.

———. "Preface." Daniel Larangé, *La Parole de Dieu en Bohème et en Moravie: La tradition de la prédication dans l'Unité des Frères de Jan Hus à Jan Amos Comenius* (Paris: L'Harmattan, 2008).

———, et al., eds. *Mistr Jan Hus 1415–2005.* Praha: Sdružení Tradice, 2005.

———. *The Encyclopedia of the Reformation,* ed. Hans J. Hillerbrand. Oxford: Oxford University Press, 1996.

———. "Luther und die Reformation in Böhmen." Michael Hrubá, Jan Royt, Petr Hrubý *et al., Sola fide—Pouhou vírou: Luterská šlechta na Ústecku a Děčínsku a její kulturní dědictví: Katalog výstavy konané na zámku v Děčíně 25. dubna - 30. září 2018,* 27–38. Dolní Břežany: Scriptorium, 2019.

———. "Christliche Vordenker der europäischen Idee in Böhmen." In *Theologen— Europäer—Brückenbauer,* ed. Jan B. Lášek, Thomas Kothmann, and Stephen James Hamilton, 20–46. Neuendettelsau: Freimund 2020.

Leff, Gordon. "Hus and Wyclif: A Doctrinal Comparison." *Bulletin of the John Rylands Library* 50, no. 2 (1968): 387–410.

Leppin, Volker, and Timothy J. Wengert. "Sources for and against the Posting of the Ninety-Five Theses." *Lutheran Quarterly* 29 (2015): 373–398.

Liguš, Ján. "Jan Hus a pražská univerzita: Její teologická a filozofická perspektiva v Husových rektorských promluvách." *Theologická revue* 87, no. 2 (2016): 151–165.

Lombard, Peter. *Petri Lombardi Libri IV sententiarum*. Ad Claras Aquas prope Florentiam: Ex Typographia Collegii S. Bonaventurae, 1916.

Loserth, Johann, ed. *Beiträge zur Geschichte der husitischen Bewegung 4. Die Streitschriften und Unionsverhandlungen zwischen den Katholiken und Husiten in den Jahren 1412 und 1413, Archiv für österreichische Geschichte* 75, 1889.

———. *Huss und Wiclif: Zur Genesis der hussitischen Lehre*. München: Oldenbourg, 1925.

———. *Wiclif and Hus*. Translated by M.J. Evans. London: Hodder & Stoughton, 1884.

Loskot, František. *Konrad Waldhauser, řeholní kanovník sv. Augustina, předchůdce Mistra Jana Husa*. Praha: Volné myšlenky, 1909.

———. *Milíč z Kroměříže: Otec české reformace*. Praha: Volná myšlenka, 1911.

Luard, Henry Richards, ed. *Roberti Grosseteste Episcopi Quondam Lincolniensis Epistolae*. Cambridge: Cambridge University Press, 2012.

———, ed. *Matthæi Parisiensis, Monachi Sancti Albani, Chronica Majora, vol. 5*. London: Longman & Co., 1880.

Lumby, Joseph Rawson, ed. *Polychronicon Ranulphi Higden Monachi Cestrensis, vol. 8*. Cambridge: Cambridge University Press, 2012.

Luther, Martin, and Johann Conrad Irmischer. *Commentarium in Epistolam S. Pauli ad Galatas*. Erlangae: Sumtibus C. Heyderi, 1843.

———. *All Become One Cake: A Sermon on the Lord's Supper*. Translated by Matthew C. Harrison. St. Louis: The Lutheran Church—Missouri Synod, 2005.

———. *D. Martin Luthers Werke: Kritische Gesamtausgabe,* 136 vols. Weimar: Hermann Böhlau, 1883–2009.

———. *Sämmtliche Werke. (Erlanger Ausgabe). (Deutsche Schriften),* 65 vols. Edited by J. G. Plochmann, J. C. Irmischer, and E. L. Enders. Frankfurt am Main; Erlangen: Heyder & Zimmer, 1862–1885.

Lützow, Franz. *The Hussite Wars*. London: J. M. Dent & Sons, 1914.

Macek, Josef. *Husitské revoluční hnutí*. Praha: Rovnost, 1952.

———. *Jan Hus: Studie s ukázkami Husova díla*. Praha: Svobodné slovo, 1963.

———. *Jean Hus et les traditions hussites (XVe–XIXe siècles)*. Paris: Plon, 1973.

Machilek, Franz, ed. *Die hussitische Revolution: Religiöse, politische und regionale Aspekte*. Wien: Böhlau Verlag, 2012.

Machovec, Milan. Bude *katolická* církev *rehabilitovat Jana Husa?* Praha: NPL, 1965.

———. *Husovo učení a význam v dějinách českého národa*. Praha: ČSAV, 1953.

Mahel, Richard. "'První česko-moravský konkordát': Fragment Dudíkova textu ke sporu pražského biskupa Ondřeje II. s králem Přemyslem I. (Příspěvek k poznání pozůstalosti II)." *Archivní sborník* 13 (2007): 18–35.

Mánek, Jindřich. "Hůsuv spor o autoritu." *Hus stále živý: Sborník studií k 550. výročí Husova upálení*, ed. Miloslav Kaňák, 20–38. Praha: Blahoslav, 1965.

Mareš, Bohumil, ed. *Listy Husovy,* 3rd ed. Prague: Hajn, 1911.

Marin, Olivier. "Hus et l'eucharistie: Notes sur la critique hussite de la Stella clericorum." *The Bohemian Reformation and Religious Practice* 3 (2000): 49–61.

Marrou, Henri-Irénée. *Svatý Augustin.* Translated by A. Ž. Řím: Křesťanská akademie, 1979.

Marsilius of Padua. *The Defender of the Peace.* Translated by Annabel Brett. Cambridge: Cambridge University Press, 2005.

Martin, R. F. "Sacra Doctrina and the Authority of its Sacra Scriptura: According to St. Thomas Aquinas." *Pro Ecclesia* 10, no. 1 (2001): 84–102.

Masaryk, Tomáš Garrigue. *Jan Hus: Naše obrozeni a naše reformace.* Prague: Čas, 1896.

———. *V boji o náboženství.* Praha: ČIN, 1947.

———. *Spisy T. G. Masaryka, vol. 6: Česká otázka. Naše nynější krize. Jan Hus,* ed. Jiří Brabec. Prague: Ústav T. G. Masaryka, 2000.

———. Spisy T. G. *Masaryka, vol. 30: Válka a revoluce I: Články—memoranda—přednášky—rozhovory. 1914–1916,* ed. Karel Pichlík. Praha: Ústav T. G. Masaryka, 2005.

———. "Hus and Czech Destiny." *The Spirit of Thomas G. Masaryk (1850–1937): An Anthology,* ed. George J. Kovtun. Houndmills: Macmillan, 1990.

Mathison, Keith. *The Shape of Sola Scriptura.* Moscow: Canon Press, 2001.

Matthiae de Janov. *Regulae Veteris et Novi Testamenti, 6 vols.,* eds. Vlastimil Kybal, Otakar Odložilík, and Jana Nechutová. Prague and Innsbruck: Universitního Knihkupectví Wagnerova, 1908–1926.

———. *Výbor z Pravidel Starého a Nového Zákona.* Translated by Rudolf Schenk. Praha: Blahoslav, 1954.

McGrath, A. E. "Justice and Justification: Semantic and Juristic Aspects of the Christian Doctrine of Justification." *Scottish Journal of Theology* 35, no. 5 (1982): 403–418.

Michálek, Emanuel. "Adjektivní neologismy v Husově jazyce." *Listy filologické* 90, no. 3 (1967): 247–250.

Migne, Jacques Paul, ed. *Patrologia Latina,* 221 vols. Paris: Migne/Garnier, 1844–1865.

———. ed. *Patrologia Graeca,* 161 vols. Paris: Migne/Garnier, 1857–1891.

Miklík, Josef. *"Mittamus lignum in panem eius. Jer. 11, 19."* *Časopis katolického duchovenstva* 9 (1923): 488–490.

Mladějovská, Aneta. "Několik písní Jana Augusty v novém kontextu." *Bohemica litteraria* 18, no. 1 (2015): 13–39.

Molnár, Amedeo. *Na rozhraní věků: Cesty reformace* (Praha: Vyšehrad, 1985).

———. *Husitské manifesty.* Translated and edited by Amedeo Molnár. Praha: Odeon, 1980.

———. "Husovo odvolání ke Kristu." *Husův sborník: Soubor prací k 500. výročí M. Jana Husa,* ed. Rudolf Říčan and Michal Flegl, 73–83. Prague: Komenského evangelická fakulta bohoslovecká, 1966.

———. "Hus et son appel à Jesus Christ." *Communio Viatorum* 8 (1965): 95–104.

———, ed. *Magistri Iohannis Hus Postilla adumbrata: liber cura Commissionis ad Hussii Opera omnia edenda ab academico Collegio historiae creatae vulgatus.* Prague: Academia, 1975.

————. *Boleslavští bratří.* Praha: Komenského evangelická fakulta bohoslovecká, 1952.

————. *Jan Hus: Testimone della verità.* Torino: Claudiana, 1973.

————. "Réflexion sur la notion de vérité dans la pensée de Jean Hus." *Listy Filologické* 88 (1965): 121–131.

————. *Pohyb teologického myšlení: Přehledné dějiny dogmatu: Skripta pro stud. účely Komenského evangelické bohoslovecké fak.* Praha: Ústřední církevní nakladatelství, 1982.

————. "Husovo místo v evropské reformaci." *Československý časopis historický* 14, no. 1 (1966): 1–14.

Molnar, Enrico C. S. "The Liturgical Reforms of John Hus." *Speculum* 41, no. 2 (1966): 297–303.

————. "Wyclif, Hus and the Problem of Authority." In *Jan Hus: Zwischen Zeiten, Völkern, Konfessionen: Vorträge des internationalen Symposions in Bayreuth vom 22. bis 26. September 1993,* eds. Ferdinand Seibt et al., 167–182. München: Oldenbourg, 1997.

Monahan, Arthur P. *John of Paris on Royal and Papal Power: A Translation, with Introduction, of the De Potestate Regia et Papali.* New York: Columbia University Press, 1974.

Morée, Peter C.A. *Preaching in Fourteenth-century Bohemia: The Life and Ideas of Milicius de Chremsir (+1374) and His Significance in the Historiography of Bohemia.* Slavkov: EMAN, 1999.

————. "The Role of the Preacher According to Milicius de Chremsir." *The Bohemian Reformation and Religious Practice* 3 (2000): 35–48.

Mulka, Arthur L. "'FIDES QUAE PER CARITATEM OPERATUR' (GAL 5,6)." *The Catholic Biblical Quarterly* 28, no. 2 (1966): 174–188.

Muller, Richard. *Post-Reformation Reformed Dogmatics: The Rise and Development of Reformed Orthodoxy, c. 1520 to c. 1725,* 4 vols. Grand Rapids: Baker, 2003.

Mundy, John Hine, and Kennerly M. Woody, eds. *The Council of Constance: The Unification of the Church.* Translated by Louise Ropes Loomis. New York: Columbia University Press, 1961.

Mussolini, Benito. *Giovanni Hus: Il Veridico.* Rome: Podrecca e Galantara, 1913.

————. "Giovanni Huss il veridico." *Opera omnia, vol. 33: Opere giovanili: 1904–1913,* eds., Edoardo and Duilio Susmel, 271–327. Firenze: La Fenice, 1961.

————. *John Huss.* Translated by Clifford S. Parker. New York: Albert & Charles Boni, 1929.

————. *Jan Huss, the Veracious.* New York: Italian Book Co., 1939.

————. *Mussoliniho kniha o Janu Husovi, muži pravdy.* Translated by Anežka Loskotová. Turnov: Jiránek, 1937.

Nechutová, Jana. "M. Matěj z Janova v odborné literatuře." *Studia minora Facultatis philosophicae Universitatis Brunensis* E 17 (1972): 119–133.

Needham, Nick. "Justification in the Early Church Fathers." In *Justification in Perspective: Historical Developments and Contemporary Challenges,* ed. Bruce L. McCormack, 25–53. Grand Rapids: Baker Academic, 2006.

Nejedlý, Zdeněk. *Dějiny husitského zpěvu,* 6 vols. Prague: ČSAV, 1954–1956.

————. *Hus a naše doba,* 2nd ed. Prague: Svoboda, 1946.

Neudorflová, Marie L. "Mistr Jan Hus v pojetí T. G. Masaryka." *ČAS: Časopis Masarykova demokratického hnutí* 23, no. 110 (2015): 17–22.

Noble, Ivana. "The Ecumenical Reevaluation of the Heritage of Jan Hus in the Czech Churches." *Lutheran Forum* 49, no. 4 (2015): 45–48.

Nodl, Martin. *Dekret kutnohorský.* Praha: Nakladatelství Lidové noviny, 2010.

Novotný, Václav. *České dějiny, vol. 1, part 3: Čechy královské za Přemysla I. a Václava I.* Praha: Jan Laichter, 1928.

————. *M. Jan Hus: Život a Učení,* 2 vols. Prague: Jan Laichter, 1919–1921.

————, ed. *M. Jana Husi Korespondence a dokumenty.* Praha: Nákladem komise pro vydávání pramenů náboženského hnutí českého, 1920.

————. "Listy Husovy: Poznámky kritické a chronologické." *Věstník Královské České Společnosti Náuk. Třída filosoficko-historicko-jazykozpytná* no. 4 (1898): 1–89.

————. *Kde se narodil Jan Hus? Přednáška proslovená 8. XI. 1923 na schůzi Historického spolku a Společnosti Husova musea v Praze.* Prague: Dědictví Husovo, 1923.

————. "Kdy se narodil Jan Hus?" *Časopis Národního musea* 89 (1915): 129–146.

————, et al. *Betlémská kaple: O jejích dějinách a zachovaných zbytcích.* Praha: Společnost Husova Musea, 1922.

Oberman, Heiko A. *The Harvest of Medieval Theology: Gabriel Biel and Late Medieval Mysticism.* Cambridge: Harvard University Press, 1963.

Oden, Thomas C. *The Justification Reader.* Grand Rapids: Eerdmans Publishing Co., 2002.

————. *The Good Works Reader.* Grand Rapids: Eerdmans Publishing Co., 2007.

Odložilík, Otakar. "The Bethlehem Chapel in Prague: Remarks on Its Foundation Charter." *Studien zur Älteren Geschichte Osteuropas [Wiener Archiv für Geschichte des Slawentums und Osteuropas 2,1].* Graz and Cologne, 1956, 125–141.

————. *M. Štěpán z Kolína.* Praha: Nákladem Společnosti Husova musea, 1924.

Palacký, František, ed. *Documenta Mag. Joannis Hus vitam, doctrinam, causam in constantiensi Concilio actam et controversias de religione in Bohemia annis 1403–1418 motas illustrantia.* Praha: F. Tempský, 1869.

Pánek, Jaroslav, and Miroslav Polívka. *Jan Hus ve Vatikánu: Mezinárodní rozprava o českém reformátoru 15. století a o jeho koncepci na prahu třetího tisíciletí.* Prague: Historický ústav AVČR, 2000.

Pasciuta, Beatrice. *Il diavolo in Paradiso: Diritto, teologia e letteratura nel Processus Satane* (sec. XIV). Rome: Viella, 2015.

Peckham, John C. "Sola Scriptura: Reductio ad Absurdum?" *Trinity Journal NS* 35, no. 2 (2014): 195–223.

————. "We Must Obey God Rather Than Men: Jan Hus on the Authority of Scripture in Relation to Church and Conscience." *Andrews University Seminary Studies* 54, no. 1 (2016): 71–102.

Pelikan, Jaroslav. *The Riddle of Roman Catholicism.* New York: Abingdon Press, 1959.

Perett, Marcela K. *Preachers, Partisans, and Rebellious Religion: Vernacular Writing and the Hussite Movement*. Philadelphia: University of Pennsylvania Press, 2018.

Petra z Mladoňovic Zpráva o mistru Janu Husovi v Kostnici. Translated by František Heřmanský. Praha: Univerzita Karlova, 1965.

Pokračovatelé Kosmovi. Translated by Karel Hrdina, V. V. Tomek, and Marie Bláhová. Praha: Svoboda, 1974.

Polc, Jaroslav V. *Tisíc let pražského biskupství: 973–1973*. Rome: Křesťanská akademie, 1973.

————, with Stanislav Přibyl, eds. *Miscellanea husitica Ioannis Sedlák*. Praha: Karolinum, 1996.

Politi, Marco. "E il papa polacco riabilita Jan Hus." *La Repubblica* (December 18, 1999).

Pondělík, František. "Ondřej, biskup pražský." *Časopis katolického duchovenstva* 7 (1862): 481–491.

Porák, Jaroslav, and Jaroslav Kašpar. *Ze starých letopisů českých*. Praha: Svoboda, 1980.

Pospíšil, Ctirad V. "Jan Hus a transsubstanciace z hlediska dogmatické teologie." *Acta Universitatis Carolinae Theologica* 5, no. 1 (2015): 9–40.

Powicke, Sir Maurice. "The Three *Studia Generale*." *Prague Ess*ays. *Presented by a Group of British Historians to the Caroline University of Prague on the Occasion of Its Six-Hundredth Anniversary*, ed. R.W. Seton-Watson, 29–52. Oxford: Clarendon Press, 1949.

Prügl, Thomas. "Dissidence and Renewal: Developments in Late Medieval Ecclesiology." *Bulletin du centre d'études médiévales d'Auxerre* (2013): 1–17.

Putna, Martin C. "Husovská omluva z Říma: přece, ale pozdě." *Mladá fronta Dnes* (December 22, 1999).

Queller, Donald E. *The Office of the Ambassador in the Middle Ages*. Princeton: Princeton University Press, 1967.

Ridder-Symoens, Hilde de. *A History of the University in Europe*, 2 vols. Cambridge: Cambridge University Press, 1991.

Roberti Lincolniensis episcopi Scriptum Innocentio papae IV a. 1250 apud Lugdunum traditum praecedente nota historica. Prague, National Library of the Czech Republic, MS IV.G.31 (Y. I. 1. n. 77.), fols. 79b–87a.

Robinson, James Harvey, ed. *Readings in European History, vol. 1*. Boston: Ginn & Company, 1904.

Roukema, Riemer. "The Good Samaritan in Ancient Christianity." *Vigiliae Christianae* 58 (2004): 56–74.

Rusnock, Paul, and Jan Šebestík. *Bernard Bolzano: His Life and Work*. Oxford: Oxford University Press, 2019.

Ryba, Bohumil. *Betlemské texty*. Praha: Orbis, 1951.

Rychterová, Pavlína. "The Vernacular Theology of Jan Hus." *A Companion to Jan Hus*, eds. František Šmahel and Ota Pavlíček, 170–213. Leiden: Brill, 2015.

Ryšánek, František J. "Husových 'Devět kusův zlatých' a jejich rozbor od Petra Chelčického." *Listy filologické* 49 (1922): 32–46, 118–134.

Schaff, David S. *John Huss: His Life, Teachings and Death after Five Hundred Years.* New York: Charles Scribner's Sons, 1915.

Schmitt, Franciscus Salesius, ed. *S. Anselmi Cantuariensis Archiepiscopi Opera Omnia.* Stuttgart-Bad Cannstatt: F. Frommann Verlag (G. Holzboog), 1984.

Schreiber, Johanna. "Devotio moderna in Böhmen." *Bohemia: Jahrbuch des Collegium Carolinum* 6 (1965): 93–122.

———. "Die böhmische Devotio moderna." *Bohemia sacra. Das Christentum in Böhmen 973–1973*, ed. Ferdinand Seibt, 81–91. Düsseldorf: Schwann, 1974.

Schröpfer, Johann, ed. Hussens Traktat "Orthographia Bohemica." *Die Herkunft des diakritischen Systems in der Schreibung slavisher Sprachen und die älteste zusammenhängende Beschreibung slavischer Laute.* Wiesbaden: Harrassowitz, 1968.

Schwanda, Tom. "The Protestant Reception of Jan Hus in Great Britain and the American Colonies." *Journal of Moravian History* 16, no. 2 (2016): 65–89.

Scott, Lisa Stith. "To Go, Stay, Tarry, and Return": Jan Hus and the Pan-European Authority of the Safe Conduct." *The Bohemian Reformation and Religious Practice* 11 (2018): 18–36.

Sedlák, Jan. *M. Jan Hus.* Prague, Dědictví sv. Prokopa, 1915.

———. "Pramen české Postilly Husovy." In *Studie a texty k náboženským dějinám českým: Studie a texty k životopisu Husovu.* Olomouc: Matice Cyrillo-Methodějská, 1914.

Seibt, Ferdinand, et al., eds. *Jan Hus—Zwischen Zeiten, Völkern, Konfessionen: Vorträge des internationalen Symposions in Bayreuth vom 22. bis 26. September 1993.* Munich: R. Oldenbourg, 1997.

Selderhuis, Herman. *Martin Luther: A Spiritual Biography.* Wheaton: Crossway, 2017.

Settari, Olga. "Jan Amos Komenský a hudba." *Studia Comeniana et historica* 45 (1991): 47–62.

———, ed. Jan Amos Komenský, *Kancionál.* Praha: Kalich, 1992.

Šimek. František, ed. *Staročeské zpracování Postily studentů svaté University pražské Konráda Waldhausera.* Praha: Česká akademie věd a umění, 1947.

Skalický, Karel. *Klasma.* České Budějovice, 2015.

Sládek, Jiří, and Johanna Grohová. "Papež: Hluboce lituji kruté smrti Jana Husa." *Mladá fronta Dnes* (December 18, 1999).

Šmahel, František. *Husitská revoluce,* 4 vols. Prague: Historický ústav, 1993.

———. *Die Hussitische Revolution,* 3 vols. Translated by Thomas Krzenck and ed. Alexander Patschovsky. Hannover: Hahnsche Buchhandlung, 2002.

———. *Jan Hus: Život a dílo.* Prague: Argo, 2013.

———, and Ota Pavlíček, eds. *A Companion to Jan Hus.* Leiden: Brill, 2015.

Smolík, Josef. "Truth in History According to Hus' Conception." *Communio Viatorum* 15 (1972): 97–109.

Souček, Bohuslav. *Česká Apokalypsa v husitství: Z dějin textu Zjevení Janova—od Konstantina ke Komenskému: Úvodem k vyd. Nového zákona Táborského.* Praha: Ústřední církevní nakladatelství, 1967.

Soukup, Pavel. *11.7.1412: Poprava tří mládenců: Odpustkové bouře v Praze.* Praha: Havran, 2018.

———. *Jan Hus: The Life and Death of a Preacher.* West Lafayette: Purdue University Press, 2020.

———. "Jan Hus as a Preacher." *A Companion to Jan Hus,* eds. František Šmahel and Ota Pavlíček, 96–129. Leiden: Brill, 2015.

Sousedík, Stanislav. *Učení o eucharistii v díle M. Jana Husa.* Praha: Vyšehrad, 1998.

Sovík, Thomas Paul. "Music Theorists of the Bohemian Reformation: Jan Blahoslav and Jan Josquin." *Kosmas* 6 (1987): 104–145.

———. "Music Theorists of the Bohemian Reformation: Translation and Critique of the Treatises of Jan Blahoslav and Jan Josquin." PhD dissertation, Ohio State University, 1985.

Spěváček, Jiří. *Václav IV (1361–1419): K předpokladům husitské revoluce.* Praha: Svoboda, 1986.

———, et al., eds. Karel IV. Vlastní životopis. Vita Karoli Quatri. Praha: Odeon, 1978.

Spinka, Matthew. *The Letters of John Hus.* Manchester: Manchester University Press, 1972.

———. *John Hus at the Council of Constance.* New York: Columbia University Press, 1965.

———. *John Hus's Concept of the Church.* Princeton: Princeton University Press, 1966.

———. *John Hus: A Biography.* Princeton: Princeton University Press, 1968.

———. "John Hus, Advocate of Spiritual Reform." In *Advocates of Reform: From Wyclif to Erasmus,* ed. Matthew Spinka, 187–195. Philadelphia: The Westminster Press, 1953.

Spitz, Lewis W. "Luther's Sola Scriptura." *Concordia Theological Monthly* 31, no. 12 (1960): 740–745.

Steed, Henry Wickham. "Jan Hus and T. G. Masaryk." *Spirit of Czechoslovakia* 4, no. 9–10 (1943): 85–86.

Stevenson, Francis Seymour. *Robert Grosseteste, Bishop of Lincoln: A Contribution to the Religious, Political and Intellectual History of the Thirteenth Century.* London: Macmillan & Co., 1899.

Štítný, Tomáš. *Knihy naučení křesťanského,* ed. Antonín Jaroslav Vrťátko. Praha: Musea království Českého, 1873.

———. *Knížky šestery o obecných věcech křesťanských,* ed. Karel Jaromír Erben. Praha: K. Jeřábkové, 1852.

———. *Sborník Vyšehradský,* 2 vols., ed. František Ryšánek. Praha: Československá akademie věd, 1960.

Štoll, Martin. "Is Kafka a Greater Czech Than Freud? The Global TV Format 100 Great Britons in Czech Translation (A Case Study)." Translated by Richard Olehla. *Czech and Slovak Journal of Humanities* 1 (2017): 68–87.

Stopa, Sasja Emilie Mathiasen. "'Seeking Refuge in God against God': The Hidden God in Lutheran Theology and the Postmodern Weakening of God." *Open Theology* 4, no. 1 (2018): 658–674.

Stump, Phillip H. *The Reforms of the Council of Constance (1414–1418)*. Leiden: Brill, 1994.

Súd Astarothóv proti lidskému pokolení. Library of the National Museum in Prague, MS III E 43, fol. 138a–150a.

Svatoš, Michal. "Das Kuttenberger Dekret und das Wirken von Magister Jan Hus an der Prager Universität." *Die Prager Universität Karls IV: Von der europäischen Gründung bis zur nationalen Spaltung,* ed. Blanka Mouralová, 45–70. Potsdam: Deutsches Kulturforum östliches Europa, 2010.

Swieżawski, Stefan. "Jan Hus—A Heretic or a Saint?" *Occasional Papers on Religion in Eastern Europe* 14, no. 2, art. 5 (1994): 36–42.

Tanner, Norman, ed. *Decrees of the Ecumenical Councils*, 2 vols. London: Sheed & Ward, 1990.

Thomson, S. Harrison. *The Writings of Robert Grosseteste, Bishop of Lincoln 1235–1253*. Cambridge: Cambridge University Press, 2013.

Tierney, Brian. *Foundations of the Conciliar Theory: The Contributions of the Medieval Canonists from Gratian to the Great Schism.* Cambridge: Cambridge University Press, 1955.

Tomek, Václav Vladivoj. *Dějepis města Prahy, vol. 3*. Prague: W komissí u Františka Řiwnáče, 1875.

Tractatus Quaestionis Ventilatae Coram Domino Jesu Christo. Inter Virginem Mariam ex una parte et diabolum ex alia parte in *Bartoli a Saxoferrato Omnium Iuris Interpretum Antesignani Consilia, Quaestiones, et Tractatus, vol. 10*. Venice: Luca Antonio Giunta, 1590.

Tříška, Josef. *Rétorický styl a pražská univerzitní literatura ve středověku: Stilus rhetoricus et litterae Universitatis Pragensis medio aevo florentes*. Praha: Univerzita Karlova, 1975.

———. *The Crisis of Church and State: 1050–1300*. New York: 1964.

Trtík, Zdeněk. "K Husovu pojetí víry." *Theologická revue* 43 (1972): 157–165.

———. "Husův odkaz a oba principy reformace." *Hus stále živý: Sborník studií k 550. výročí Husova upálení*, ed. Miloslav Kaňák, 38–44. Praha: Blahoslav, 1965.

Urban, Rudolf. *Die tschechoslowakische hussitische Kirche*. Marburg/Lahn: J.G. Herder-Institut, 1973.

Vanhoozer, Kevin. *Biblical Authority after Babel: Retrieving the Protestant Solas in the Spirit of Mere Protestant Christianity*. Grand Rapids: Brazos Press, 2016.

Vašica, Josef. *Staročeské evangeliáře*. Praha: České akademie věd a umění, 1931.

Ververková, Kamila. *Bernard Bolzano: A New Evaluation of His Thought and His Circle*. Translated by Angelo Shaun Franklin. Lanham: Lexington, 2022.

———. *The Four Articles of Prague within the Public Sphere of Hussite Bohemia: On the 600th Anniversary of Their Declaration (1420–2020)*. Translated by Angelo Shaun Franklin. Lanham: Lexington Books, 2021.

———. "Co a proč stojí u Husa za další bádání?" *Theologická revue* 86, no. 2 (2015): 152–157.

Vidmanová, Anežka. *Laborintus: Latinská literatura středověkých Čech*. Praha: KLP, 1994.

———. "Hus als Prediger." *Communio viatorum* 19 (1976): 65–81.

—————. "Kdy, kde a jak psal Hus českou Postilu." *Listy filologické* 112 (1989): 144–158.

—————. "Ke spisku Orthographia bohemica." *Listy filologické* 105 (1982): 75–89.

Voleková. Kateřina, ed. *Orthographia Bohemica*. Praha: Akropolis, 2019.

—————. *Česká lexikografie 15. století*. Praha: Academia, 2015.

de Vooght, Paul. *Hussiana*. Louvain: Bureaux de la Revue: Publications universitaires de Louvain, 1960.

—————. *L'hérésie de Jean Huss,* 2nd ed. Louvain: Publications Universitaires de Louvain, 1975.

de Voragine, Jacobus. *The Golden Legend: Readings on the Saints*. Translated by William Granger Ryan. Princeton: Princeton University Press, 2013.

Vos, A., et al., eds. *Duns Scotus on Divine Love: Texts and Commentary on Goodness and Freedom, God and Humans*. New York: Routledge, 2003.

Wagner, Murray L. *Petr Chelčický: A Radical Separatist in Hussite Bohemia.* Scottsdale: Herald Press, 1983.

Walter, Ferdinand, ed. *Corpus Iuris Germanici Antiqui, vol. 2*. Berolini: Impensis G. Reimeri, 1824.

Weber, Reid S. "A Preacher's Priorities: Jan Hus and Late Medieval Homiletics." PhD dissertation, University of Florida, 2014.

—————. "The Knowledge and Eloquence of the Priest Is a Gift from God." The Homiletic Self-Promotion of Jan Hus." *The Bohemian Reformation and Religious Practice 10* (2015): 28–48.

Weis, Martin. "M. Jan Hus v ideologii Komunistické strany Československa ve světle díla Zdeňka Nejedlého a archivních dokumentů." *Studia Theologica* 17 (2015): 113–123.

Weltsch, Ruben Ernest. *Archbishop John of Jenstein (1348–1400): Papalism, Humanism and Reform in Pre-Hussite Prague*. The Hague: Mouton, 1968.

Werner, Ernst. *Jan Hus. Welt und Umwelt eines Prager Frühreformators*. Weimar: Hermann Böhlaus, 1991.

Wernisch, Martin. "Ratio voluntatis M. Johannis Hus. Zur Rolle von Vernunft und Willen in der Lehre Hussens." In *Jan Hus: Zwischen Zeiten, Völkern, Konfessionen: Vorträge des internationalen Symposions in Bayreuth vom 22. bis 26. September 1993, 139–155*. München: Oldenbourg, 1997.

Wilken, Robert Louis. "*Fides Caritate Formata*: Faith Formed by Love." *Nova et Vetera* 9, no. 4 (2011): 1089–1100.

Wilks, Michael. "The *Apostolicus* and the Bishop of Rome, I." *The Journal of Theological Studies NS* 13 (1962): 290–317.

—————. "The *Apostolicus* and the Bishop of Rome, II." *The Journal of Theological Studies NS* 14 (1963): 311–354.

—————. "Legislator divinus-humanus: The Medieval Pope as Sovereign." Pierre Guichard et al., *Papauté, monachisme et théories politiques, vol. 1: Le pouvoir et l'institution ecclésiale, 181–195*. Lyon: Presses universitaires de Lyon, 1994.

—————. *The Problem of Sovereignty in the Later Middle Ages: The Papal Monarchy with Augustinus Triumphus and the Publicists*. Cambridge: Cambridge University Press, 1963.

William of Ockham. *Philosophical Writings: A Selection.* Translated by Philotheus Boehner. Indianapolis: Hackett Publishing, 1990.

Williams, D. H. "The Search for Sola Scriptura in the Early Church." *Interpretation* 52, 4 (1988): 354–366.

Wojtyla, Karol. *Sources of Renewal: The Implementation of Vatican II.* Translated by P.S. Falla. San Francisco: Harper & Row, 1980.

Workman, Herbert B., and R. Martin Pope. *The Letters of John Hus.* London: Hodder and Stoughton, 1904.

Wratislaw, Albert Henry. "John of Jenstein, Archbishop of Prague, 1378–1397." *Transactions of the Royal Historical Society* 7 (1878): 30–57.

Wyclif, Johannes. *Tractatus de Civili Dominio, vol. 1.* Edited by Reginald Lane Poole. London: Trübner & Co., 1885.

———. *Tractatus de Logica,* ed. Michael Henry Dziewicki. London: Trübner & Co., 1893–1899.

———. *Opera Minora.* Edited by Johann Loserth. London: C.K. Paul & Co., 1913.

———. *Opus Evangelicum.* Edited by Johann Loserth. London: Trübner & Co., 1895.

———. *Tractatus de Ecclesia.* Edited by Johann Loserth. London: Wyclif Society, 1886.

———. *Sermones, vol. 1: Super Evangelia Dominicalia.* Edited by Johann Loserth. London: Trübner & Co., 1887.

———. *De veritate Sacrae Scripturae,* 3 vols. Edited by Rudolf Buddensieg. London: Wyclif Society, 1905–1907.

———. *Tractatus de potestate papae.* Edited by Johann Loserth. London: Trübner & Co., 1907.

———. *De eucharistia tractatus maior: Accedit tractatus De eucharistia et poenitentia sive de confessione.* Edited by Johann Loserth. London: Trübner & Co., 1892.

———. *Sermones, vol. 4: Sermones Miscellanei.* Edited by Johann Loserth. London: Trübner & Co., 1890.

———. *Trialogus: Cum Supplemento Trialogi.* Edited by Gotthard V. Lechler. Oxford: Clarendon Press, 1869.

———. *Tractatus de Potestate Pape.* Edited by Johann Loserth. London: Trübner & Co., 1907.

Zachová, Jana. "Waldhauser a Hus." *Husitství—reformace—renesance: Sborník k 60. narozeninám Františka Šmahela,* 3 vols. Praha: Historický ústav AV ČR, 1994.

Zbožínek, Jaroslav. "Papež vyjádřil lítost nad upálením Jana Hus." *Právo* (December 18, 1999).

Zeman, Antonín. "K biblickému textu Husovy postily." *Listy filologické* 101 (1978): 13–16.

Žemlička, Josef. *Přemysl Otakar I. Panovník, stát a česká společnost na prahu vrcholného feudalismu.* Praha: Svoboda, 1990.

———. *Počátky Čech královských 1198–1253: Proměna státu a společnosti.* Praha: Lidové noviny, 2002.

———. *Století posledních Přemyslovců: Český stát a společnost ve 13. století.* Praha: Panorama, 1986.

————. "Spor Přemysla Otakara I. s pražským biskupem Ondřejem." *Československý časopis historický* 29, no. 5 (1981): 704–730.

Zilynská, Blanka. "Mistr Jan Hus a pražská univerzita: Několik zamyšlení nad možnostmi poznání jejich vzájemného vztahu a Husovy pedagogické činnosti." *Acta Universitatis Carolinae: Historia Universitatis Carolinae Pragensis: Příspěvky k dějinám Univerzity Karlovy* 58, no. 1 (2018): 209–221.

Index

Guttenstein, Andreas von, 35

Haberkern, Phillip N., 90
Hagen, K., 91
Hahn, Scott, 96
Halík Tomáš, xiv
Hamilton, Stephen James, xii
Hanuš of Mühlheim, 105
Harrison, Matthew C., 101
Havel, church of St., 4
Havlík (priest), 61, 68, 122
Havránek, Bohuslav, 103
Hefele, Karl Joseph, 35, 96
Helan, Pavel, xiii
Herold, Vilém 8, 16.90, 120
Heřmanský, František, 70
Heydrich, Reinhard, 130
Heymann, Frederick G., 70
Higden, Ranulf, 38
Hill, Peter C., 91
Hillerbrand, Hans J., xii
Hilsch, Peter 35, xix
Hlaváček, Ivan, 70
Höfler, Konstantin K.A. von, 19
Holeček, František J., xiii, xix,
    67, 90, 129
Holeton, David R., 8, 16, 39,
    70, 122, 124
Holý, Ladislav, 131
Horský, Rudolf, 110, 115, 121, 122
Hrabák, Josef, 67, 103
Hrdina, Karel, 35
Hrdlička, Jaroslav, 90
Hrejsa, Ferdinand, 120
Hrubá, Michaela, xii
Hrubý, Petr, vii
Hudson, Anne, 16
Huijgen, Arnold, 92–94
Hünermann, Peter, 68

Innocent IV, pope, 36–38
Innocenzo, Master, 36
Isidore of Sevila, 48
Izbicki, Thomas M., 67

Jakoubek of Stříbro (Jacobellus de
    Misa), 61, 116, 122
Jan (martyred disciple of Hus), 14
Jan of Chlum, 29, 31, 38, 54, 60, 128
Jan of Jenštejn, archbishop of
    Prague, 5, 8, 52
Jan of Luxemburg, king, 3
Jan of Ústí, 57
Janz, Denis R., 6
Jaroslav (monk), 63
Jerome (Hieronymus) of Prague, 10,
    50, 122, 123
Jerome (Church father), 31, 77, 122
Jesenice, John of 38, 43, 44
Jeschke, J. B., 66, 123
John XXIII, anti-pope, 13, 14,
    19, 20, 24, 28, 29, 42–44, 46,
    50–53, 116, 123
John of Paris. *See* Quidort, Jean
John Paul II, pope, 60, 68, 126, 129
Josquin, Jan, 124
Jukl, Jiří Jakub, 129
Justinian, emperor, 49

Kadlec, Jaroslav, 7, 8
Kalivoda, Robert, 123
Kambartel, Friedrich, 130
Kaminski, Howard, 70
Kaňák, Miloslav, 8, 10, 16, 72, 91, 93,
    96, 121, 122
Kardinál Jan of Rejnštejn, 30, 42,
    50, 90, 129
Kašpar, Jaroslav, 51
Kašpar, Josef, 129
Kafka, Franz, xx
Kavka, František, 18
Kejř, Jiří, viii, xiii, 20, 36, 43, 44,
    47, 89, 90
Kelly, J. N. D., 35
Klein, Ernest, 121
Klassen, John Martin, 70
Knápek, Aleš, 70
Knouse, Nola Reed, 124
Knox, Ronald, 7
Kohnle, Armin, xii, xix

Kolesnyk, Alexander, 16
Kolpakoff, Deane Jennifer, 5
Komenský (Comenius), Jan Amos,
	vii, 119, 124
Konrád, archbishop of Prague, 45, 68
Kothmann, Thomas, xii
Kotowski, Norbert, xi, xviii, xix
Kotyk, Jiří, 90
Kouba, Jan, 124
Kovář, František, 126, 130, 131
Kovtun, George J., xiv
Krása, Josef, 7
Krmíčková, Helena, 144
Krofta, Kamil, 16, 36, 91, 120
Krügelgen, Constantin von, 69
Krzenck, Thomas, xii, xix, 16, 70
Křišťan of Prachatice M., 32, 39,
	55, 95, 96
Kříž, Jan, 105
Kubíček, Alois, 120
Kučera, Zdeněk, xi, xiv, xviii
Kyas, Vladimír, 147
Kybal, Vlastimil, 8, 20, 90

Lacembok, Jindřich, 60
Ladislav of Naples, 14
Lamport, Mark A., 67
Lane, Anthony N. S., 14
Langpaul, Ladislav, 70
Larangé, Daniel, xii
Lášek, Jan B., vii, viii, ix, xi, xii, xiv,
	xv, xviii, xix, 7, 16, 20, 90, 129
Lefebvre, Marcel-Francois,
	archbishop, 60
Leff, Gordon, 16
Lefl of Lažany, 59
Lechler, Gotthard V., 147
Leppin, Volker, 21
Liguš, Ján, 16, 95, 98
Loomis, Louise Ropes, 67
Lochman, Jan Milíč, 78, 89, 96
Lombard, Peter, 52, 74, 77, 78, 81,
	82, 99, 145
Loserth, Johann, 16, 17, 29, 37,
	59, 67, 146

Loskot, Franrišek, 7, 8
Loskotová, Anežka, xiii
Loužek, Marek, xi, 20
Luard, Henry Richards, 36, 38
Loužil, Jan, 130
Lumby, Joseph Rawson, 38
Luther, Martin, vii, 6, 15, 21, 67, 74, 75,
	77, 81–83, 86, 91, 94, 97, 101, 102
Lützow, Franz, 70

Macek, Josef, 123
Macek, Ladislav, 70
Mahel, Richard, 36
Machilek, Franz, 7, 70
Machovec, Milan, xix, 123
Mánek, Jindřich, 96
Mantello, F. A. C., 37
Marc, P., 6
Marcion, 31
Mareš, Bohumil, 69
Marin, Olivier, 16
Marrou, Henri-Irénée, 7
Marsilius of Padua, 2, 6
Martin V (Oddo de Colonna), pope,
	39, 117, 123
Martin, Francis R., 97
Martin (martyred disciple of Hus), 14
Martin of Volyně, 122
Masaryk, T. G., ix, x, xiv, xvi
Maur, Eduard, 18
Matěj of Janov, 5, 7, 8, 112
Mathison, Keith, 91
Matthew of Paris, 38
McGrath, A. E., 97
Merick, John, 94
Michael de Causis, 24, 38, 39, 107, 148
Michálek, Emanuel, 145
Miklík, Josef, 31
Milíč of Kroměřížm, 5, 78,
	105, 112, 120
Mladějovská, Aneta, 124
Molnár, Amedeo, xii, xix, 20, 67, 68,
	88, 89, 91, 103, 121, 124, 131
Molnár, Enrico C. Selley, 93, 124
Monahan, Arthur P., 6

About the Authors

Angelo Shaun Franklin is an independent researcher who works as a translator and educational consultant in Prague. He is currently translating several works in modern Bohemian history, theological texts by Jan Hus, and other medieval Bohemian works.

Prof. ThDr. Jan Blahoslav Lášek is the vice-dean for science and research at the Hussite Theological Faculty of Charles University in Prague. He has authored and edited numerous works in the fields of theology and church history.